DANTE AND AUGUSTINE:
LINGUISTICS, POETICS, HERMENEUTICS

At several junctures in his career, Dante paused to consider the process of writing and what it means to be a writer. The questions he posed were both simple and wide-ranging: How does language, in particular 'poetic language,' work? Can poetry be translated? What is the relationship between a text and its commentary? Who controls the meaning of a literary work? In *Dante and Augustine*, Simone Marchesi re-examines these questions in light of the influence that Augustine's reflections on similar issues exerted on Dante's sense of his task as a poet.

Examining Dante's lifelong preoccupation with Augustine, Marchesi goes beyond traditional inquiries to address more technical questions related to Dante's evolving ideas on how language, poetry, and interpretation should work. In this engaging literary analysis, Dante emerges as a versatile thinker, committed to a radical defence of poetry and yet always ready to reconsider, revise, and rewrite his own positions on matters of linguistics, poetics, and hermeneutics.

(Toronto Italian Studies)

SIMONE MARCHESI is an associate professor in the Department of French and Italian at Princeton University.

SIMONE MARCHESI

Dante and Augustine

Linguistics, Poetics, Hermeneutics

UNIVERSITY OF TORONTO PRESS
Toronto Buffalo London

© University of Toronto Press 2011
Toronto Buffalo London
utorontopress.com

Reprinted in paperback 2021

ISBN 978-1-4426-4210-2 (cloth)
ISBN 978-1-4875-2618-4 (paper)

Toronto Italian Studies

Library and Archives Canada Cataloguing in Publication

Title: Dante and Augustine : linguistics, poetics, hermeneutics / Simone Marchesi.
Names: Marchesi, Simone, author.
Series: Toronto Italian studies.
Description: Series statement: Toronto Italian studies | Paperback reprint. Originally published 2011. | Includes bibliographical references and index.
Identifiers: Canadiana 20210122544 | ISBN 9781487526184 (softcover)
Subjects: LCSH: Dante Alighieri, 1265–1321 – Criticism and interpretation. | LCSH: Dante Alighieri, 1265–1321 – Technique. | LCSH: Augustine, of Hippo, Saint, 354–430 – Influence.
Classification: LCC PQ4390 .M37 2021 | DDC 851/.1–dc23

This book has been published with the assistance of a grant from Princeton University.

University of Toronto Press acknowledges the financial assistance to its publishing program of the Canada Council for the Arts and the Ontario Arts Council, an agency of the Government of Ontario.

Canada Council   Conseil des Arts
for the Arts   du Canada

ONTARIO ARTS COUNCIL
CONSEIL DES ARTS DE L'ONTARIO
an Ontario government agency
un organisme du gouvernement de l'Ontario

Funded by the   Financé par le
Government   gouvernement
of Canada   du Canada

For Dadi – both the one who'll never read this and the one who, maybe, one day will

Contents

Preface ix
Acknowledgments xv

Introduction 3
1 Linguistics 19
2 Poetics 65
3 Hermeneutics 107
4 Augustine in Dante: Three Readings 154

Notes 197
Works Cited 229
Index 247

Preface

This book is about the dialogue between Dante's minor works and his poem. It focuses on three interrelated areas: poetics, linguistics, and hermeneutics. Taken together, these aspects of Dante's reflection on his work form what one may call 'the task of the poet,' as Dante perceived it at various stages of his career. In the title and body of this book, these three terms are presented and studied in what is hoped to be a logical succession. As we shall see, when he most attentively and systematically reflected on his work as poet, Dante presented these core concepts in the same hierarchical order: in the years in which he was composing *Convivio* and *De vulgari eloquentia*, he defined poetry as the product of the interplay between language and rhetorical colours and figures, and he approached hermeneutics as an authorial encroachment upon poetry. In that framework, interpretation was designed to extract meaning from poetic texts and poetry was the result of adding some special ingredient to ordinary language.

In my investigation I pay particular attention to the presence of Augustinian ideas in Dante's thinking. The main argument threading through the book is that Augustine was a constant presence, at times accompanying and, at times, even prompting Dante's reflection on linguistics, poetics, and hermeneutics. In his writings, Augustine was an often encumbering, if sometimes silent (or silenced) interlocutor. We know that his theories on language, rhetoric, and hermeneutics, as they may be glimpsed primarily but not solely through his treatise *On Christian Doctrine*, were a permeating element of Dante's culture. The task of this book is to show how Dante found in these theories a constant reference point for his reflections, whether he wilfully silenced Augustine's voice, as he did sometimes, or he confidently recuperated it and let it echo in his work, as he did at other times.

When Augustine's presence as one of Dante's interlocutors is not taken into account, three foundational elements of what will become Dante's poetics in the *Commedia* may be accounted for only with difficulty. Augustine provided him with a model for the essence and goals of human language that could counteract Dante's own professed reliance on the conceptualist linguistic framework that he advocated most strongly in *De vulgari eloquentia*; a radical alternative to the reductionist philosophical poetics that he avowedly evoked in *Convivio*, a theory of poetry based on the split between artistic form and intellectual content; and finally a hermeneutic model coherent with a poetics of inspiration that could endow his texts with a higher authority than the limited, all-too-human prestige of its author, a notion that may be found in embryo in *Vita nuova*, but that only the *Commedia* fully develops. When we look diachronically at Dante's intellectual history, Augustinian ideas may be found at the root of three easily observable (and often observed), interconnected phenomena: first, the shift from his experimentations with self-commentary to the writing of independent prose and poetry; second, the shift from his (strategically invoked) skepticism about the ability of poetry to communicate fully with its readership to his investiture of the reader with the production of an active and ultimately salvific reading of his text; and third, the shift from his reliance on the authority of the author to the profession of a poetics of inspiration, in which poetic texts are products to which 'heaven and earth have set their hands.' Augustine's meditations on language, style, and interpretation helped achieve all three transitions.

My reconstruction of this technical facet in Dante's evolving thought may appear to be little more than 'grist from the old mill' of Dante studies. After all, it is true that my arguments will tend to confirm the existence of three large phases in Dante's life as a poet and thinker: a period up to the exile that finds its culminating text in *Vita nuova*, the mid-career treatises which sharply depart from several key notions of the *libello*, and finally the *Commedia*, a text that goes back to the acquisitions of the first period, bypassing (without eliding them) the positions Dante had taken in the midway texts. These are, notably, the same three large partitions in Dante's intellectual history that quite recently Barański has insisted upon, suggesting, incidentally, that they are perhaps not as old as one may think (2000, 30). The contribution that this book aims to make to the understanding of Dante's thinking in action is twofold, consisting in an attempt both to provide further support to the present view of Dante's intellectual history and to nuance it. On the one hand, by extending to matters of poetics in addition to the philosophical issues that are commonly seen as the guiding factors for Dante's transitions from one phase to the next, my arguments support the currently accepted intellectual profile of Dante as a writer. In my view, Dante's shifting involvement with the 'philosophical' and 'theological' or the 'exegetical' strain of his culture was accompanied by a change of course in matters of poetics. Dante's successive adoption of different models for thinking about language (radical Modistic and Augustinian theories), his wavering between privileging the philosophical clarity of prose and the strenuous advocacy of his poem's power to cross into ethics, his initial insistence on the authority of the author and his eventual and surprising staging of reader-oriented hermeneutics – these changes in perspective are not just the tell-tale signs of Dante's shifting intellectual allegiances from a rationalist or theological approach to philosophy to a biblical and hermeneutic one. They may be seen, rather, as their triggers. On the other hand, my attempt to nuance this periodization comes from the care with which I will highlight areas in Dante's reflection on poetry in which continuities across the three phases do seem to exist: while, for instance, the break between the poetics of *Convivio* and of *Vita nuova* is sharp, it does not seem to affect the balance that both works establish between the prose of commentary and the commented poetry; similarly, while *Convivio* is, as a project, definitely coherent with Dante's mid-career theorizations, it contains, especially in book 4, several elements that connect it with the poetics of the *Commedia* – especially the renewed interest in the historicity of poetry's plots.

If Dante's flirting with a rationalistic poetics in the *Convivio* and *De vulgari eloquentia* was neither representative of his praxis in those works nor destined to have an import on the poetics of the poem, why should we take his arguments seriously? The underlying principle of my sally into Dante's theory of language, poetry, and interpretation is that some arguments do have a force of their own: not only for the points they make, but also for the cultural associations they evoke in the audience. Today, keywords such as 'class struggle' or 'struggle for life' evoke distinct resonances: Marxism, Darwinism, social Darwinism, perhaps. I may be an old-style liberal, or a creationist, or a combination of both, but if I use these words in my argument, it will not serve my ideas without resistance. Dante's arguments in the mid-career treatises appear to be no exception to this rule. The terms he uses (mostly, as has recently been noted, traditional) do have some weight in his reasoning. Their import may not be irresistible (and, more often than not, Dante will actually resist them), but they tend to orient the reading towards specific conclusions – or, at least, they frame the argument in a specific reasoning mode.

In his seminal contributions to the study of Dante's poetics and intellectual history, Barański is certainly right when he underscores the essentially unsurprising quality of Dante's thinking in matters of linguistics and poetics, and to connect his conservative attitude to a desire to mediate between the revolutionary quality of much of his poetic output and the traditional expectations of his audience. Yet, mediation is not all there is at stake in Dante's choice of words. Dante certainly does seek recognition with an audience of literary experts who are ultimately unprepared to deal with the novelty of his works, but the language that he uses does more than grant him that recognition: it actually comes close to having his literary theory coincide with traditional understandings of the task of the poet. Not even Dante, in other words, is immune from the eventual (or, at least, potential) backfiring of some of his arguments.

Let me provide a few examples of notions that Dante explicitly defended at one time and then was eventually compelled to review, reframe, or reject. First, as I will argue in the first chapter of this book, it is difficult to say that language is designed to convey concepts (as Dante explicitly and unambiguously does in *Convivio* and *De vulgari eloquentia*) and then assign a primarily expressive or adumbrative function to it in one's poetry (as he did in *Vita nuova* and will do in the *Commedia*). It similarly is difficult to say that content and form are always mixed discretely in language (and that what really matters, in the end, is content), as both *Convivio* and *De vulgari eloquentia* seem to propose, and then bracket the question of the legitimacy of poetic form. Finally, it is difficult to state that the author is the only person legitimately in charge of retrieving meaning from a poem (as *Convivio* unmistakably, if strategically, declares), and then invoke for the *Commedia* (and at least one crucial section of *Vita nuova*) a poetics of inspiration that unloads the burden of interpretation onto the reader and subordinates the author to a higher source. One could even say that Dante could not have become the author of the *Commedia* had he stayed faithful to some of the points he made in the years leading up to it. Simply put, by adhering to those principles, Dante should not have written that kind of poem. When theoretical arguments are framed in a certain way, in other words, it is difficult to defend a practice that contradicts them. Difficult, but not – it is good to remember – impossible. Apparently Dante was up to the task: he was able to claim and achieve continuity throughout his career. By isolating the areas of friction, however, my book tries to assess what local adjustments he implemented in order to do so, what tactics he called upon at distinct junctures in his intellectual career, and what strategies he put in place in order to design and transmit to his readers a coherent, if complex, intellectual self-portrait.

A point of method: by studying some elements in Dante's changing sense of his task as a poet, their prehistory in the *Vita nuova*, and their eventual deployment or abandonment in the *Commedia*, I will often be forced to separate Dante's theory from his practice and contrast them. In order to highlight what notions he had held onto from those that he eventually had to refute, what elements he had considered and introduced as crucial into his systematic thinking from those that he eventually downplayed or redefined, my study will strategically privilege explicit statements over silent behaviours. It will look more to 'what Dante says he does, rather than what he actually does' – as Teodolinda Barolini put it, advocating the opposite direction of investigation for the *Commedia* (1992, 16). The principle by which my reading of the pre-*Commedia* works will abide should not, however, be taken as absolute. I do not choose theory over and to the exclusion of practice. Evaluating the development of Dante's reflection on language, poetry, and interpretation often means, rather, that readers are called to decide on matters of emphasis. In theoretical statements that appear to run counter and work at cross-purposes to Dante's practice, readers are called to choose where they would place more interpretive weight. They may follow the theory and downplay the discordant elements in the practice, or vice versa they may privilege practice and relegate his theory to the rank of an afterthought. Let me provide one example of these sorts of question. When it comes to defining the basic components and essential limits of Dante's understanding of the nature of the Latin language, we have on the one hand his repeated statements that Latin is an artificial human construct, perfect (that is, apt to embody and transmit rational philosophical ideas) and immutable (that is, stable in both its lexicon and syntax). On the other hand, in this traditional, scholastic-modistic peaceful picture of the language, Dante finds a way to insert an unsettling element: a statement, based on the authority of Horace's *Ars poetica*, suggesting that mutability and flux do indeed affect Latin as well. Is there a way of thinking about the apparent – and perhaps even real – *aporia* in Dante's systematic thinking that does not betray the complexity of his reflections?

The take that this book will have on this and similar problems is to acknowledge that both statements are true, even if contradictory. Rather than excising one side of the question, we should accept them both, but still be able to appreciate and account for their divergence. For instance, in order to deal with the contradictory views on Latin to which Dante subscribes in *Convivio* and *De vulgari eloquentia*, it may actually help to think that Dante treated the language in question the same way as modern physics deals with the study of gases. By assuming, for the sake of some arguments (not all of them) and some calculations (not all of them), that gases are 'perfect' or 'ideal,' physicists predict their behaviour according to a simple equation linking pressure, volume, number of moles, absolute temperature, and a universal gas constant for all of them. Of course, to respond to different conditions (relatively high pressure and low temperatures are the discriminating element in physics), scientists are always ready to go back to a finer, more complex, and in the end truer treatment of individual substances. Similarly, as we shall see, in Dante's thinking Latin could be treated, for the sake of some arguments (but not all of them), as a limit-language. Dante could have felt the need to do similar adjustments and develop different arguments in different contexts: Latin should be understood as a perfectly stable and artificial language for certain purposes, as caught in the perpetual flux of natural languages for others. Both pictures of Latin, then, would be true under their own conditions, and the contradictions between statements that are close in time would be a matter of Dante's argumentative agility and ductility rather than 'confusion' or 'evolution' in his thought. Such an approach, in sum, may help reduce the effects of the two opposed (and yet similarly judgmental) attitudes embedded in the words highlighted above: neither indicting nor hagiographic, the study of Dante's linguistics, poetics, and hermeneutics does not need to turn into a systematic search for coherence. Coherence at all costs was not a prominent trait in Dante's profile.

Acknowledgments

The roots of this book extend back to my 2002 doctoral dissertation at Princeton University. It was then and there that I first engaged many of the texts on which I have worked ever since and developed most of the arguments presented in these pages. Throughout the years I have accumulated a vast debt of gratitude with teachers, colleagues, and friends, who have kindly agreed to read, provide criticisms, and patiently re-read my evolving arguments. Their sheer number prevents me from even attempting a comprehensive list, but I want to acknowledge at least three names. Without the generosity, time, and advice of Bob, Teo, and Zyg, this book would simply not exist. Or, rather, a much worse one would. They all have tried to curb what Dante, in Augustinian language, would call my hermeneutical 'consuetudo deviandi.' Any reading gone 'in perversum' is totally my own.

To Christian Moevs, whose name did not make it into the previous shortlist only because cutting it down to three letters would put him beyond recognition, goes my gratitude for having gotten the whole project unstuck at a critical juncture.

Princeton University generously provided support for this project, in the form of a Bicentennial Preceptorship leave. The months I have spent in Italy between 2008 and 2009 were crucial for the completion of my rethinking and rewriting of this manuscript. I also consider myself fortunate for having had Ron Schoeffel as editor at University of Toronto Press; he believed in this book even before I did.

My wife Ilaria gets, as usual, the last word. Thank you.

DANTE AND AUGUSTINE:
LINGUISTICS, POETICS, HERMENEUTICS

Introduction

My work locates itself at the crossroads of two distinct but not unrelated approaches to Dante: on the one side, the investigations into the internal articulation and theoretical foundations of Dante's meta-poetic thinking and, on the other, the studies of Augustine's influence on Dante's praxis as a poet. One of the aims of this book is to bring these two strains together. To that effect, I focus on Dante's dialogue with Augustine-the-theorist of language, literature, and interpretation in addition to the confessional Augustine, who has been traditionally taken as Dante's main reference point in a series of seminal studies in North America. This explains my frequent discussion of passages from Augustine's *De doctrina christiana*, a text that Dante most likely encountered late in life, but which often offers intriguing conceptual parallels with his works. Two advantages, it is hoped, will derive from the critical cross-pollination I attempt: first, by looking into Augustine's treatment of 'technical' questions that may be of interest for a poet, a larger context will be made available for some of Dante's Augustinian 'moments' in the *Commedia* – a context in which meta-poetic issues may be allowed to play a larger role than they have been up to now; second, to the welter of influences proposed to gloss Dante's reflection on poetry a new authoritative voice will be added – one with whose complexity he arguably had significant familiarity. In other words, when the influence of the two Augustines – the 'doctrinal' and the 'poeto-logic' – is brought to bear on the interpretation of Dante's self-conscious poetic thinking and poetic making, we may have a further indication and perhaps a better sense of how these two areas of his work as a poet are intertwined.

Steps in this direction have been taken in the recent past, both thanks to a new attention to Dante's poetics and to a constant interest in reading Dante with an Augustinian filigree. To both these lines of inquiry the argument I develop owes a considerable debt, both for their local interpretive contributions and, more generally, for the proactive way they have responded to the challenging, almost complete, silence that Dante's *Commedia* keeps on Augustine: as is well known, the Bishop of Hippo only gets a belated mention in *Paradiso* 32.35, one canto short of the end of the poem.[1] To studies that have matched Dante's puzzling choice with a supplement of investigation rather than an acquiescent distraction, we owe crucial notions for our understanding of the poem. Several aspects of Dante's poem have been illuminated by Augustinian intertexts. For instance, that the narrative impulse of the *Commedia* conforms to and is patterned on an essentially Augustinian conversion paradigm; that, in its bringing together Christian and classical elements, the poem is a surprisingly solid compound of Virgil and Augustine (or a frail edifice, showing all its cracks, depending on personal critical inclinations); that it embodies and transmits a sense of history at once tragic and redemptive (again, a Virgilian and Augustinian product); that Dante's text is inviting an active hermeneutic engagement on the part of its readers and, in so doing, negotiates its fictional status are all stable acquisitions of the current critical discourse, thanks to studies such as those by John Freccero (collected in Freccero 1986), Giuseppe Mazzotta (1979), Charles T. Davis (1984), Teodolinda Barolini (1992), and Peter Hawkins (1999), among others.[2]

There are other areas in which Dantean paradoxes have triggered critical interest. The chasm between Dante's theory of poetics and his praxis has offered another field, on which a series of seminal contributions have recently focused, and my argument is no less indebted to them. In the field of poetics, Barolini's survey of Dante's tendentious narrative strategies in the *Commedia* (1992), Barański's series of contributions on the cultural background of Dante's meta-literary discourse (1995a, 2000, 2001), and Ascoli's painstaking exploration of the de-historicizing techniques Dante adopted to construct authority (1989, 1990, 1993, culminating in 2008) all have in common a critical auscultation of the text that does not take as final Dante's word about his poetry making. Rather, these studies systematically match what Dante declares with earlier and contemporary traditions by which Dante's work was shaped and with which it necessarily, if polemically, came into contact.[3] By moving past the conciliatory surface of Dante's texts and refusing to accept his attempt to de-contextualize his writing, these inquiries have opened up a line of research into which my work follows: there is something to be gained hermeneutically by focusing on the internal contradictions in Dante's thinking and on the incongruities across neighbouring projects or even neighbouring sections of the same work. As we know, Dante is not a systematically linear thinker – neither in matters of philosophy, nor in the matters that most closely relate to his *fare poesia*.

My survey of Dante's metapoetic thinking begins by assigning central relevance to the two major projects he undertook in the early years of his exile. The centrality of *Convivio* and *De vulgari eloquentia* is not merely chronological. They actually preserve the clearest traces of Dante's attempt to reflect on poetry: they are not just mid-career or mid-life texts; they represent his period of most sustained and most explicitly articulated meta-poetic thinking. Quite consistently, it is in these works that Dante treats for the first time several of the issues that are of interest here. Of course, the statements he made there were neither born in a vacuum nor definitive: when he reaches *Convivio* and *De vulgari eloquentia*, Dante's thinking about language, poetry, and interpretation already has a history, which I will sketch out in due course, by going back to the few self-reflexive paragraphs of *Vita nuova*; he will also continue thinking about the questions he addressed in the treatises – in some cases, as we will see, along alternative if not incompatible lines. As systematic, if unfinished and unpolished works, however, *Convivio* and *De vulgari eloquentia* brought to the fore some of the principles underlying Dante's reflection on his task as a poet.

Dante's thinking about poetry and his providing a theory for it appear to have an essentially defensive quality. It is perhaps not merely a rhetorical ploy that Dante, when he moved from writing lyrical poetry to engaging in his first experiment with a *prosimetrum*, phrased his first deployment of meta-critical language in the form of a response to an objection: *Vita nuova* 25 opens with the famous tag 'potrebbe qui dubitare persona degna da dichiararle ogne dubitatione' (At this point it may be that someone worthy of having every doubt cleared up could be puzzled; 25.1). And it is not surprising that the first reflection on poetry penned by Dante be phrased in such terms. Dante knows that the tradition he could count upon to justify his poetic enterprise was both new and grounded on a slim collection of texts, as he acknowledges in that chapter. Beyond its lack of positive authority, however, vernacular poetry had other problems: it had explicitly come under attack from a specific component in Dante's own culture. His theorizing and his choosing a specific terminology and a particular set of issues to be tackled is a response to the potential theoretical weakness of his practice. In particular, it appears to be informed by the debates on the value of poetry that had been articulated in the theological-philosophical camp. In discussions on the status and value of literature in Dante's age, a line of argument had been developed which indicted poetry from a strictly theological-philosophical standpoint. A convenient authoritative formulation of the issue may be found in an often-cited passage by Aquinas. In the ninth article of the first *quaestio* in his *Summa theologica*, devoted to the 'literary' features of Scripture, Aquinas incidentally notes that poetry is the least informative, least truthful of the arts. While discussing the limits and procedures for interpreting biblical texts, he states that 'Procedere autem per similitudines varias et repraesentationes, est proprium poeticae, quae est infima inter omnes doctrinas' (It is typical of poetry, which is the lowest among the sciences, to proceed by way of varied similes and descriptions; *ST* 1.1.9).[4] The charge, we should note, is not of small weight, since it targets the specific difference of (allegorical) poetry from ordinary discourse: its working with images and 'surrogates.' To this line of argument Dante responds in different ways at different stages of his career.

Having been branded as a mode of writing that made of the *alieniloquium* its distinctive element, poetry could be championed in two ways: either by arguing that under its appealing veil of fiction poetry did indeed contain a worthy core of philosophical truth, or bracketing the role of *similitudines* and *repraesentationes* (thus mounting a defence of the historical truthfulness of the narrative) and insisting that poetry was a direct representation of reality, a genre that could accommodate the relation of *res* to *res*. The former, in the case of classical authors (but not only), was the route most travelled – by Dante himself, as we will be able to observe, in his mid-career treatises; the latter he adopted for the *Commedia*. Some of the principles that Dante espouses in *Convivio* and *De vulgari eloquentia* may be read in light of this defensive move. As I will argue, Dante's definition of language as primarily designed to convey concepts, his predicating a disjunctive theory of content and style, his tendency to privilege prose over poetry, and his insistence on the authority of the author as originator and controller of meaning in poetic fiction, all are principles in tune with a philosophically bent defence of poetry. At a certain point, Dante apparently entertains the idea of accepting this field of discussion and defending his work with arguments that could be well received in the philosophical camp; his aligning with the positions of the philosophers, however, is not a permanent solution.[5] When he provides the *Commedia* with a theoretical framework (one inherent in the poem itself), Dante chooses the alternative strategy. With ammunition drawn from Augustine, as I will suggest, Dante increasingly draws closer to the side of the exegetes, producing a new kind of argument in defence of his own poetry. The first element to acquire new meaning in this new theoretical configuration is the claim to historical truth that the text of the *Commedia* repeatedly, though subtly, stakes out for itself.[6] The ensuing redefinition of the notion of *fictio*, which was central for both *Convivio* and *De vulgari eloquentia*, has some corollaries that extend to the basic components of poetic texts. Coming to balance Dante's former emphasis on the communicative aspects of language, the *Commedia* appears to go back to a theory that values its expressive and ethical qualities; in matters of style, the severing of content from form that the mid-career treatises established by leaning towards prose gives way, in the poem, to a search for a model in which 'beauty and goodness' could be intrinsically joined; in a coordinated move, to the author-centred hermeneutics, apparently privileged in *Convivio*, the *Commedia* now joins a new attention to the authority of the reader as interpreter and the poetics of inspiration for his text.

In the course of my argument, I will often bring back these notions which Dante explored and exploited in the *Commedia* to texts by Augustine: these ideas were of course not unique to Augustine, but they are conveniently available to us (as they were to Dante) in a small set of Augustinian texts which we know he knew and openly cited. Augustinian ideas, if not Augustine's own texts, helped Dante to counter the arguments against poetry that came from the Scholastic component of his culture; they were also inspirational in Dante's reassessment of Scripture's role in defining his poetics. The two processes go hand in hand. In the context of the *Commedia*, Dante's recuperation of the biblical model results from the interplay of the same factors we have just surveyed: his option in favour of the rhetorical rather than dialectical function of language (which de-emphasized the centrality of 'concepts' in language), his appreciation of biblical stylistics (in particular of its poetics), his renewed interest in a theory of meaning that valued the reader over the author (and, correspondingly, literal readings over allegorical ones), his insistence on the historical truth of narratives (to bridge, sometimes artificially, the gap between secular epic and Christian canon). Once again, all these factors have one element in common:

they all respond well to the accusations levelled against poetry in the philosophical camp because they defend poetry by association with the human component in Holy Writ. After having tried to have the linguistic, poetics, and hermeneutics designed to accompany his poetry be sensitive to the point of view of the 'philosophers' (and align itself with it), Dante tried a different way of responding to their critique of poetry: he instilled in his readers the notion that biblical writing could be considered a model for his own. This process, as this study will show, is both gradual and carefully conducted.

In evaluating Dante's progress in matters of linguistics, poetics, and hermeneutics, I use the platform of the 'minor,' more explicitly metapoetic works to look forward to Dante's *Commedia*; I do not do so, however, in teleological terms. The poetics of the *Commedia* are not the point of arrival – a logically necessary one – of Dante's itinerary; rather, in practical terms, they are a new response to the same questions that the pre-*Commedia* works had posed and attempted to answer. The poem's answers are neither better nor the necessary outcome of Dante's development. They are different answers. By looking at the 'minor' works in retrospect, I try to keep two aspects of their relation to the *Commedia* in mind: on the one hand, they are its necessary antecedent, in the sense that we understand better what the *Commedia* does in matters of poetics by looking at what they did (and at the consequences of what they did) in the same field; on the other hand, they are its peers – the poem's solutions, no matter how strongly it claims it has any, have no metaphysical advantage over the ones Dante entrusted to his earlier experiments. In sum, the solutions Dante offers in the poem are no less contingent answers to questions of poetics than were those advanced in the pre-*Commedia* works. If they have been treated otherwise, and if the temptation to imbue them with a sense of finality is always open, this is because Dante frames them in a more cogently authoritative and authoritarian mode.[7]

Having noted this, however, we need to be able to appreciate the fact that equality does not mean unanimity or identity of views: Dante's way of going about advocating and theoretically justifying his making poetry changes over time, and it does so, I maintain, because on some points the cure Dante envisages in his theory appeared to be worse than the illness. The solution that Dante prescribes in the pre-*Commedia* works is, in fact, not without problems, and if in the *Commedia* he advances solutions that are different from those of the treatises, there is a chance that he does so because of these problems. Theoretical crossroads in Dante's career do exist and they act sometimes as points of departure for diverging lines of thought. For instance, one would be ill advised to try to mend the almost complete break between the poetics of *De vulgari eloquentia*, in the fields of both linguistics (Book 1) and stylistics (Book 2), and Dante's linguistic and stylistic practices in the poem. The definition of the high style (the 'stilus tragicus' of *De vulgari eloquentia* 2.iv.5) as the only style to which the use of the illustrious vernacular is fitting, and the corresponding choice of precisely that style and that language in Dante's *canzoni*, can only with difficulty be brought into agreement with the stylistic theory of the *Commedia* and its practice. Both the theory sketched out in *Epistle* 13 and the declarations made in this direction by the poem function as a reminder that the poetics of *De vulgari eloquentia* cannot be brought into play in the poem straightforwardly.[8]

Another wide and profound gap seems to exist between the ideologically coherent block of the two treatises and the *Commedia* on the function of poetry and its troubled relationship with prose. The bulk of the poem's poetics is destined to appear as an absurd construction if judged with the yardstick of *De vulgari eloquentia* – just as the final stance Dante takes there cannot be used to illuminate his previous pronouncements. As readers of the poem have long recognized, the style of the *Commedia* is essentially and programmatically mixed;[9] poetry is only limitedly a *fictio*;[10] and the model of writing proposed for imitation is no longer the poetry of the *regulati poete*, but rather Scripture.[11] What is more, the role of the poet no longer coincides with the communication of a philosophical truth, but rather with the re-presentation of the unified order of nature and history in God. Dante's poetic praxis in the *Commedia* suggests that both the metapoetic statements he advanced in *Convivio* and *De vulgari eloquentia* and the model of poetry that these treatises defended have undergone a careful re-examination.[12] When measured with the prescriptive and proscriptive rule of the poetics laid out in *De vulgari eloquentia* and underwritten by *Convivio*, the *Commedia* appears as a text (and a project) that has gone astray. On the surface of the text, for instance, the linguistic colour (*patina*) of the poem does not shun pronounced regionalisms in the vernacular that it uses;[13] stylistically, the poem shows a systematic lowering of tone from the 'high style' of the tragic *canzoni* prescribed in the treatise to the 'mediocre style' (with notable incursions into the 'lowest');[14] more generally, in the place that the poem chooses for itself in the system of literary genres, the *Commedia* revises what *De vulgari eloquentia* had prescribed and *Convivio* most explicitly attempted. As I will propose at several junctures in my argument, there are additional issues that divide the theory of poetry that Dante advanced in the treatises and the praxis of his poem – further crucial and similarly technical choices that Dante, the poet turned self-critic, made as he decided to turn (or circle back) to the practice of self-sufficient (i.e., 'prose-less') poetry once more. One of the goals of my work is to point out these elements of discontinuity and suggest a possible set of reasons for their existence.

In exploring Dante's poetics, the cultural roots of his thought, and the ultimate consequences of his reasoning, this book reviews some key notions in Dante's defence of (his) poetry and classicism and provides a rationale for the choices of poetics that he made in his poem – a set of strategic and often polemical decisions that shaped the poetry of the *Commedia*. In chronological (but not, as noted, teleological) perspective, my work brings into focus Dante's thinking about his task as poet at various stages in his career and proposes to see it as based on an intermittently polemical, but never abandoned, dialogue with Augustine. In Augustine's theories, Dante found both confirmation for some of the principles he had adopted in his reflection on literature and invitations to rethink some of them. These alternative strands deserve to be dissected, but before that, one should confront directly the philological question of Augustine's influence on Dante.

As the central chapters argue in detail (chapters 2, 3), Dante's revision of his poetics took place during his post-exilic experiments with prose, and passed through a reactivation of Augustinian principles. Of course, the coincidence of some basic arguments that Augustine develops in *De doctrina christiana* with solutions that Dante gives in the *Commedia* to several questions of poetics and hermeneutics can be read in a 'weak' or in a 'strong' way. In the weak sense, the similarities appear as a purely 'coincidental' convergence between Dante's developing poetics and Augustine's philosophical investigation, both insisting on the same set of problems and situating themselves at the confluence of the same traditions of classical and biblical writing. From a philological point of view, Paul Zumthor was probably right in noting that, in medieval textual culture, works are 'hardly claiming for themselves the status of individuality.'[15] Augustine's hermeneutic model could thus be similar to Dante's simply on account of Dante's independent 'discovery' of the biblical stylistic and hermeneutic model for the *Commedia*. Dante's reflection on linguistics, poetics, and hermeneutics could, in sum, have been triggered and guided more by widespread discussions on the same questions that were, so to speak, in the air than by one central text. This is a possibility, and my insistence on Augustine as a specific model might result in a doubly unfaithful account of both Dante's personal wide-reaching reading habits and of the multi-focal dynamics of his culture.

However, there are some essential philological data that point to Dante's receptive reading of Augustine's *De doctrina christiana*. We know that Dante cites Augustine's work. The dating of his reading is, of course, tricky, but a convincing attempt at achieving chronological precision has been recently made by Barański. The *terminus ante quem* for Dante's knowledge of and engagement with Augustine's treatise is certain: Dante quotes *De doctrina christiana* in *Monarchia* 3.iv.6 ('circa sensum mysticum dupliciter errare contigit' [one can make two kinds of error when dealing with the mystical sense]), and the whole argument in the paragraph depends on Augustine's discussion of biblical semantics (see chapter 3). The *terminus post quem* poses a more delicate problem: in *Convivio* 1.xii.1 Dante's discussion of the relationship between natural signs and the things they signify appears to be unaware of Augustine's terminology. Dante takes fire and flames as examples of univocal and natural signs ('Se manifestamente per le finestre d'una casa uscisse *fiamma di fuoco*, e alcuno dimandasse *se là dentro fosse il fuoco* …'), while Augustine used for the same relationship smoke and flames (2.i.2: 'Naturalia [signa] sunt quae sine voluntate atque ullo appetitu significandi praeter se aliquid aliud ex se cognosci faciunt, sicuti est *fumus significans ignem*'). What makes this example particularly interesting is that Dante appears to have changed his focus and come closer to Augustine in *Purgatorio* 33.97–9, when he writes, *in persona Beatricis*, '*E se dal fummo foco s'argomenta,* / codesta obblivïon chiaro conchiude / colpa ne la tua voglia altrove intenta.'[16] An argument can be made that this last passage, on account of its lexical proximity to *De doctrina christiana*, marks the true earliest *terminus ante quem* for Dante's reading. Augustine's text is either unknown or, at least, dormant in Dante's mid-career treatises, but it is 'discovered' or, at least, deemed again worthy to be used as an authority in the years of the *Commedia*.[17]

There are additional, larger contextual considerations that seem to point to Dante's engaged reading of *De doctrina christiana*; however, beyond establishing whether Dante read Augustine's treatise or not, and picking a point in his career when this reading may have taken place, I suggest that a precise set of problems and notions that intermittently reach the surface of Dante's thought can indeed be found in Augustinian texts. Even if he did not get them from Augustine, Dante could hardly be unaware that notions such as those outlined above were Augustinian in origin or, at least, that they were Augustinian in quality. Put in another way, *De doctrina christiana* might not be the source of some of Dante's choices in matters of linguistics, poetics, and hermeneutics, but the formulations that we can find in that text often represent a clear and fitting parallel to illuminate the cultural implications of those choices. Postulating an encounter with Augustine may, thus, be only one among many solutions to the problem of determining Dante's points of reference, but it certainly figures among the most economical ones.

By illuminating its Augustinian background, this book attempts to measure the impact that Dante's constantly moving reflection on linguistics, poetics, and hermeneutics had on his praxis as a poet. Chapter 1 focuses on Dante's constant interrogation of the conceptual nature of poetic language and proposes to evaluate his alternative stressing of the semiotic and expressive sides of communication in the context of Augustine's complex reflection on language acquisition, as it was developed in the *Confessions* and taken up again in *De doctrina christiana*. After having established the centrality of the definition of language as conceptual in the mid-career treatises, my argument moves on to trace the roots of the redefined role Dante assigns to 'concepts' in his poem and contrasts it with the theories advanced in both *Convivio* and *De vulgari eloquentia*. Whereas in the pre-*Commedia* treatises Dante assigned to language the task of conveying the writer's concepts (and adds that language is to do so, in spite of the obscurities that poetic form has added), the poem progressively marginalizes and eventually transcends this crucial notion. The notion Dante eventually embraced in the *Commedia* – namely, that in poetry language is not designed solely to transmit concepts – may not be exclusively Augustinian, but it certainly is attuned to his linguistics. Several instances in the poem suggest that Dante rethought the theoretical parameters defining language and came closer to Augustine's inclusive definition. In the context of several of the poem's invocations, Dante speaks of concepts in a new way, suggesting that the concepts that his poem is communicating either are perceived (through experience) or received (through poetic inspiration), not autonomously 'conceived' in the mind of the author. What is more, coming again into contact with Augustine, he also often pairs the linguistic concept with a different kind of 'conception' – incarnation. One of the consequences of the 'new' linguistics explored in the *Commedia* is that the conceptual mediation between the reality that the protagonist experiences (and the author purports to relate) and the stylistically elaborate words that make up the fabric of the text is systematically downplayed. Dante's redefinition of a keyword in his linguistics is matched by an adjustment in the poetics of the poem. For the linguistics and the poetics of the *Commedia* poetry is no longer a distracting and distorting veil for truth but the only suitable vehicle for it.

Following a similar strategy of argumentation, chapter 2 focuses on Dante's appreciation of the stylistic quality of biblical writing and compares it to Augustine's mapping of his initial struggle with and final embracing of the anti-classical style of Scripture. Dante's poetics follow apparently the same trajectory. His qualified reliance on biblical models, which is practised in the *Commedia*, is not native to his poetics. In *Convivio*, both his theory and his practice as vernacular writer were indifferent to the poetic potential of the Holy Writ. Such a reorientation in matters of stylistics also involved a revaluation of earlier statements Dante had made about the sweetness of biblical poetry. Moving from a subtle reference to *Convivio* 1.vii.14–16 (a passage discussing the effects of translation on the 'verses of the Psalter') that may be read in *Inferno* 31, and touching upon several passages (mostly meta-poetic addresses to the reader) in which psalms are by implication labelled as 'sweet,' my argument registers Dante's changing position on this point. The poetics of the *Commedia* return to and revise Dante's earlier dismissal of biblical stylistics, moving the poetics of the poem towards acknowledging the aesthetic quality of the psalms: the potential sweetness of biblical poetry, which *Convivio* deemed as lost in translation, is fully active in the *Commedia*.

As can be reconstructed from his autobiographical and theoretical works, Augustine's intellectual trajectory, which moved from a preconversional and deeply classicizing refusal of Scripture's stylistics to advocating and promoting the 'different rhetoric' of Christianity, provides us with a precedent that may illuminate what was at stake when Dante returned to thinking about translation and reached different conclusions from his mid-career treatises. Augustine's proposal of a 'different rhetoric' for biblical writing may have had an impact on the author of the *Commedia*. Resting on the indissoluble connection between the text's outward aspect and both the moral stance of its author and its revolutionary, deeply paradoxical content, Augustine's theory of Christian eloquence came to undermine the idea that content and ornamentation (both rhetorical and allegorical) were separable – in Dante's terms, that *verba* and *sententia* are only *discretive mixta* (that is, mixed without dissolving into one another, as *De vulgari eloquentia* 2.i.10 and *Convivio* 1.x.12 put it).[18] If Dante was looking for a theoretical model of poetry alternative to the one he advanced in his pre-*Commedia* works, he could find it adumbrated in Augustine's prose.

When Dante abandoned his programmatic indifference towards the poetic potential of Scripture, he also opened a larger trend in his poetics. His rediscovery of biblical writing as an essentially poetic artefact had two consequences, both of which may again be shown to be in tune with Augustine's own meditations on the same points. Dante's rethinking of biblical stylistics produced a shift in the relationship he established with his classical Latin models. What in the pre-*Commedia* works could be described as a rapport of emulation is turned by the poem into a clear, repeated statement of the intrinsic superiority of the new, comic, Christian poetic experiment over the old, tragic, and pre-Christian tradition of poetry.[19] The poem registers and fosters, in other words, Dante's detachment from the idea of the viability of importing 'tragedy' into vernacular poetry, his negotiation of what Harold Bloom called the 'anxiety of influence' with the classics.[20] Second, Dante's re-evaluation of biblical poetry also allowed him to model his new project on a poetics of inspiration that thus far had been the essential patrimony of scriptural poetics and hermeneutics.[21]

With the final step in my argument (developed in chapter 3), I move into the exploration of the interdependence of Dante's poetics and hermeneutics, again in an Augustinian light. Here too a chronological survey of Dante's ideas on how to read a poetic text and how to compose one shows that his pre-*Commedia* tenets may only limitedly be taken as a guide to his treatment of the same questions in the poem. My focus is on the episode of Statius's active misreading of Virgil's texts at the centre of *Purgatorio* 22, and I suggest that the principles of hermeneutics Dante espoused in his minor works cannot in any way account for Statius's creative reading of Virgil's works. Even a rapid survey of the many instances in which Dante prescribes a reading method for his poems shows that no text by Dante before the *Commedia* ever supported the related notions that Dante advances using Statius as his intermediary. That meaning can be divorced from the intention of the author and that it should be brought back to a different agency is something that only the poem implicitly accepts. Dante's vernacular *prosimetra*, notwithstanding the many differences between them, had both been designed to promote the authority of the author, and they had done so by isolating authorial intention as the only meaning that readers ought to retrieve from his poems. On the contrary, Statius surprisingly claims that he had found a salvific meaning in two passages from Virgil's *Aeneid* 3 and *Eclogues* 4 that had remained unknown to their author.

The hermeneutic model presented in Statius's episode is unprecedented in Dante's pre-*Commedia* works. It had, however, some currency in the critical discourse of his time: Augustine's *De doctrina christiana* contained all the elements of the model Dante adopted in the *Commedia*. Although focused on the interpretation of Scripture, Augustine's treatise is a pertinent antecedent for the new hermeneutics appearing in action in the *Commedia*. Both texts share a basic principle: the *regula caritatis*, the principle according to which any interpretation of Scripture, in order to be correct, must construct the double love for God and one's neighbour. In the Statius episode, Dante's reliance on Augustine's hermeneutic theory as applied to pre-Christian texts allowed him to propose a new 'writerly' approach to reading in his work.[22]

The reading method advocated in the *Commedia* impacts the poetics of the poem too. By granting the works of pre-Christian authors, on account of their openness to interpretation, a *rhetorical* status equivalent to that of Scripture, Dante, by implication, allows the text of his vernacular poem to be considered as partaking in the potentially salvific action of Scripture, thanks to its rhetorical equivalence with certain pagan texts, and with the method of interpretation that Dante invites his readers to deploy there.[23] The Statius episode suggests, in other words, that the radical and drastic change of perspective we witness in the author of the *Commedia* on matters of interpretation is part of a larger strategy of promotion of his work as a poet which involves another change. By relying on Augustine's sense of Scripture as a collaborative work of human and divine authors, Dante could claim for his poem the ambitious status of a divinely inspired work of art. The text of Dante's *Monarchia* insists on the very passage in *De doctrina christiana* in which Augustine granted legitimacy to a constructive hermeneutic approach. Augustine uses for the inspired nature of the Scriptures the same lexicon that was and will be deployed in two key metapoetic sections of the *Commedia* (respectively *Purgatorio* 24.52–4 and *Paradiso* 10.26–7). Through this chain of references Dante conveys a sense of his poem that is related to the active hermeneutic Statius practises *en abîme* on Virgil (a pagan text), but betters it on the basis of the inspirational (Christian) poetics developed in the second and third *cantiche*. Framed in Augustinian terms and treated as a corollary of his hermeneutic principles, Dante's vindication of a poetics of the Spirit for his poem may also have been more easily accepted by his readers. By evoking Augustine's treatment of hermeneutic questions, Dante could defuse, at least in part, the potential for heresy contained in the idea that his texts did not derive their authority from their author, but from their potential to point to something beyond themselves. As rhetorical artefacts, they allude to the ultimate reality of Being; metaphysically, they foreshadow it.[24]

My book will end with three readings of passages from the *Commedia*, in which Augustine's presence can be most distinctively felt. They are all moments in which Dante balances his adherence to Augustinian principles with moments of qualified scepticism. They each come from one of the three *cantiche* and are all centred on Virgil – perhaps the most difficult element in Augustine's negotiation of his own classicism. They deal with three points of Virgilian tangency with Dante's text in three areas in which Dante's dissent from Augustine was perhaps most acute: Cato and the historical-political role to be assigned to the Roman Empire in a poem, Dido and the role that erotics play in the development of ethical poetry, and Aeneas and the status of the souls in the afterlife (an exquisitely theological point about the resurrected body). In all these cases, I will argue, Dante will not have to circumvent or abandon Augustine's authority: if Augustine the polemicist had consistently attacked Virgil, his poetry, and the culture it stood for, most memorably in his *Confessiones* and *De civitate Dei*, he had also opened the way, in *De doctrina christiana*, to a mediated reclamation of classical knowledge.

In reviewing the moments of open and allusive treatment of Cato's character in the *Commedia*, I will focus on one crucial interaction, the nexus between Pier della Vigna's apology and Augustine's polemical take on Rome's pseudo-martyr 'virtuous suicides.' By engaging Augustine's anti-classical polemic through allusion and open treatment (linking, that is, *Inferno* 13 and *Purgatorio* 1), Dante enters into a dialectical dialogue with Augustine on the role of Rome in providential history. Beyond the local consequences it may have for our reading of individual figures in the poem, a reconsideration of Cato's surprising, if allusive, appearance in the intertextual filigree of *Inferno* 13 may serve as an entry point into the broader problem of Dante's dissent from the main polemical thrust of Augustine's indictment of all things Roman. Addressing Dante's disagreement with Augustine on matters of history does not constitute a digression in a book that explores the evolution of

Dante's poetics. In tackling, by way of Virgil, the most un-Augustinian theme of the Empire and accepting its internal contradictions, Dante is able to dissolve Augustine's ostracizing of imperial Rome and reabsorb the Roman Empire into a providential plan. His response is, as I will insist, not merely political, but poetic as well. Together with the Rome that Augustine had attacked in *De civitate Dei*, Dante defends the semiotic productivity of Virgil's texts, the poetry in which Rome's providential mission was made manifest.

Similarly, when I look at the heightened density of Virgilian allusions and explicit citations that marks *Purgatorio* 30, the point at which the poem bids farewell to the character of Virgil, I propose to use again an Augustinian lens to evaluate this phenomenon. I focus on Beatrice's first words to Dante, which contain both the only mention of his name in the poem and a threefold invitation not to cry (*Purgatorio* 30.55–7). In these lines, in addition to the Virgilian and Ovidian passages usually associated with them, I propose to see also the trace of a climactic passage from Augustine's *Confessions* (1.xiii.21), which contains Augustine's famous indictment of Virgil's poem as a distraction from the Christian imperative of self-knowledge. Two elements make the *Confessions* text a pertinent target of allusion for Dante's lines: it is not surprising to find an echo of Augustine in a context that, like *Purgatorio* XXX, entails the protagonist's and author's confessional self-naming, nor it is strange that a passage in which Augustine focuses on the pathos of Dido's trials may be called to balance the clearest re-citation in the poem of Dido's most famous line 'agnosco veteris vestigia flammae': 'conosco i segni de l'antica fiamma' (ibid., 48). Beatrice's allusively Augustinian reprimand follows up on Dante's tendentious translation of Virgil's *vestigia* with the technically Augustinian *segni* and balances it. By evoking, in the short span of two tercets, two different sides of Augustine's attitude towards Virgil, Dante forces them to collide. Having learned from Augustine how to deploy a more articulated and effective strategy of reading, one that could accommodate a salvific betraying of the original's intentions, Dante now corrects the stern poses of his teacher.

Finally, in *Paradiso* 31, by exploring the theme of resurrection of the flesh and describing the initial appearance of the souls and angels in the Empyrean as a swarm of bees, Dante comes back to a passage from *Aeneid* 6 that contains both the theme of reincarnation and the bee simile. At first sight, Dante's passage apparently resonates with the traditional and negative patristic interpretation, which blamed Virgil's text both for having included in his poem a treatment of reincarnation (a smacking 'pagan' move) and for having attributed to Aeneas an astounded, uncomprehending response in front of the souls' desire to go back to their bodies: *unde tam dira cupido?* (Whence such a cruel desire?). The passage, which had been cited by Augustine in a similar anti-Manichaean context in *De civitate Dei*, however, contains more than just an occasion to indict Virgil's authorial inability to grasp the 'real' meaning of his poetic treatment of reincarnation. It is true, as has been noted, that Dante's evocation of the *Aeneid* is here contrastive, with Virgil being cast in the 'tragic' light of an unwitting and blind prophet. It is also true, however, that in combining a theological point with a simile, one of the most technically poetic features distinctive of the epic genre, Dante also redresses the balance of his theological poetry, by suggesting that the state of the resurrected souls is a theme that poetry may treat with authority, one that perhaps only poetry, by the force of its similes (and metaphorical reasoning), may address to the fullest extent. By showing that poetry, insofar as it proceeds by similes and representations, has the potential to tell the truth about Being and move beyond appearances – in short, to cross into metaphysics – he is able to suggest how limiting was the philosophers' intransigent (and his own momentary) scepticism about the specific powers of poetic texts. By showing that the language of poetry may represent reality as it is Dante recognizes how ill advised had been also his attempt to subject it to the strictures of prosaic rationality.

Taken together, these three readings constitute a continuation and a response to traditional approaches to Augustine's influence on Dante. While, with few exceptions, exegetical work targeting Augustinian intertexts in Dante has focused on the 'textual meaning' that is produced when Augustinian material is indirectly evoked or immediately cited in the *Commedia*, my readings focus on the 'meta-poetic significance' of Dante's dialogue with Augustine for the poet's own investigations on the nature and use of language, poetry, and interpretation. This difference may appear slight, but it is essential. My readings are intended as a continuation of the theoretical work of the preceding chapters: though textually oriented, they still focus on Dante's *ideas* on the making of poetry, rather than on the poetry itself; they relate to Dante's *processes*, rather than to his achievements; they point to areas of his poem in which poetry *harks back* to its reasons for being (and to its own making as a poem), rather than proceed boldly with the exploration of the imagined afterlife. They are, in sum, devoted to an exploration of the poetics of a 'prose-free' poem.

1 Linguistics

> Wovon man nicht sprechen kann, darüber muß man schweigen.
> L. Wittgenstein, *Tractatus Logico-Philosophicus*, prop. 7

1. Cum ipsi appellabant rem aliquam et cum secundum eam vocem corpus ad aliquid movebant, videbam, et tenebam hoc ab eis vocari rem illam, quod sonabant, cum eam vellent ostendere. Hoc autem eos velle ex motu corporis aperiebatur tamquam verbis naturalibus omnium gentium, quae fiunt vultu et nutu oculorum ceteroque membrorum actu et sonitu vocis indicante affectionem animi in petendis, habendis, reiciendis fugiendisve rebus. Ita verba in variis sententiis locis suis posita et crebro audita quarum rerum signa essent paulatim colligebam measque iam voluntates edomito in eis signis ore per haec enuntiabam.

When they [my elders] named some object, and accordingly moved towards something, I saw this and I grasped that the thing was called by the sound they uttered when they meant to point it out. Their intention was shown by their bodily movements, as it were the natural language of all peoples; the expression of the face, the play of the eyes, the movement of other parts of the body, and the tone of the voice which expresses our state of mind in seeking, having, rejecting, or avoiding something. Thus, as I heard words repeatedly used in their proper places in various sentences, I gradually learnt to understand what objects they signified; and after I had trained my mouth to form these signs, I used them to express my own desires.

Augustine, Confessions 1.8

1. These words, it seems to me, give us a particular picture of the essence

of human language. It is this: the individual words in language name objects – sentences are combinations of such names. – In this picture of language we find the roots of the following idea: Every word has a meaning. The meaning is correlated with the word. It is the object for which the word stands.

2. That philosophical concept of meaning has its place in a primitive idea of the way language functions. But one can also say that it is the idea of a language more primitive than ours ...

3. Augustine, we might say, does describe a system of communication; only not everything that we call language is this system. And one has to say this in many cases where the question arises 'Is this an appropriate description or not?' The answer is: 'Yes, it is appropriate, but only for this narrowly circumscribed region, not for the whole of what you were claiming to describe.'

L. Wittgenstein, *Philosophical Investigations* 1.1–3

In this passage on the mechanics of language learning, Wittgenstein isolates the basic elements of a philosophy of language that he places, in his thinly veiled polemic, under the sign of Augustine. In his reading, the core of this outlook on language is that 'Every word has a meaning. The meaning is correlated with the word. It is the object for which the word stands.' This three-member definition of language forms the core of a logical neo-positivist approach to language, which becomes the object of much of Wittgenstein's three-pronged philosophical critique: things, meanings, and words (nature, intellect, and language) are placed in a relationship of mutual correspondence; they are said to mirror one another.

Wittgenstein's reading was designed to introduce a meditation on language that would break the system of correspondences so neatly organized by the generation of philosophers preceding him; hence the selective partiality in its treatment of Augustine's account.[1] Instrumental to his advancing a new, problematized, and potentially self-critical understanding of how language is learned and how it actually works, Wittgenstein's reading focuses on what feels most 'natural' (i.e., philosophically 'traditional') in Augustine's account. In so doing, however, it turns Augustine's thought into something more monolithic than it actually is. In particular, Wittgenstein downplays the simultaneous presence of two equally essential points of view in Augustine's recollection and reconstruction of his own experience in language apprehension.

The crucial element to which Wittgenstein's commentary apparently devotes no attention is the balance achieved in Augustine's passage between the expressive and semiotic elements in language. The full context from which Wittgenstein excerpts makes clear that together with 'words,' the building blocks of rational (adult) language, Augustine considered essential to language also non-linguistic acts – the expressions (e.g., those issuing from the body). He calls these acts that always accompany language 'verba naturalia omnium gentium' (almost natural words [common] to all languages), and he presents them as the necessary operators in communication: without them – that is, without something like a universal system for encoding the motions of the soul – pure semantic language would simply be impossible, or worse, useless. There would be no point in knowing the 'name' for each object on earth, were there not a system to understand and communicate what the relation between this object and the speaker might be.

By insisting on the role that volitional indicators play in language acquisition, Augustine opens up a doubly ethical dimension in language, which Wittgenstein elides. On the one hand, Augustine insists that will is the engine of communication. The word *velle* and its derivatives recur often in the passage, standing for the subject's own will to communicate, to be understood, which does not mean only 'conceptually' understood but, more essentially, 'practically' answered. In Augustine's account, language is the result of a primal impulse, one which aims not so much at the description of reality but at its modification. Communication is born from this need. On the other hand, Augustine stresses the strict interconnection of learning and an ethically inflected use of language. Learning to decipher as well as to encode meaning into language is functional for the articulation of a system of basic ethical dichotomies: the speakers from whom Augustine learns to speak 'seek, possess, reject, or avoid' the things that they name. Language is, in other words, ethical because it refuses to do away with the non-linguistic indicators that accompany every word its speakers utter, which in turn classify reality according to the traditional (Stoic) fourfold ethical system of the passions: desire, pleasure, pain, and fear. In Augustine's Latin, the fourfold option 'petere, habere, reiciere, fugere' mobilizes loaded ethical terms.[2]

In sum, by concentrating on the 'what' and 'how' of language, Wittgenstein's (counter-)commentary to Augustine bypasses its equally important 'why.' In order to focus on the risk that modern thinkers will be seduced by and eventually remain entangled in Augustine's rudimentary outline of language as semiosis, he chooses to de-emphasize the complexity of Augustine's picture of what it means to learn how to speak.³ In the following pages I will address Dante's changing position on the nature and use of language, as this emerges from his texts at three stages in his career. As we shall see, Dante will at different moments behave just as Wittgenstein did – choosing to emphasize one side of Augustine's account of language acquisition over another. In his mid-career treatises, as Wittgenstein did in the passage quoted above, Dante decided to present language as mainly a matter of conceptual communication, of semiosis. And, just as Wittgenstein did so with a self-correcting agenda, so too did Dante: in the prose treatises he revised and reversed intuitions he had had (and principles he had abided by) in *Vita nuova*, a work in which language had been introduced as a means of expression together with (or, better, rather than) rational communication. Correspondingly, having reached a new stage in his career with the *Commedia*, Dante again chose to emphasize the side of Augustine's treatment of language that values volition and ethics over communication and dialectics, and in so doing redefined the principles guiding his activity as a poet.

1.1 The Nature of Language and the Common Project of *Convivio* and *De vulgari eloquentia*: *Enucleare aliis conceptum*

The earliest attestations of Dante's interest in formulating a theory of language are found in his mid-career treatises. For their stance on the issue these two can be taken as a coherent block. The first time that Dante tackled with systematic attention the intertwined issues of linguistics, poetics, and hermeneutics was when he worked through the arguments of *Convivio* and *De vulgari eloquentia*. For a series of both ideological and chronological reasons the two treatises can be shown to run in an almost perfectly parallel direction. They tackle similar, if not identical, problems and, what is more, to the problems they raise, they offer the same solutions.⁴ They can be taken, in short, as representative of the same phase in Dante's thinking about his task as a poet. In spite of the difference in the ranking they apparently give to Latin (*gramatica*) and the vernacular (for which see below), *Convivio* and *De vulgari eloquentia* share the same understanding of the nature and goal of language, the same attention to situating the activity of literary figures of the recent and distant past in their socio-political context, and finally the same cultural milieu from which they both set forth and which they ultimately aim to address.

These similarities exist in spite of the blatant and much discussed contradiction between Dante's pronouncement in *Convivio* 1 and *De vulgari eloquentia* 1, when he defines the relative status of 'nobility' of Latin and the vernacular. A survey of the issues raised by this contradiction will serve to reveal several features of the image of language that both treatises together create. As is well known, the treatises offer two radically divergent assessments of the languages in which they are not written. *Convivio* 1.v.7 defends Latin's worth: '(Lo latino) non era subietto ma sovrano, e per la sua nobiltà e per vertù e per bellezza' ([Latin] would not have been subject but sovereign, because of its nobility, its virtue, and its beauty); whereas *De vulgari eloquentia* 1.i.4 trenchantly declares: 'Nobilior est vulgaris' (The more noble is the vernacular).[5] *Convivio* and *De vulgari eloquentia* indicate in a similar manner the basic features that oppose vernacular and grammatical languages. In Dante's thought, the vernacular and *gramatica* consistently possess different abilities to withstand the passing of time; they are apprehended in different ways; they differ in their geographic articulation; they display a different relationship with other cultural languages (both with grammatical ones and with others only 'capable of being grammaticized').

The order in which they arose is also an axiological order, determining the relative worth of *gramatica* and vernacular languages:

> Hinc [the ever-changing nature of human language through time] moti sunt inventores gramatice facultatis: que quidem gramatica nichil aliud est quam quedam inalterabilis locutionis ydemptitas diversis temporibus atque locis. (*De vulgari eloquentia* 1.ix.11)[6]

> This was the point from which the inventors of the art of grammar began; for their *gramatica* is nothing less than a certain immutable identity of language in different times and places.

In Dante's way of thinking, vernaculars are superior to grammatical languages on account of both the chronology and the logic of their creation. Any grammatical language, whether Latin or Greek or Hebrew, comes later than and is positioned below the vernaculars, the 'fall' of which it is designed to counter.[7] On the timeline, grammatical languages come after Babel and are no less the by-product of Babel's fragmentation of language than the vernaculars. In addition, artificial languages have been devised to supplement natural idioms, and not in any way to replace them. They are artificial tools, prosthetic limbs designed to carry out a function that natural languages can no longer perform. Their remedial and supplementary nature also establishes their rank. Both in the phylogenetic mechanics of their fabrication and in the ontogenetic modalities of their apprehension, the various grammars display their character of technical artefacts. Thus, the greatest shortcoming of *gramatica* is that it can neither replace the vernaculars it supplements, nor is there any possibility of it existing independently from them; what is more, it does not have any reason to exist independently from them.

De vulgari eloquentia is particularly direct about the double phylo- and ontogenetic secondariness of *gramatica*. Latin is constructed with the building blocks of the Romance languages, mainly with those of the *vulgare Latium* (Italian). However surprising this reversed genealogy might be for modern readers, Dante is clear in asserting the notion. 'Gramatice positores inveniuntur accepisse "sic" adverbium affirmandi: quod quandam anterioritatem erogare videtur Ytalis, qui "sì" dicunt' (Those who devised the rules of *gramatica* are known to have chosen the word *sic* as an adverb of affirmation: and this fact would seem to confer a certain pre-eminence on the Italians, who say *sì*; *De vulgari eloquentia* 1.x.1). The present argument in favour of the Italian vernacular is in itself rather weak; Italian is somewhat superior to the other Romance languages because the way Italians say 'yes' has been taken as the *adverbium affirmandi* in Latin. While it is essentially circular – after all, it is only Dante who makes the word for 'yes' such a central element to a definition of individual idioms – Dante's argument is also extremely telling. Logic dictates that, if the *gramatice positores* have chosen *sic* as an affirmative particle privileging the Italian *sì* over the available *oc* and *oïl*, it follows that the Italian word *sì* was there before the Latin *sic*. From Dante's statement, in other words, only one inference is possible – that the process of formation of grammatical languages has moved from the fully formed Romance 'triad' to its artificial distillation, Latin.[8]

On the level of linguistic ontogenesis the two treatises align with one another as well. When it comes to how languages are learned, *Convivio* and *De vulgari eloquentia* outline the same method. Latin is secondary to the vernacular because it is acquired through a schooling process that relies on the natural, 'primary,' and nobler vernacular. The relevant *loci paralleli* in the two works mutually reinforce their respective claims:

> Questo mio volgare fu introduttore di me ne la via di scienza, che è ultima

perfezione, *in quanto con esso io entrai ne lo latino e con esso mi fu mostrato:* lo quale latino poi mi fu via a più innanzi andare. (*Convivio* 1.xiii.5)

This vernacular of mine was what led me into the path of knowledge which is our ultimate perfection, *since through it I entered upon Latin and through its agency Latin was taught to me*, which then became my path to further progress.⁹

What in *Convivio* is an argument based on Dante's individual experience becomes in *De vulgari eloquentia* a general principle. The stress of the Latin treatise is on the common progression in time from the immediate, natural vernacular we learn from our maternal proxy (the wet nurse) to the secondary, artificial, and paternal language of intellectual communication:

Vulgarem locutionem asserimus quam sine omni regula nutricem imitantes accipimus. Est et inde alia locutio secundaria nobis [...] Ad habitum vero huius pauci perveniunt, quia non nisi per spatium temporis et studii assiduitatem regulamur et doctrinamur in illa. (*De vulgari eloquentia* 1.i.3)

I declare that vernacular language is that which we learn without any formal instruction, by imitating our nurses. There also exists another kind of language [...] Few, however, achieve complete fluency in it, since knowledge of its rules and theory can only be developed through dedication to a lengthy course of study.[10]

In short, even though *Convivio* and *De vulgari eloquentia* contain a paradox in their initial arguments, this contradiction does not affect the main trajectory of their coordinated arguments.

A further element reinforces the sense of proximity that is derived from a parallel reading of the two works: the definition of language that Dante gives in them is not only perfectly compatible, but almost the result of a literal translation. Before even starting to treat individual idioms and their respective ranking, *Convivio* and *De vulgari eloquentia* agree in endorsing the same philosophy of language. They share the same functional definition of what it means to speak and assign to this activity the same object and the same goals. Both works treat language as the most human of human characteristics, the vehicle for the social manifestation of mental realities, and the means of rational exchange by way of material signs. The last feature of this definition – as a sign of

Dante's commitment to a specific philosophical conception of language – eventually proves to be the most problematic as well.[11]

The two parallel definitions of language in the treatises are actually the same. In *Convivio*, in the context of the instrumental assertion of Latin's greater nobility and virtue, Dante notes:

> Così lo sermone, lo quale è ordinato a *manifestare lo concetto umano*, è virtuoso quando quello fa, e più virtuoso quello che più lo fa. (1.v.12, emphasis added)

> Thus language, which is constituted to *convey human thought*, is virtuous when it does this, and the more completely it does this, the more virtuous it is.[12]

The same concept is repeated in the conclusion of the syllogism:

> Onde, con ciò sia cosa che lo latino *molte cose manifesta concepute ne la mente* che lo volgare far non può ... più è la vertù sua che quella del volgare. (ibid.)

> Therefore, since Latin *conveys many things conceived in the mind* which the vernacular cannot ... its virtue is greater than that of the vernacular.

Again, still in a crucial programmatic passage justifying the project of *Convivio*, Dante returns to the same terms, *manifestare* and *concetto*, the keywords of his definition:

> E noi vedemo che in ciascuna cosa di sermone *lo bene manifestare del concetto* sì è più amato e commendato: dunque questa è la prima sua bontade. (1.xii.13)

> Now we see that in all things relating to speech *the apt conveyance of thought* is most loved and praised: therefore this is its prime goodness.[13]

Moving to the Latin treatise, we find Dante taking up the exact same notion, with the same vocabulary, insisting that

> Si etenim perspicaciter consideramus quid cum loquimur intendamus, patet quod *nichil aliud quam nostre mentis enucleare conceptum*. (*De vulgari eloquentia* 1.ii.3)

Now, if we wish to define with precision what our intention is when we speak, it is clearly *nothing other than to expound to others the concepts formed in our minds.*[14]

These definitions of language per se are perfectly parallel and they reverberate in both works. *Convivio* returns to the definition at 1.x.12, when it states that 'by means of this commentary the great goodness of the vernacular of *sì* will be seen, because its virtue will be made evident, namely how 'it conveys the loftiest and the most unusual conceptions almost as aptly, fully, and gracefully as Latin.'[15] Similarly, *De vulgari eloquentia* also comes back to the definition of language as the means for the rational communication of concepts, arguing that 'language is nothing other than *the vehicle indispensable to our thinking*' (2.i.8).[16]

We will return to these parallel passages more than once in the course of this book, approaching them from different perspectives and illuminating the various implications they have for Dante's linguistics and poetics. What is of interest here is the place that Dante's concurrent definitions of language occupy both in his career and in the cultural horizon of his time. The apparently neutral and balanced definition of language reviewed above has one corollary, which derives from the object – the 'what,' if you will – of human speech. By focusing on the power of language to manifest concepts, Dante's definition limits language to being a tool for transmitting mental contents – rational ideas – to other human beings. In the treatises, in other words, language is presented as primarily, if not exclusively, a matter of semiosis.[17] The point is not inconsequential and it actually helps to see the coordinates of Dante's thinking as he was composing *Convivio* and *De vulgari eloquentia*. The definition he gives in the treatises is neither intuitive nor to be taken for granted; rather, it points in a specific cultural direction at the expense of other ones. As we shall see in the next section, what the two treatises so firmly agree upon is not the only possible definition of language circulating in Dante's culture, nor has it always been the same one – not even for Dante himself.

Judging from his definition of language, Dante's linguistic philosophy was solidly bound to a theory that made of language, thought, and being three interrelated spheres and treated linguistics, gnoseology, and ontology as three reciprocally mirroring disciplines.[18] When considered as a tool for signification, a means for manifesting concepts, the grammatical language that Dante seems to have in mind is the same the Modistae were actively studying and constructing: a language that would reflect in its *modi significandi* the mirroring relationship between the modalities in which reality exists and those in which it is conceptualized (the reflection of the *modi essendi* into the *modi intelligendi*).[19] Insofar as it is the syntactically organized manifestation of concepts, the language system is subject to the laws of logical coherence that regulate the syntax of mental processes. When the logical coherence of 'conceived meanings' is what an utterance can communicate, it follows that any utterance is to abide by the norms of correct (that is, congruous) syntactic combination. These norms, in turn, reflect the rational structure of reality and of its mental perception (conceptualization).

In the first part of *De vulgari eloquentia*, Dante paints a neatly contrasted portrait of vernacular language and Latin grammar. The vernacular has a natural origin while grammar is a purely artificial, conventional, and rational construct; vernacular is multiform and subject to change, while grammar is stable through time and in space. The former has lost the capacity of accurately representing 'truth,' while the latter is a perfect tool for representing reality, based on the correspondence between the modes of being (*modi essendi*), the modes of understanding (*modi intelligendi*) and the modes of signifying (*modi significandi*). To use Dante's own terms, the vernacular was born from the confusion of Babel and is the mirror of fallen human nature, while the *gramatice positores* (the grammarians/philosophers of language) have developed Latin as a vehicle for conceptual truths, in order to remedy the instability that affects any human product. This situation of strained symbiotic coexistence of vernacular and grammatical languages perhaps deserves a second look – one which should bring to the fore some of its implications for Dante's linguistics.

1.2 The Quest for a Perfect Language: Latin as Grammar

A brief consideration of Dante's theory of Latin may help to show what was at stake in his approach to language in the mid-career treatises. In *De vulgari eloquentia*, Latin is presented, in a radical move, as the tool for an ideally perfect transference of meaning across geo-linguistic and chronological borders. The treatise clearly states that the *gramatice positores* – the philosophers who have come up with the language(s) of culture in the Judeo-Greco-Roman tradition – devised grammar for a precise reason:

> ... ne propter variationem sermonis arbitrio singularium fluitantis, vel

nullo modo vel saltim imperfecte antiquorum actingeremus autoritates et gesta, sive illorum quos a nobis locorum diversitas facit esse diversos. (*De vulgari eloquentia* 1.ix.11)

... they did so lest, through the changes in language dependent on the arbitrary judgment of individuals, we should become either unable, or, at best, only partially able, to enter into contact with the deeds and authoritative writings of the ancients, or those whose difference of locations makes different from us.

Dante's lexical choice is revelatory: the Western cultural *koine* is the means that allows the *perfect retrieval* of 'the deeds and authoritative writings of the ancients.' In his view, the world of the past *can* be retrieved through Latin – and the process of translation is both successful (as it corrects the *nullo modo*) and exhaustive (as it negates the *saltim imperfecte*). Designed to bridge gaps in time and distances in space, the ideal function of Latin is performed when it embraces transparency. To be sure, full disclosure would mean that Latin would have to accept a loss of its poetic density, and with it any residue of non-translatability; yet this is apparently not a problem for Dante. In his systematic thinking, the limit condition of Latin is paradoxical: Dante's ideal language is conceived as a self-effacing vehicle for non-historical and non-local meaning. Insofar as it is a tool for translation, Latin exists only as a field traversed by constant currents of multidirectional translation – vertically, from past to present (and forward to the future), as well as horizontally, across coeval linguistic borders. The perfect idiom for temporal and spatial transference, Latin becomes a transparent language: in postmodern terms, an absurd non-language; in Dante's terms, however, an ideal and yet historically viable one.[20]

The optimistic aspect of Dante's philosophy of language has often been overlooked by critics, perhaps obscured by other features, apparently more in tune with modern thinking and expressing what could be interpreted as Dante's distrust of the ability of language to be transparent. To be sure, the widespread modern pessimistic view of human language as an embodiment of and tool designed to wield power quite naturally harmonizes with Dante's notion that translation is a complicated affair, one in which the betrayal of original intentions, for example, is physiological.[21] And yet, in Dante's foundational hypotheses on language, there is little that thinkers may find appealing today. Even when he discusses the problems inherent in translation, Dante proves far from being *à la page* – beginning with the ways he approaches the question of translatability. Not only is Dante's faith in translation essentially immune from our modern scepticism; the conclusions we tend to draw today about the nature of language from our questioning the process could not be more foreign to his thought. Dante's notion of the perfect translatability of conceptual language preventively eliminates many of our doubts about the natural power of language to signify. If inter-language translation is always possible, so also is the interpersonal transference of meaning, which is at the root of communication. (As we shall see in the next chapter, translation is a sensitive area of Dante's reflection on poetry – one in which it is not difficult to observe the shifting of his theoretical allegiances.)

But there is one more point to be made about Dante's portrait of grammar as a model language. As we have noted, stability in time and perfect transparency are bound in a single conceptual knot in Dante's argument about Latin. There is one interesting corollary to this point: in language, both stability and transparency depend on the removal of the disturbing agency of the individual user.[22] The argument of *De vulgari eloquentia* is unambiguous: as an *in vitro* language, Latin is rendered immune from the essential agent of change, namely, individual 'discretion.' One should pause to note that, in general, discretion (*piacimento* in *Convivio* or *arbitrium* in *De vulgari eloquentia*) is the same agent that makes communication (the basic form of interpersonal translation) a problem. Dante seems to be unproblematically confronting the issue that in the history of philosophy has been labelled the private-language problem. As set up by Wittgenstein in his *Philosophical Investigations*, the core of the private-language argument is that there could not exist a language the words of which 'are to refer to what can be known only to the speaker; to his immediate, private, sensations' (paragraph 243). The implication of such a principle is that we are wrong when we assume, as we generally do, that communication is based on a process of word-to-concept matching. The assumption is that communication takes place when, in order to talk about things (the world), we refer to them by words that match a concept we have in our head, so that any utterance involves for the speaker a process of encoding things into concepts and concepts into words which the hearer will retrace, reversing its order, from words to concepts to things. In this framework, in fact, while the experience of things and words may be shared, there is no guarantee that different users of the language share perfectly matching concepts.[23]

Dante, like Wittgenstein, will take a 'social' way out of the impasse: if no private language can exist, all we have is public language – the result of interpersonal, non-binding negotiations and interactions. Dante's social way out is, however, not the same as Wittgenstein's. As we are about to see, Dante's attempt to solve the problem insists on the conceptual quality of language, to the point of actually reinforcing it. His apodictic reasoning in *De vulgari eloquentia* leaves little unspoken on the position of the problem. For him, language is born from the need to overcome individuality and its ideal purpose is to remove it altogether:

> Cum igitur homo non nature instinctu, sed ratione moveatur, et ipsa ratio vel circa discretionem vel circa iudicium vel circa electionem diversificetur in singulis, adeo ut fere quilibet sua propria specie videatur gaudere, per proprios actus vel passiones, ut brutum animal, neminem alium intelligere opinamur. Nec per speculationem, ut angelum alterum alterum introire contingit, cum grossitie atque opacitate mortalis corporis humanus spiritus sit obtectus. (*De vulgari eloquentia* 1.iii.1)

> Since, therefore, human beings are moved not by their natural instinct but by reason, and since that reason takes diverse forms in individuals, according to their capacity for discrimination, judgment, or choice – to the point where it appears that almost everyone enjoys the existence of a unique species – I hold that we can never understand the actions or feelings of others by reference to our own, as the baser animals can. Nor is it given to us to enter into each other's minds by means of spiritual reflection, as the angels do, because the human spirit is so weighed down by the heaviness and density of the mortal body.

Animals have no need of language because their intentions cannot but coincide with the common instinct of their species; neither do angels nor demons because their collective wills have perpetually been fixed on a single point, and divergence from that point is for both classes of beings unthinkable. On the contrary, human beings do need language because they do not share the same instinctual perception of reality, and their wills are at constant variance. Men are individuals because they are endowed with reason that guides them in the threefold process of discrimination (*discretio*), judgment (*iudicium*), and choice (*electio*) according to personal parameters. This process of individualization has, for Dante, the result that each human being is a species unto him- or herself:

Oportuit ergo genus humanum ad communicandas inter se conceptiones suas aliquod rationale signum et sensuale habere: quia, cum de ratione accipere habeat et in rationem portare, rationale esse oportuit; cumque de una ratione in aliam nichil deferri possit nisi per medium sensuale, sensuale esse oportuit. (*De vulgari eloquentia* 1.iii.2)

So it was necessary that the human race, in order for its members to communicate their conceptions among themselves, should have some signal based on reason and perception. Since this signal needed to receive its content from reason and convey it back there, it had to be rational; but, since nothing can be conveyed from one reasoning mind to another except by means perceptible to the sense, it had also to be based on perception.

However, when correctly used – which is to say, when it is used transparently – language guarantees that the opacity of human (animal) bodies can be traversed and human beings attain the (angelic) attribute of reciprocal understanding. Language is called upon to reduce Man's individuality, and it can do so because, in addition to being rational and perceptible at the same time, it is also both individual and collective.

We can review the problem from a different but related point of view. When, in *De vulgari eloquentia*, Dante insists that language is one of the *simplicissima signa* (simplest of signs) that define a community and the position of an individual in it, he apparently is simply developing the ascending pyramidal reasoning which informed the dialectological picture of the speaking community outlined in the first book. Three passages at the end of his survey of Italy's municipal and regional vernaculars illuminate Dante's notion of a gradual ascent and grouping from the smallest to the largest circle of human community. The general principle is spelled out quite explicitly:

In quantum homines latini agimus, quedam habemus simplicissima signa et morum et habituum et locutionis, quibus latine actiones ponderantur et mensurantur. (*De vulgari eloquentia* 1.xvi.3)

Insofar as we act as human beings who are Italians, there are certain very simple features, of manners and appearance and speech, by which the actions of the people of Italy can be weighed and measured.

Dante's point of view then gradually recedes to embrace increasingly larger social bodies, each possessing fewer and fewer specific linguistic markers:

> Nam, sicut quoddam vulgare est invenire quod proprium est Cremone, sic quoddam est invenire quod proprium est Lombardie; et sicut est invenire aliquod quod sit proprium Lombardie, <sic> est invenire aliquod quod sit totius sinistre Ytalie proprium; et sicut omnia hec est invenire, sic et illud quod totius Ytalie est. (1.xix.1)
>
> For, just as one vernacular can be identified as belonging to Cremona, so can another that belongs to Lombardy; and just as one can be identified that belongs to Lombardy, so can another that belongs to the whole left side of Italy; and just as all these can be identified in this way, so can that which belongs to Italy as a whole.

The plan Dante outlines at the end of the first book of the treatise confirms the foundational value of the principle at work in the passage. When he promises that he will gradually descend from the illustrious, tragic, and all-embracing vernacular to the analysis of the lower regional, municipal, and local vernaculars – down to the lowest speech, shared by a single family – he is continuing the same thought:

> Quibus illuminatis, inferiora vulgaria illuminare curabimus, gradatim descendentes ad illud quod unius solius familie proprium est. (1.xix.3)
>
> Having clarified all of this [namely, the conditions for the usage of the illustrious vernacular, the one that defines our actions as 'Latini'], I shall attempt to throw some light on the question of the less important vernaculars, descending step by step until I reach the language that belongs to a single family.

The resulting image is that of a progression of concentric circles (*oikeosis*), moving from the smallest group of speakers using a familial idiolect to the population and language of a district, to those of a city, of a region, and, finally, of a nation. Human beings take part in a linguistic process that defines them progressively as members of larger groups. They belong to a family insofar as they share the active and passive competence of the same idiolect, to a city for their municipal speech, to a region for their dialect, and to Italy because they are able to use what Dante calls the unifying illustrious vernacular. Incidentally, this is the same pyramidal structure that one encounters in *Convivio* 4.iv.1–4, growing in scope in the progression 'individual-household-village-city-kingdom-universal empire' (*uomo-casa-vicinanza-cittade-regno-impero*). In *De vulgari*, the progression is inflected in linguistic rather than political terms, but in both cases Dante's reasoning appears to move between the same poles of the individual and the collectivity.[24]

For Dante, to the process of inclusion in the increasingly wider circles corresponds the ability that individuals should possess for shedding, step by step, idiosyncratic traits of 'private' language (personal, familial, municipal, and so on), that is to say, their ability to partake in the progressively wider order of humanity. It is significant that Dante stresses that the few approved practitioners of the illustrious vernacular are those poets who have been able to transcend the limited linguistics of their municipality: the most hallowed case in point being Guido Guinizzelli (and a few others), whom Dante notes had chosen to forsake his 'vulgare ... proprium,' that of the city of Bologna, to adopt the larger *koine* of the illustrious vernacular (*De vulgari eloquentia* 1.xv.6). Human beings can belong to the smaller linguistic circles, therefore, only because they belong also to the widest circle possible, that of mankind. This widest circle, the base of the linguistic cone (to give a third, axiological, dimension to Dante's image), does not have a common 'positive' (that is, actualized and distinct) language.[25] The *simplicissimum signum* of human beings as such is not their accidental language, but the faculty of speaking, which is also the foundation of and scaffolding for their rationality.

Located as individuals at the tip of the definitional cone, we each are those irreducible individuals who are a species unto themselves, of which Dante spoke in defining the need of humanity for language, but we also form the basis for the cone by sharing the same *simplest sign* of our humanity – our potential for language. The double placement of individuals at the bottom and the top of Dante's imaginary cone pre-emptively solves the modern philosophic conundrum issuing from the potential existence of a 'private language.' Just as it does away with any inter-language translation problem, so the actual or potential existence of a stable *gramatica* (or grammaticized vernacular) also solves the problem of the privileged access to and discretional control that each individual has over his or her own semantics. Even when caught in the process of individualization and dispersion, human beings resolve in practice the paradox of interpersonal communicability. They may be 'private' individuals, with their mental processes hidden under the thick cover of their bodies and actions subjected to the law of instability. Their language, however, insofar as it can be made more 'stable,' does not remain 'private.' Human beings may be in possession of a private language, but they also possess and practise a shared understanding of what is real. On this common understanding, the perpetual process of interpersonal translation can rest.

But let us return to Latin. From Dante's treatment, Latin emerges with a grammatical perfection, which makes it the ideal tool for the communication of concepts. This feature also makes of Latin the model on which a new, perfected vernacular should be based. The model of language Dante envisions for his vernacular is not oriented towards facilitating the 'expression of an experience' (as Nardi put it). On the contrary, the theory developed by Dante in De vulgari eloquentia aims at identifying and strengthening a language for rational communication – for protocol description, if one wants to interpolate the terminology of a more modern line of research and speculation about purely rational linguistics.[26] He strives for a language in which a community of *doctores* (both poets and *literati* – in the modern sense of the word) can exchange knowledge. And this language, one may infer, is the more perfect the closer it comes to becoming transparent, to becoming the imperceptible vehicle for the exchange of ideas.

In perfect accordance with his general theory, Dante's rational view of language includes the notion that a *forma locutionis* is also the form of human understanding and of the orderly arrangement of being. In this perspective, whatever may be spoken about is rational, and whatever is rational is also real. As will be true for both Hegel's discussion of the Absolute and Wittgenstein's concluding remark on rational linguistics in his *Tractatus*, the threefold correspondence of reality, rationality, and language is as much foundational as it is instrumental to the practice of a strictly controlled, and sharply delimited, rational discourse. There are things to which language does not grant access, and they need to remain unspoken. In his post-exilic treatises, Dante takes a logical neo-positivist stance *avant la lettre*. He restricts his field of investigation to what comes before metaphysics. The restriction is simultaneously gnoseological and linguistic: just as *Convivio* contains no indication that language may fail in the process of signifying, so it also has no room for arguments that may fall beyond the grasp of dialectics. Similarly, in *De vulgari eloquentia*, Dante never intimates that a particular language system (what we may call a 'national' vernacular) is in any way impervious to translation.

What we have reviewed above, however, is only part of the picture – even of the picture merely outlined in Dante's mid-career treatises. Dante's theory of Latin, which appears to assert itself in such incontrovertible terms in *De vulgari eloquentia* and the first book of *Convivio*, does not prevent him from rephrasing the question of what is *gramatica*, and radically reframing it, in the chronologically identical (or nearly so) context of *Convivio* 2. Apparently ready to contradict himself on the essential issues of Latin's stability through time, Dante comes back to a brief treatment of *gramatica* and adds a crucial detail. Now seen as one of the seven liberal arts with each of which the second book of *Convivio* proposes to associate a specific heaven, *gramatica* is assigned the heaven of the Moon, the heaven dominated by change. The reasons Dante gives for this surprising association is double:

> E queste due propietadi hae la Gramatica: ché per la sua infinitade li raggi della ragione in essa non si terminano, in parte spezialmente delli vocabuli; e luce or di qua or di là, in tanto [in] quanto certi vocabuli, certe declinazioni, certe construzioni sono in uso che già non furono, e molte già furono che ancor saranno: sì come dice Orazio nel principio della Poetria, quando dice: 'Molti vocabuli rinasceranno che già caddero.' (*Convivio* 2.xiii.10)

> These two properties Grammar possesses; for because of its infinitude the rays of reason are not terminated, especially in the particular of words; and it shines now on this side, now on that, insofar as certain words, certain declensions, and certain constructions are now in use which formerly were not, and many were formerly in use which will yet be in use again, as Horace says at the beginning of his Poetics, when he says: 'Many words shall be reborn which have long since fallen out of use.'

In his learned entry on *gramatica* for the *Enciclopedia dantesca*, Mengaldo labels the passage 'problematic' on account of the blatant contradiction of the core principles of Dante's clearly stated assessment of what Latin is. In order to remove the inconsistency, he agrees with Grayson's proposal to see two different notions of *uso* at work in Dante's thought: on the one hand, there is one type of 'use,' one that negatively affects the vernacular by subjecting it to the arbitrary taste of the speakers, and on the other hand a less detrimental type that simply operates periodical selections in the *gramatica* without permanently damaging it. The former notion would be operative in the passages where Dante establishes the relative worth of the two idioms, the latter in this particular passage.

Mengaldo's and Grayson's concerted attempt to solve the problem has one advantage, but is not without problems itself. It has some merit because it explains the unbalance of tenses in the *Convivio* passage just quoted and puts that imbalance to the service of a general interpretation: the first oppositional sentence juxtaposing present versus preterite (*sono ... che già non furono*) actually appears to signal a momentary act of selection in an apparently stable system, the stability of which is actually well expressed by the second sentence that connects preterite with future (*già furono che ancor saranno*). The main problems that this conciliatory argument raises, however, probably outweigh its advantages. First, by invoking as pertinent a second passage from *Convivio* 4.iv.3, in which Dante speaks of 'uno verbo molto lasciato da l'uso in gramatica' ('a verb that has very much fallen out of use in Latin'), it rules out the possibility that in discussing Latin's variability he may be thinking about that language as including also a 'natural' dimension, one subject to the usage-prone arbitrariness of the speakers. The current interpretation thus severs this passage from other statements on linguistics that will be typical of the *Commedia*, as for instance *Paradiso* 26.136–8, in which Adam, the first language-maker, alludes to the same passage from Horace's *Ars poetica* that Dante cites here, and reinforces the notion that any natural language is subject to flux. Second, by insisting on a search for coherence, Mengaldo ends up framing Dante's inconsistency as the result of his 'struggling with a web of conceptual difficulties' ('impigliato in alcune difficoltà concettuali') preliminary to his elaboration of a final and allegedly peaceful notion of Latin as *gramatica*. In so doing, he attempts to construct a monolithic, black-and-white theory out of Dante's thought, ruling out the possibility that here the question is one of argumentative ductility. In other words, it may be the case that Dante still is unclear about some aspects of what he thinks about Latin and that his argument is here reaching particularly rough conceptual waters. However, it might also be the case that Dante may want his notion of Latin to play different roles at different argumentative junctures in his treatises: he wants Latin to play the role of a model language for the vernacular, but he also is ready to see the complexities of its history and use them to other argumentative purposes. It might be possible, in sum, that Dante has intimations that Latin is also what we would today call a 'living language,' mutable because 'natural': a language that one may learn outside of schools, by imitation and not study, for immediate existential rather than philosophical reasons. As we shall see in the next section, it is true that this is not the aspect he chose to emphasize in his treatises; there will be a time, however, when he will return to the problem, reassess his position, and reactivate also some of the texts from which he had drawn that sense of Latin as a potentially un-grammatical language.

Whatever the eventual position Dante will take in the *Commedia*, whatever the emphasis he will put on either aspect of his understanding of Latin, in *Convivio* and *De vulgari eloquentia* Dante privileges only one of the two alternative pictures of that language outlined above. In the treatises, Latin is singled out for its stability and transparency. It actually is presented as a limit-language, one on which vernaculars may model themselves. If vernacular languages are condemned to perpetual flux and to coexist geographically in different, incommunicable forms (language, one in essence, is divided *in diversas prolationes*, as stated in *De vulgari eloquentia* 1.i.4), the way to produce a 'grammaticized' vernacular is always open (in theory for the Modistae, in practice for Dante). The idea of producing (the rules for) a new language, simultaneously natural and perfected by literature, and thereby acting as the poet-grammarian for his own language, is part of Dante's aims in *De vulgari eloquentia*. Indeed, a telling note about the exemplary role that Latin writers should be allowed to play in the new vernacular poetry, for the keywords it mobilizes, shows that for Dante the connection of literary and linguistic aspects in the illustrious vernacular cannot be severed. In a short digression on the legitimacy of calling 'poets' those who composed vernacular poetry, he asserts the almost complete equivalence of those *qui vulgariter versificantur* and those who have written poetry in Latin (2.iv.2). As was already implicit in the restrictive clause 'secondo alcuna proporzione' (according to some proportion; i.e., 'not immediately') of *Vita nuova* 25.4, there is one crucial difference between these two classes of writers:

> Differunt tamen a magnis poetis, hoc est a regularibus, quia magni sermone et arte regulari poetati sunt, hii vero casu, ut dictum est. (*De vulgari eloquentia* 2.iv.3)

> Yet they differ from the great poets, that is, those who obey the rules, since those great ones wrote their poetry in a language, and with a technique, governed by rules, whereas these write casually, as I said above.

Latin, that is 'grammatical,' poets relied on more than a set of stabilized poetic rules in their works; the regularity of their language was no less fundamental for their excellence than were the *doctrinatas poetrias* that

Dante mentions immediately after the passage just quoted. Dante's invitation to model the new vernacular poetry on them involves, therefore, linguistic as well as stylistic choices. The knot of regular language and regularized compositional techniques is an apparently indissoluble compound, a *synolon*. The same conceptual core animates *Convivio*. One need only look at the convergent argument that the vernacular treatise develops around Dante's poetic attempt to stabilize language through poetry. In both treatises, poetic rules and linguistic matters are interdependent, and the dynamics of natural 'transmutation' that affect language are always subject to the regularizing action of poetry:

> Ciascuna cosa studia naturalmente a la sua conservazione: onde, se lo volgare per sé studiare potesse, studierebbe a quella; e quella sarebbe acconciare sé a più stabilitade, e più stabilitade non potrebbe avere che in legare sé con numero e con rime. E questo medesimo studio è stato mio, sí come tanto è palese che non dimanda testimonianza. (*Convivio* 1.xiii.6)

> Everything by nature pursues its own preservation; thus if the vernacular could by itself pursue anything, it would pursue that; and that would be to secure itself greater stability, and greater stability it could gain only by binding itself with meter and with rhyme. This has been precisely my purpose, as is so evident that it requires no proof.

Stability, as clearly stated in an earlier passage of *De vulgari eloquentia* (1.ix.6), was the primary motive behind the invention of grammatical language. Dante's argument is syllogistically cogent: the sin at Babel turned the God-given language of humanity into a merely human artefact; since Man is an ever-changing being (*instabilissimum animal*), it follows that his language can only be unstable (*instabile*). The conclusion of the argument in paragraph 11 is not surprising: *Hinc* (that is, having realized that any human language is unstable) *moti sunt inventores gramatice facultatis*. Latin, the *regularis sermo* of *De vulgari eloquentia* 2.iv.3, was invented as a corrective to the instability of all the vernaculars. As we learn from *Convivio* 1.xiii.6, Dante's poetry has had the same purpose – and, in a way, the same effect. Once again, in Dante's argument, poetics and linguistics go hand in hand, and the poet acts as his own language's grammarian.

Of course, Dante never intended to write a purely grammatical treatise for the *volgare di sì*. In *De vulgari eloquentia*, he is isolating a single, ideal (or, if one will, utopian) linguistic strain in the widely varied and always varying vernaculars of the Italian peninsula.[27] The *vulgare illustre, cardinale, aulicum*, and *curiale* that he, a handful of Florentine and Bolognese, and most of the Sicilian poets had used in their poetry, is the only one suitable for grammaticizing. For the author of *De vulgari eloquentia* the process of geographical and temporal stabilization of this vernacular seems to have already been initiated, since the texts of the Sicilians appeared to have travelled, intact, for more than five decades and across several of the geopolitical and linguistic borders dividing Italy. The selection of its suitable lexicon is also well under way, and Dante contributes to its theorization in the second book of the Latin treatise, by isolating phonetically and rhythmically poetic and unpoetic words. Finally, the poetry it produced has by now achieved cultural pre-eminence; and the treatise may be seen as compiling its canon in both survey and catalogue form (in books 1 and 2, respectively).

As we shall see in the next chapter, Dante's coherent and cogently argued linguistics had one crucial implication for his poetics. The illustrious vernacular Dante envisions in the prose treatises is a language that undeniably has its origin in his own vernacular poetry, but that is still attracted by the gravitational field of intellectual, Latinizing prose. The idea that prose is the final touchstone to test both the beauty and virtue of his language – a notion that is undeniably present on the surface of *Convivio* – depends on the role as a transparent conveyor of 'altissimi e novissimi concetti' that Dante attributes to his vernacular in the same work (and the definition of language – as we have noted – does not change in *De vulgari eloquentia*). The next chapter will explore the poetics that stemmed from Dante's crossing of these two oppositional pairs: Latin and vernacular, prose and poetry. Before this, however, the cultural background of Dante's definitions and their corollaries require further investigation.

1.3 An Alternative Model: Augustine Again

If in the two treatises Dante is perfectly coherent to his own linguistic program (to the point of self-translation), he is also surprisingly at odds with at least one very authoritative definition of language available in his day. Dante's consistency in the treatises has obscured the fact that his insistence on semiosis as the essence of language is both new for him and the result of a partisan choice. When Dante treats language as the answer to the need to transfer concepts from one mind to another, he certainly sides with the mainstream philosophical culture of his time, but not with all of it. Alternative definitions and conceptualizations of language existed, and one in particular he had already (if implicitly and indirectly) made use of in his work.

When, in *Convivio* and *De vulgari eloquentia*, Dante defines language as pure semiosis, the vehicle for transmitting concepts from mind to mind, he moves away not only from his previous treatment of the same issue in *Vita nuova* (as we will soon see), but also from an authoritative model to which he had access. An alternative and more balanced assessment of the expressive and semantic character of language, similar to the one we have found in Dante's poem, may be found in the definition of the nature and purpose of language that Augustine gives in the frame of his discussion of biblical linguistics in *De doctrina christiana*. At the opening of book 2, Augustine distinguishes between signs that are intentional (*signa data*) and signs that are 'automatic' (*signa naturalia*). Under the heading of the *signa data*, the central concern in his treatise, he includes all the signs 'produced by living beings' (*viventia*). To this quite ample definition of intentional signs, comprehending those issued by any living being capable of sensing (animal, man, angel, God), Augustine immediately adds a fundamental restriction. He does not want to treat the question of whether animals also produce intentional signs with their voices. 'It is not part of the present endeavor,' he writes, 'to ascertain whether their signs are only a reflex given without the purpose of signifying, just like the facial expression or the cry of a person suffering.'[28] At the bottom of the linguistic ladder of being he thus places the signs produced by animals and avoids discussing them. Similarly, at the top of the ladder he reserves no special treatment for the intentional production of signs by the other intellectual beings who communicate with man – that is, angels and God. His focus is on human beings and on the conditions in which they operate linguistically.[29]

It is with human beings in mind that Augustine offers a comprehensive definition of language:

Data vero signa sunt quae sibi quaeque viventia invicem dant ad demonstrandos, quantum possunt, motus animi sui vel sensa aut intellecta quaelibet. (*De doctrina christiana* 2.ii.3)

Conventional signs, on the other hand, are those which living beings mutually exchange for the purpose of showing, as well as they can, the feelings of their minds, or their perceptions, or their thoughts.

The difference between Dante's pre-*Commedia* notion of language and Augustine's is remarkable and hinges on two key notions: first, for Augustine language is designed to transfer more than pure meaning from the mind of the speaker to that of the addressee: and, second, language can perform its function only in determinate circumstances. Dante's and Augustine's lexical choices are significant in their divergence. Dante assigns language the sole function of signifying (*intendemus ... nihil aliud quam ... enucleare aliis conceptum*), whereas Augustine insists on its dual goal of 'transferring the motion of the soul' even before becoming the vehicle for 'the things one has either perceived or understood.' Furthermore, if for Dante transference of meaning is ideally straightforward and complete, Augustine is sensitive to the inadequacy and the frequent failures of language, its constitutional fallibility (*quantum possunt*). Finally, whereas Dante locates the origin of the conceived meaning in the mind of the speaker (*nostre mentis ... conceptum/conceputa sentenza*), Augustine writes in wider terms of the *animus* of the speaker:

> Nec ulla causa est nobis significandi, id est signi dandi, nisi ad depromendum et *traiciendum in alterius animum id quod animo gerit* qui signum dat. (ibid.)

> Nor is there any reason for giving a sign except the desire of drawing forth and conveying into another's mind (*animus*) what the giver of the sign has in his own mind (*animus*, again).

The current English rendering as 'mind' of both Latin nouns *mens* and *animus* should not prevent us from noting that the terminological difference in the original points to a remarkable conceptual divergence: *mens* and *animus* are not the same thing. For Augustine and for general scholastic understanding, *animus* is a term that indicates a specific part of the human psyche, namely, the seat of the will.[30] Augustine's insistence on *animus* in *De doctrina christiana* echoes the stress he puts on volition in the passage from the *Confessions* that we have briefly considered at the start of the present chapter.

As it is easy to see, not much of what Augustine has to say about language finds an echo in Dante's theorizations in *Convivio* and *De vulgari eloquentia*. What would then be the relevance of his model? Why even mention him here? The answer is simply that whereas *Convivio* or *De vulgari eloquentia* appear impervious to Augustine's nuanced definition of language's powers and conditions, the linguistic theory and poetic practice implicit in Dante's *Vita nuova* were at least compatible, if not in essential accordance, with Augustinian ideas. For instance, while neither of the mid-career treatises even remotely mentions the possibility that language could be born from a need to *express* rather than *signify*, in *Vita nuova* Dante had hinted at the possibility that language, particularly poetic language, could be more than a means of communicating rational ideas.[31] In *Donne ch' avete intelletto d'amore*, a poem to whose re-conceptualization Dante returned most often, he had treated poetic language as a means of expression rather than communication.[32] In *Vita nuova* 19, poetic language was explicitly cast as a failing semiotic tool and was assigned the role of expressive agent for the lyric self. Inaugurating his new 'poetics of praise,' Dante wrote:

> Donne ch'avete intelletto d'amore,
> i' vo' con voi de la mia donna dire,
> non perch'io creda sua laude finire,
> ma ragionar per isfogar la mente.
>   (*Vita nuova* 19.4.1–4)

> Ladies, who have an understanding of Love, / I wish to speak with you about my lady, / not thinking to exhaust her praise, / but conversing, which perhaps may ease my mind.[33]

The way Dante handles the topos of ineffability in *Vita nuova* 19 is significant for the clear antecedent it evokes and the figural connection it invites its readers to establish. The central notion expressed in the opening stanza, namely, that the poet may not exhaust the praise of his beloved, contains an intertextual clue that may help shed light on the larger context of the passage. It finds a notable verbal and conceptual parallel in the traditional treatment of a different, more technical, ineffability – the one relating to theological matters. Isidore of Seville posits a distinction that resonates profoundly with Dante's text:

> Dicitur autem ineffabilis non quia dici non potest, *sed quia finiri sensu et intellectu humano nullatenus potest*, et ideo *quia de eo nihil digne dici potest*, ineffabilis est.

> God's name is said to be ineffable not so much because it cannot be uttered, *but because in no way it can be exhausted by human sense and intellect*;

thus, it is ineffable, *since of it nothing worthy can be said*. (*Etymologiae* 8.1; my translation)

In tune with Isidore's conceptualization of ineffability, in *Donne ch'avete intelletto d'amore* Dante opens an analogical dimension for Beatrice that the *libello* explores with increasing acuity in the following chapters and rephrases in the summative, if temporary, renunciation of speech on which it closes. Significantly, Dante here deploys technical language drawn from the sphere of linguistic and theological thinking: unlike in the later prose works, in the *libello* Dante conceptualizes his linguistics in poetic terms. For him, the power of language coincides with that of a specific poetic genre, *laude* – the poetry of praise. The transcendental quality of his poetry's object determines his immediate reasons for speaking just as it delimits the power of language to signify. Not only is the dynamics of the expression crucial for the poetic persona authoring the text, but the programmatic *canzone* of Dante's post-Cavalcantian style also establishes a related topos of ineffability that will recur at the close of the book. In both places, language approaches Beatrice along an unfinished path. Both poetry (here) and prose itself (in *Vita nuova* 42) stop before having treated all her worth. Poetry, the result of a need to relieve the poet's mind rather than manifest the concepts it contains, suggests a meaning – Beatrice's meaning – in the history of Dante's life that the accompanying prose will clarify but never exhaust. Prose, in its turn, will reach the same conclusion, the work coming to a close with a promise – deferring a fuller treatment of Beatrice's worth to a later text – that draws a bridge between the necessary finitude of a linguistic act and its admittedly inexpressible object.[34]

Several essential corollaries follow from this notion. In the framework of *Vita nuova* 19, the language of poetry has its goal in itself: the words of poetry, even in their most logical and formalized setting, are not designed to convey an idea but to re-present an object. Their object is not conceptual but historical, and poetry is what allows a transcendent reality to be spoken, without claiming the power to constitute or substitute for it. Poetry is the record of the temporal and spatial manifestation of a creature, the historicity of which it aims to preserve. The role of the poet depends on his relationship with the subject: he moulds poetry in order to express a nucleus of truth that he does not own, but of which he invites his readers to partake. The prose of *Vita nuova* 19 specifies that the incipit of the *canzone* was not dependent on authorial intention but rather on inspiration: 'Allora dico che la mia lingua parlò quasi come per sé stessa mossa, e disse: *Donne ch'avete intelletto d'amore*'

(Then my tongue, as though it moved of its own accord, spoke and said: 'Ladies who have understanding of love').

Accordingly, as the next chapter will elaborate, the prose of *Vita nuova* never attempts to exhaust the meaning of Beatrice. In the *libello*, prose might delimit the meaning of poetry and orient the reader's interpretation, as it will be called to do in the pretextual framework of *Convivio*'s commentary, but it never claims to replace it. The prose of the *libello* twice calls attention to the inadequacy of the hermeneutics others have provided for its enigmas or that the author has left for others to produce (especially the first dream in *Vita nuova* 3.15 and the final vision in 41.9). As we will see in more detail in the next chapter, *Convivio* appears to operate under a rather different set of principles. For the linguistic theory advanced in the treatise, as we have seen, language does not express, but signifies; as we soon will see, the prose of the commentary does not contribute to the historical truth of the poems, but allegedly attempts to resolve it; finally, as will be argued in yet a further section of this book, the task of the poet is to originate and convey meaning in a language that has the power to treat exhaustively its subject.[35] The neat system of oppositions outlined above is, of course, not so neat when we look at what *Convivio* does, rather than what it claims it is doing. However, one thing seems clear: in the years in which Dante conceived the core principles of *Convivio*, the poetic scepticism of *Vita nuova*, which was implicit in the topos of ineffability surveyed above, appears to have receded into the background. For the Dante of *Convivio* and *De vulgari eloquentia*, language should (and, if properly handled, can) exhaustively describe reality. In other words, the two treatises appear to locate Dante's reasoning at a considerable distance from both his own earlier understanding of language's purpose and limitations as well as from Augustine's.

What then of the *Commedia*? Where does it stand in matters of linguistics? Where are we to look to find in it Dante's definitions of language that may be compared and contrasted with those we have traced in the 'minor works'? If we look at one word, the term *concetto*, and trace the fortune of this keyword from Dante's mid-career linguistics in the poem, we may begin to address the question at hand. Dante's usage of the term *concetto* in his definition of language in *Convivio* and *De vulgari eloquentia* may serve as a litmus test for his linguistics. In the *Commedia*, this most sensitive term undergoes a thorough redefinition and transvaluation. In the time between the treatises and the poem, much appears to have changed in Dante's outlook on language: to the 'conceptual' function that language was asked to perform in the prose work corresponds, in the poem, a marginalizing redefinition of the role played by 'concepts.' This move reorients both Dante's linguistics and his poetics. In particular, it shows that his indifference to Augustine's theory in the prose treatises was not his final stance. The implicit linguistics of the *Commedia* will once again be compatible with Augustinian texts.

1.4 *Concetto:* The Redefinition of Conceptual Speech in the *Commedia*

The first notable feature of the history of the word *concetto* is that it is distributed rather unevenly in the three parts of the *Commedia*. It appears once in *Inferno* (32.4) in a fundamental metapoetic statement, never in *Purgatorio*, and ten times in *Paradiso*.[36] Here it is consistently associated with the ability of the poet's (or the pilgrim's) language to negotiate an ineffable *au delà*. More precisely, when it is used to describe what one may call – with some degree of approximation – the Poet's/Pilgrim's mental images, the term seems to appear increasingly in conjunction with poetic invocations and to acquire a precise technical value. The term is still part and parcel of Dante's metaliterary language and constitutes the central object of the poem's communication. In spite of the metapoetic continuity, however, the connotations the word assumes in the poem have changed from the time of the prose treatises. In the *Commedia*, the notion of *concetto* is increasingly displaced from the central role as object of communication and condition of communicability. Rather, from *Inferno* 32 on, a slight but significant shift takes place: as the 'conceived meaning' of an utterance, concepts are now the result of an initial passivity (they result either from experience or inspiration) and they actually become a recessive trait in Dante's new sense of what is needed in order for *poetic* communication to work. In other words, in several metapoetic passages of the *Commedia*, the principle that controls the adequacy of the message has ceased to be the correspondence of poetic language and intended meaning (words and concepts); its place has been taken by a new poetic imperative: the direct correspondence of poetic language and reality, be it the truth of the pilgrim's experience or that of the message the poet has received. Accordingly, as chapter 3 will return to illuminate, the relative merit or demerit of the poet no longer coincides with his ability to originate meaning – his (rhetorical and poetic) task is now to mediate it.

In the *Commedia*, *concetto* is something that is not 'conceived' by the author's mind. It certainly resides there and it needs to be put on the page, traversing the narrative space and reaching his audience, but only because it has been received (in a process of poetic inspiration that may even take the form of a full-fledged dictation) or experienced (in the time and space of the narrative through which the character of the pilgrim moves) by an individual. In both cases, the 'content' of Dante's poetry comes from outside him and it needs to be related rather than 'enucleated' or 'made manifest.' According to the fictive non-fictional status of the poem, in other words, the author has been granted an experience and has drawn a concept of it; he now needs to encode it into a message that may reproduce (rather than translate) that experience in his readers. At this juncture, the authorial voice in the *Commedia* insists, poetry is needed, in its full force and with its peculiar way of signifying, so that the individual's experience may be shared among his readers.

A close reading of the *Inferno* passage, in which Dante most explicitly comes back to and re-evaluates the basic tenet of his prose treatises, will clarify the point. Dante's invocation at the opening of *Inferno* 32 strongly suggests that the term *concetto* has now been put to a different use. Facing the task of relating his experience in the lowest section of hell (the frozen floor of Cocytus), Dante pauses to reflect on the power of his poetry to represent the negative:

> S'ïo avessi le rime aspre e chiocce,
> come si converrebbe al tristo buco
> sovra 'l qual pontan tutte l'altre rocce,
>   Io premerei di mio concetto il suco
> più pienamente; ma perch' io non l'abbo,
> non senza tema a dicer mi conduco;
>   Ché non è impresa da pigliare a gabbo
> discriver fondo a tutto l'universo,
> né da lingua che chiami mamma o babbo.
>   (*Inferno* 32.1–9)

If I had verses harsh enough and rasping / as would befit this dismal hole / upon which all the other rocks weigh down, / more fully would I press out the juice / of my conception. But, since I lack them, / with misgiving do I bring myself to speak. / It is no enterprise undertaken lightly – / describing the center of the universe – / nor for a tongue that cries 'mommy' and 'daddy.'

The first gesture of the canto is one bordering on the classical *recusatio*: a profession of poetic and linguistic insufficiency balanced by an actual adequate performance. The harshest possible subject matter challenges the poet to find adequately harsh rhymes; but the difficulty is overcome in the same breath as it is stated. Dante's virtuoso display of unusual rhyme patterns *-occe, -uco, -abbo, -erso* (but also, later in the canto, *-icchi, -ecchi, -azzi, -ezzi*) gives proof that he actually has the needed rhymes. Similarly, the language that the text deems inadequate to the task at hand – the Florentine vernacular ostracized in *De vulgari eloquentia* – is the same language in which the canto is written. In the Latin treatise, puerility and 'municipalism' were enough to ban a word or an idiom from the high-style and tragic poetry Dante was recommending. Now that very same puerile and municipal tongue that calls (or spells out) *mamma* and *babbo* is the actual language of the poem.[37] The ambiguity of this metapoetic rhetorical move, affecting idiom and style, only prepares for the further ambivalent gesture contained in the actual invocation that follows it.

The paradox of not possessing adequate linguistic means in order to reproduce the horror of reality is entrusted to a conditional counterfactual clause (*s'io avessi … premerei*) hinging on the centrality of the author's *concetto*. The ultimate dystopia of hell is described as threatening the process of communication, because the poet is said to be unable to bridge the gap between his conception and the language of poetry – traditional *convenientia* would call for extreme linguistic and poetic measures.[38] The author's conceived meaning, in other words, becomes technically unspeakable: the absolute otherness and absurdity of the reality he experienced are said to render poetry insufficient for the task at hand. The situation thus set up is the same as that of the prose treatises, but two essential elements have been reconfigured. First, the nature of the *concetto* that needs to be expressed has changed; second, Dante indicates in poetry the means by which it will be expressed. Both elements are featured in the ensuing invocation: here the apparent wavering of the poet's faith in his poetic and linguistic means becomes an assertion of a modest self-assurance. The job can be done:

> Ma quelle donne aiutino il mio verso
> ch'aiutaro Anfïone a chiuder Tebe,
> sì che dal fatto il dir non sia diverso.
> (ibid. 10–12)

But may those ladies who aided Amphion / to build the walls of Thebes now aid my verse, / that the telling be no different from the fact.

What is striking – and new – in this poetic invocation is that while Dante asks for aid in expressing his concept, he also does so by eliding precisely that word. Rather than asking for help in matching (intellectually) what he has experienced with adequate mental notions and these, in turn, with adequate poetic forms, he focuses on the immediate action of the Muses on his verses and on their direct relation with the action. They should help his poetry (*verso*) to perform its mimetic function (*fatto*). In order to represent the final zone of hell, Dante's poetry and the reality of the hereafter must correspond directly, independently of the mediation of the poet's semantics. The exact interlocking of conceived meaning and words is no longer what matters the most, as the theory of the prose treatises recommended; direct correspondence of poetic words and reality has taken the central role in the process of communication. The poet's task is no longer the encoding of meaning into language, and thus the mirroring of his conception of reality, but the production of a controlled poetic environment, in which his experience of evil could be re-enacted by his readers.

As the next chapter will elucidate more fully, in the perspective of *Convivio* and *De vulgari eloquentia* it would be at best ill conceived, if not plainly absurd, to ask for 'rhymes' (the specific feature of poetry) in order to communicate a concept and, by way of a concept to point to a thing in the real world. For the combined arguments of the two treatises, the rhetorical elaboration (and belabouring) of ideas that poetry is in itself bound to produce may, rather, end up acting as a hindrance to communication. Dante's strategic, and yet uncanny, questioning of *le accidentali adornezze* of poetry in *Convivio* 1.x.12–13 (and, with the same metaphoric system, in *De vulgari eloquentia* 2.i.10) singled out 'rhymes, rhythm, and meter' as responsible for poetry's opacity. As noted in passing above, in the argument of *Convivio*, which instrumentally advocates a revaluation of prose, rhymes are precisely what should be removed from the message in order for it to be able to transmit, unhindered, its meaning: '*manifestare conceputa sentenza*' (the '*altissimi e novissimi concetti*' of philosophy), or, for *De vulgari eloquentia*, '*enucleare aliis conceptum.*' According to the new model of poetic utterance sketched out in the poem, poetry replaces conceptual mediation with direct connection.

The invocation just reviewed, which preludes the character's immediate (and unmediated) experiencing of the worst sins in hell, begins to suggest an answer to two interrelated questions springing from the linguistics of the poem and affecting its poetics. The first question concerns the content of the *Commedia*: is the conceptual truth of the poem *ultimately* what poetry communicates? The text appears to say no. Dante needs an understanding, a conceptualization, of the events that he is called to witness – and we can assume that he is granted it. What his poem is called upon to express, however, is not so much that mental object he has formed, but the fragment of (fictional) reality in which that experience originated. The second question concerns the form: can the poem be *translated back* into its concept? Again, the invocation suggests that it cannot; and it discourages any attempt in this direction: the Muses (the mythological code name for the poet's craft) are put in charge of expressing that concept and their work can apparently not be undone. The conceptual truth of the poem, though necessary for its creation, is not what the poem aims at communicating. The poem, qua poetry, claims that it establishes a direct relationship with the events it recounts, and de-poeticizing poetry would not grant access to the author's concepts. Any attempt to *reduce* the meaning of the *Commedia* to its underlying conceptual core will be frustrated by the poetic nature of the text.

When Dante asks for the Muses' aid in order to convey this conception, in other words, the context in which he does so makes clear that he is not dealing in philosophical notions, but providing access to an experienced reality, the understanding of which cannot do without the poetic medium he adopts. When he asks for technical aid in shaping his poetry, and bypasses its conceptual stage, he also signals that his poetry is not the dressing-up of concepts in pleasant rhetorical paraphernalia (as he put it in arguments advanced in *Convivio* and *De vulgari eloquentia*), but the relation of events through poetry. As chapter 2 will argue in detail, this position represents a breaking away in poetics from a line of argument with which Dante experimented in the early years of his exile. In Dante's new framework, poetry cannot be translated into conceptual prose (and its figurality cannot be reduced) simply because the text was not produced through the dressing up of conceptual meaning in rhetorical colours and figures. Rather, as we have seen, its meaning was produced through experience and, as we are about to see, Dante's poetry will locate its origin on the linguistic threshold between human and divine – the locus of incarnation. Once it will have reached the last stretch of its narrative, Dante's poetry will allude to this threshold by evoking repeatedly the double meaning of the verb 'conceive' (mental as well as maternal), and thus embed in its own language the paradigm of its ultimate liminality.

1.5 *Concetto* Again: Dante's Incarnational Poetics in *Paradiso*

Dante's point of arrival in *Paradiso* coincides in one fundamental way with his beginnings in *Vita nuova*: it is again in tune with Augustine. We have seen how in the *libello* he had courted the option of treating language as a tool for the expression rather than the transmission of concepts – an option he ended up downplaying in the prose treatises. We have also noted that, in embracing a philosophical theory of language, Dante departed from Augustine's linguistic theory to align his research with that of the *Modistae*. Leaving behind the experiments of the minor works, in the *Commedia* Dante goes back to Augustine. The essentially poetic play on the ambivalence of the word *concetto*, a term that equally applies to the conceiving of ideas and the conception of a child, is a clear, if allusive, signal of this return. While discussing his hatred for second-language (Greek) literature, Augustine incidentally revisits, in a recapitulative mode, his theory on language acquisition:

> Didici vero illa sine poenali onere urgentium, *cum me urgeret cor meum ad parienda concepta sua*, et †qua non essett, nisi aliqua verba didicissem non a docentibus sed a loquentibus, *in quorum et ego auribus parturiebam quidquid sentiebam*. (*Confessiones* 1.xiv.23)

> When I had learnt the Latin language I had been free from the menacing burden of people who compelled me, *while it was my heart that compelled me to give birth to its concepts*. In order for me to do so, however, there was no other way but to learn some words – not from teachers, but from those speakers, *in whose ears I was giving birth to what I felt*.[39]

A few elements are worth noting: first, it is Augustine's heart, not his mind, that compels him to express himself and thus acquire linguistic competence; second, the content of his utterances is treated more as the signal of a need to establish a connection than as the transmission of an idea; finally, the internal realities (*concepta*) that are born by the heart and made to be born in the ears of listeners are embodied by language, rather than encoded into it. It is perhaps the daring metaphor Augustine chooses to structure his diction that most cogently prefigures Dante's final approach to language in the poem: the nexus of language and childbearing that Augustine creates is the same that the poetics of *Paradiso* finally reaches. In its technical and poetic sense, Dante's conceptual poetry ultimately surrenders and yields ground to ineffability; in so doing, however, it also opens up the poem to the possibility of expressing the ultimate truth of language, the Word becoming flesh.[40]

One preliminary observation is in order as we move into the linguistics of *Paradiso*. The narrative presuppositions in force throughout the third realm establish a peculiar state of affairs when it comes to communication: in Paradise, communication is not really about the transference of any mental content from a speaker to an addressee. In the poem's fiction, blessed souls already know (because they see it in God) what the speaker has to say. Speaking, then, is all about expression – manifesting more the disposition of the soul than any conceived meaning. In the area of the poem that is dominated by a semantics of expression, which Dante places under the aegis of the verb *spirare*, it only makes sense that *concetto* is marginalized.[41]

The following example will serve to recall the basic dynamics of communication in *Paradiso* and the role that meaning plays in some of the cantos. In the unrecorded part of the *proemium* to his dialogue with the blessed soul of Cacciaguida, Dante has his ancestor speak a language that is commensurate to the charity that ignites him and is thus ultimately incomprehensible. Dante's text reads:

> Indi, a udire e a veder giocondo,
> giunse lo spirto al suo principio cose,
> ch'io non lo 'ntesi, sì parlò profondo;
>   né per elezïon mi si nascose,
> ma per necessità, ché 'l suo concetto
> al segno d'i mortal si soprapuose.
>   E quando l'arco de l'ardente affetto
> fu sì sfogato, che 'l parlar discese
> inver' lo segno del nostro intelletto,
>   la prima cosa che per me s'intese,
> 'Benedetto sia tu,' fu, 'trino e uno,
> che nel mio seme se' tanto cortese!'
>   (*Paradiso* 15.37–48)

Then, a joy to hear and a joy to see, / the spirit added to what first he said / words so profound I could not understand them. / Nor did he hide his thoughts from me by choice / but by necessity, for his conceptions / were set beyond our mortal limit. / And when his bow of ardent love / relaxed enough to let his speech descend / down toward the limits of our intellect,

/ the first thing I could understand was: / 'May you be blessed, Threefold and One, / who show such favor to my seed!'

The lexicon that the poem deploys is familiar at this point: the soul speaks in order to express his love (*l'ardente affetto / fu sì sfogato*) with such ardour that Dante cannot understand him. The obscurity of the message, grounded on the depth of the conception that the speaker bears in mind (*il suo concetto*), however, does not prevent Dante from understanding its connotations. If the 'what' of the message is beyond reach, in other words, the 'how' is still able to bear meaning: the failed communication cannot prevent the exchange from being 'a udire e a veder giocondo.' Concepts are not, in short, the only currency that *Paradiso* allows.

The redefinition of *concetto* is not merely linked to the imaginary conditions of the narrative. In *Paradiso*, *concetto* is also treated as a keyword in meta-poetic sections: it is not only the characters that under certain circumstances have little or no need of it; the poem itself stops several times to re-evaluate the role that concepts should play in its own making. Dante's ascent through the heavenly spheres is placed from the start under the balanced constellation of ineffability and mediation. Two passages contribute to articulating the paradox of preliminarily admitting failure and necessarily overcoming it. At the beginning of *Paradiso*, Dante makes clear that conceptual reasoning cannot solve the riddle of his presence in the flesh in the heaven of the Moon, and that human language can give no full account of his condition for the last stretch of the journey. From the outset the poem is confronted with the problem of transgressing the limits of its author's humanity and giving a linguistic account of his new condition. The language that Dante deploys is technical:

> Trasumanar significar *per verba*
> non si poria, però l'essemplo basti
> a chi esperïenza grazia serba.
> (*Paradiso* 1.70–2)

To soar beyond the human cannot be described / in words. Let the example be enough to one / for whom grace holds this experience in store.

Words cannot convey the meaning of Dante's new condition to those who have not experienced it. Only the exemplary Ovidian myth of Glaucus becoming more than human by tasting a magical grass can foreshadow the reality of Dante's transformation for those who will eventually be granted his same experience.[42] Similarly, in crossing the physical threshold of the heaven of the Moon, the ability of the mind to conceive the paradox of two bodies occupying the same space at the same time is called into question. Dante and Beatrice penetrate the Moon without disturbing it, as a ray of light penetrates a body of water without stirring waves in it. The poem glosses the absurd physics of the passage by entertaining the question of whether Dante was really in the body during his flight:

> S'io era corpo, e qui non si concepe
> com'una dimension altra patio,
> ch'esser convien se corpo in corpo repe;
>   accender ne dovea più il disio
> di veder quella essenza in che si vede
> come nostra natura e Dio s'unio.
> *(Paradiso* 2.37–42)

> If I was there in flesh – and here on earth we can't conceive / how matter may admit another matter to it, / when body flows into, becomes another body – / that, all the more, should kindle our desire / to see the very One who lets us see / the way our nature was conjoined with God.

The answer to the question of the presence of Dante's body in Paradise is an implied 'yes,' and the problem originating from it – the inability of those on earth to conceive a violation of the laws of earthly physics – should act as a trigger for the desire to experience what lies beyond the reach of earthly minds. As will be true of the failure of the word to communicate 'transhumanate' reality, Dante denounces the limits of human understanding only to elicit the desire to transgress them. Propelled by desire (a desire kindled by poetry) the journey beyond 'mortal' concepts and towards a new and higher conceiving has one specific goal and one specific destination, as the poem indicates in so many words: the direct experience of the hypostatic union of the Divine.

Having been perhaps sidetracked by the question of Dante's bodily presence in the heavens, critics have devoted little attention to the second tercet.[43] In seamlessly moving from marking the limits of human intellectual powers to evoking the force of desire to propel one's soul to blissful contemplation, Dante's tercets anticipate the exploration of the lexical and mystical resonances of the word *concepire* that will be developed later in the poem. Anticipating the same polysemous resonance that will be explored in the invocations at the end of the *cantica*, the first use of the word 'conceive' in *Paradiso* 3 opens a new semantic dimension for the term. Introduced here for the first time, and for the first time inextricably linked, we find the two notions that will recur in the same constellation in the authorial voice: the necessarily failing conceptualizations of the human mina and the union of divine *logos* and human nature through the conception of Christ. Dante never articulates this connection explicitly – just as he understandably never conceptualizes the ultimate object of heavenly desire in rational terms. However, at several crucial moments in *Paradiso* he expresses what the shortcomings of conceptual thinking and linguistics are supposed to produce: the poetic experience of crossing the threshold between human and divine through incarnation.

In the heaven of Jupiter, when Dante needs to relate the political message that the souls of the Just literally spell out for him in their 'alphabet dance,' the specific terminology of conceptualization and poetic production surfaces again. Before starting to relate the words of the message (*diligite iustitiam qui iudicatis terram*), Dante requests the aid of the Muse:

> O diva Pegasea, che li 'ngegni
> fai gloriosi e rendili longevi
> ed essi teco le cittadi e ' regni,
>   illustrami di te, sì ch'io rilevi
> le lor figure com' io l'ho concette:
> paia tua possa in questi versi brevi.
>   (*Paradiso* 18.82–7)

O divine Pegasean, who bestow glory / and long life on genius, as, with your help, / it gives life to towns and kingdoms, / inspire me with your light so that I may set down / their shapes as I conceived them in my mind. / May your power appear in these few lines.

The message that the souls mediate to Dante needs to be understood by the poet and the poet needs to relate it. The letters that spell out God's message are 'the figures' that Dante needs to conceptualize and reproduce in his poetry. The model of communication the passage sets up apparently resembles Dante's customary reliance on his conceptions to inform and give substance to his poetry – one might even add that a hint of self-promotion is contained in the first tercet, in which the poet expresses his striving for poetic longevity. Nevertheless, it is clear that the conception of these signs in Dante's mind is far from autonomous. It might even be better described as their 'reception.' Dante casts himself as the medium for a message that is dictated to him. His transcription of God's command may well be what grants the poet perpetual fame in time, but the power that will be conveyed in his verses is not his own.[44]

That the word 'conceive' is now used in such an emphatic scene of dictation and faithful transcription of a message shows the transvaluation that the term has undergone in reaching *Paradiso*: dictation is the process most alien to the authorial encoding of rational concepts into poetic language. Dictation, in other words, is incompatible with the principles on which the poetics of the mid-career treatises were based. Technically, the words that the souls spell out, and that Dante's poem relates, do not originate with him: they are not the linguistic translation of a concept residing in his mind. Rather, they are given to him in the most literal and transparent fashion. The task of the author is here at its least active: the situation the poem sets up involves the reception of the message and the appeal to the power of poetry to relate it.[45] What the poem thematizes is most certainly not the power of the author to conceptualize reality and articulate it in language; rather, what is at stake is the power inherent in poetic language – as *poetic* language – to become the vehicle of God's truth. Dante's transcription of the souls' message to the rulers of the earth, together with the meaning God has entrusted to it, will achieve an effect that is not limited in any way by the artistic medium through which they are conveyed.[46] Quite the contrary: the term *versi* is brought to the fore in order to signal that poetry is the only means that allows it to be delivered. God's everlasting power passes through the fleeting form of the poem's text.

Before we move to the reading of the last stretch of *Paradiso*, devoted to the narrative exploration of the Empyrean, and conclude this survey of Dante's use of the term 'concetto' across his linguistics and poetics, it may be useful to pause and take into consideration a related term in Dante's definition of language. In *Paradiso*, the notion of 'making manifest,' which was central to the prose-treatises' account of language as semiosis, can be shown to have followed a similar path of evolution. The verb 'manifestare' undergoes a radical revision in two related ways. On the one hand, 'manifestare' is used as a technical verb for the transcription into language of a vision, in particular, but not only, Dante's own; on the other hand, it is used to indicate the ethical stance that a subject takes by speaking. Three instances of the word are crucial to understand the former usage. First, the invocation at *Paradiso* 1, in which the Divine power is asked to provide aid so that Dante may report what he has been shown: 'tanto che l'ombra del beato regno / segnata nel mio capo *manifesti*' (enough that I may show the merest shadow / of the blessèd kingdom stamped within my mind, vv. 23–4); second, Cacciaguida's mandate to Dante to give a faithful account in *Paradiso* 18 [17]: 'tutta tua visïon fa *manifesta*' (reveal all that you have seen, 128); third, in *Paradiso* 15 [25], a different vision, the one John was granted of the resurrected bodies as clothed in white robes (as per Apoc. 7:9), is listed as an aid to Dante's and all Christians' hope for the resurrection of the body: 'questa revelazion ci *manifesta*' (explains to us / this revelation with still greater clarity, 96). In all three cases, the verb 'manifestare,' which used to be associated with the act of conveying a mental concept (a 'conceputa sentenza'), is now tied to the need to relate an experience that may reside in the mind, but certainly does not originate there.

The second meaning in which Dante uses the word in *Paradiso* may be illuminated by looking at a single moment in the poem: the context of Peter's examination of Dante on matters of faith in *Paradiso* 24. In this case, the verb 'manifestare' and its related adjective 'manifesto' are explicitly connected to their former associate, the word 'concetto,' but they appear to establish a new relation to it: the act of 'manifesting' is not solely related to the communication of mental realities, but it is connected to the performative power of language to let the subject take a stance in the world by speaking. In the canto, the terms 'concetto' and 'manifesto' appear twice in relation to one another, each time ascribed to a different speaker and semantically balancing their respective values. The examination starts with Peter's issuing of an order that assigns an ethical charge to language: 'Dì, buon Cristiano, fatti *manifesto*' ('Speak up, good Christian, and make your declaration,' v. 52); before addressing the question in doctrinal terms, Dante avails himself of an intradiegetical quasi-invocation, which points to the conceptual quality of language: 'La Grazia che mi dà ch'io mi confessi / ... da l'alto primipilo / faccia li miei *concetti* ben *espressi*' (May the grace that allows me to make confession / ... to the great centurion grant clear expression to my thoughts, 58–60).[47] The same dialectics between the task of conveying ideas and manifesting one's own internal disposition is again at work in the second phase of the examination later in the canto. This time, however, Dante is asked to convey information rather than to prove himself directly: 'Ma or convien *espremer* quel che credi' (But now you must declare what you believe, 122); to this charge, however, he responds by rephrasing the demand in terms of an ethical stance: 'Tu vuo' ch'io *manifesti* / la forma qui del pronto creder mio' (you would have me here declare / the substance of my ready faith, 127–8). The nature of the question – What is Faith? – brings the two goals of language into harmony. Faith has a conceptual core that both needs to be enucleated and can be put into language; at the same time, however, the act of articulating into language the doctrinal core of the first theological virtue has ethical implications for the subject. What Dante is asked to do is not to define Faith, but to profess it, and the question 'What is it that you believe as a Christian?' elicits an answer that potentially reduces the distance between the speaker and what he says. Dante's 'confession' – that is, technically, his statement of belief – is not limited to the exposition of a speculative content; it is also a moral act.[48]

But let us return to the keyword 'concetto.' The same situation of ineffability outlined above, with an even higher degree of self-consciousness, can be found in the final invocation of the poem in *Paradiso* 33. The final vision of God that the poet claims he has been granted is literally impossible to tell. Yet, the poem will attempt it. The author's understanding, his bearing in his mind the trace of his experience, is the starting point of his work as a poet. The meaning of what poetry is to convey is not *his* meaning (intention, *sentenza*), nor is the final merit his. On account of both elements in this poetic economy, the concept that God grants the Pilgrim and that the poet will transmit is radically different from what the word 'concetto' indicated in the minor works. The invocation that opens the final segment of *Paradiso* is not addressed to the Muses but to the divine light itself:

> O somma luce che tanto ti levi
> da' concetti mortali, a la mia mente
> ripresta un poco di quel che parevi,
>   e fa la lingua mia tanto possente,
> ch'una favilla sol de la tua gloria
> possa lasciare a la futura gente:
>   chè, per tornare alquanto a mia memoria
> e per sonare un poco in questi versi,
> più si conceperà di tua vittoria.
>   (*Paradiso* 33.67–75)

O Light exalted beyond mortal thought, / grant that in memory I see again / but one small part of how you then appeared / and grant my tongue sufficient power / that it may leave behind a single spark / of glory for the people yet to come, / since, if you return but briefly to my mind / and then resound but softly in these lines, / the better will your victory be conceived.

The object of the vision and of the poetry is the light that exceeds understanding: this, the text makes clear, is beyond mortal minds and technically inconceivable. Only when dimmed and perceived as a trace will it again visit the mind of the writer. If the experience of vision was unique, the memory of it may be communicated – at least in part and vicariously.

As the two tercets underline, sharing the memory of the experience with his readership, albeit imperfectly, is the task of the poet. Once again, the chosen vehicle of communication is specifically poetry; and, once again, the effect of the communicative act is not the transmission of an idea from the writer to the reader, but the engendering in the reader of God's victory. What exactly this victory is has been the object of debate among commentators: Scartazzini observed that it certainly is neither Christ's victory over the devil; nor is it retrospectively God's exceeding of human conceptions; rather, it is the victory of the highest power and infinite excellence, with which and through which God's light overcomes all things.[49] Carroll refined Scartazzini's reading by shifting the focus from the metaphysics to the poetics of the poem, and glossed that the victory is not 'the infinite greatness and excellence of God by which he conquers or transcends the universe,' but 'the way in which the vision of God conquered all [Dante's] mortal powers.'[50] This last line of interpretation is perhaps most convincing: by framing God's victory in terms of His overcoming ineffability, it best captures the technical quality of Dante's invocation. It too, however, may be refined further: what shall be conceived in the readers' minds is not simply the possibility of the vision in Dante's mind, but its verbalization on the poem's page. God's victory is not only over the created universe or human minds (Dante's among them), but over silence.

As framed in the invocations surveyed above, Dante's poetry agrees to become a docile medium for a meaning that its author does not originate. By juxtaposing them with the 'concetti mortali,' the poem isolates the immortal 'concetti' to which God has given Dante experiential access: these he now shares with us through the mediation of poetry. Accordingly, the final effect of the reception of this poetry does not concern its intermediate author, but its ultimate issuer. Discarding the option he had resolutely taken in the past, Dante now accepts that the decoding of his text will take place outside its textual borders, outside authorial control, and to the greater glory of God – not the promotion of its writer. Neither the poet nor the poem itself will have won 'a victory' if the words carry across the message entrusted to them. The victory will be God's, insofar as He has overcome both author and language by defeating their resistance to signify what lies beyond the limits of 'mortal' conception and of linguistics. Displaced from its role as origin and goal of any communicative act, the concept is now marginalized – in the same measure as the author has abandoned his role as source for the ultimate meaning of his poetry and accepted becoming a vehicle for a transcendent truth.

One last passage helps to measure how far Dante has come from the authorial ethics he had practised in his mid-career treatises. In *Paradiso*, the ultimate goal of poetry is to produce in the reader the experience of an excess. The last self-reflexive moment of Dante's poem phrases this experience in terms of a double failing: that of language to represent concepts and that of concepts to represent experience. With its technical quality, Dante's argument (and the language that he uses) brings us back to the utter inadequacy of any neo-positivist gnoseological and linguistic attitude to deal with metaphysics: in the Empyrean – which is to say, in God – conceptual knowledge is not the mirror of things and language is not the mirror of knowledge. Having been granted direct vision of the Trinity, Dante first records his experience in geometrical terms:

> Ne la profonda e chiara sussistenza
> de l'alto lume parvermi tre giri
> di tre colori e d'una contenenza;
>   e l'un da l'altro come iri da iri
> parea reflesso, e 'l terzo parea foco
> che quinci e quindi igualmente si spiri.
>   (*Paradiso* 33.115–20)

In the deep, transparent essence of the lofty Light / there appeared to me three circles / having three colors but the same extent, / and each one seemed reflected by the other / as rainbow is by rainbow, while the third one seemed fire, / equally breathed forth by one and by the other.

The theological coherence of the image that the poem evokes of the triune God is remarkable. The second circle, the Son, is the reflection of the first circle, the Father, in accordance with (and as a rendering of) the theological notion of generation; the third circle, the Holy Spirit, is breathed forth equally from both circles, in accordance with the Latin Church's creed that also includes, through the debated *filioque* clause, the Son along with the Father as sources of procession for the third person of the Trinity. Completed by the following evocation of the 'eternal light,' which inflects the mutual relationships of subsistence, intellection, and love that bind the persons of the Trinity, Dante's account of the Trinity is so theologically and poetically precise that the metapoetic tercet wedged between these two moments, and containing one of the several professions of poetic inadequacy marking the last stretch of the poem, has appeared to some (Romantic) readers as a purely rhetorical ploy. Far from being rhetorical, however, the tercet recapitulates the poem's internal debate on the mechanisms (and the limits) of communication – and it does so by going back to the keyword *concetto*:

> Oh quanto è corto il dire e come fioco
> al mio concetto! e questo, a quel ch'i' vidi,
> è tanto, che non basta a dicer 'poco.'
> (124–6)

O how scant is speech, too weak to frame my thoughts. / Compared to what I still recall my words are faint – / to call them little is to praise them much.

Phrased as a profession of poetic inadequacy, we find here all the elements of the customary neo-positivist attitude towards language: forced to reckon with the objective limitations that metaphysics imposes on its instruments, poetic language (*dire*) is for Dante insufficient to communicate fully (*corto*) and effectively (*fioco*) what his mind has conceived – or, better yet, received. In turn, his conceptions (*concetto*) – what he has brought back with him of his direct vision (as *Paradiso* 1.7–9 had preliminarily established) – are now utterly inadequate to the realities his intellect has experienced ('quel ch'io vidi'). Object, concepts, and language appear to be ordered in the usual threefold relationship that makes of mind the mirror of nature and of language the mirror of mind. Something essential has, however, changed in Dante's outlook on this relationship: faced with what is technically ineffable, Dante does not ask for any correction of the situation. He does not ask to be able to render the idea fully (his poetry is in charge of that) or to maintain a full conceptualization of the truth.

Far from being the necessary and sole content of communication, concepts appear now unable to incorporate the ultimate experience of reality. Rather than trying to correct the gnoseological and poetic impasse, by invoking – for example – a higher subtlety for the author's mind or for the poem's language (a move that readers of the pre-*Commedia* Dante might have expected from the self-appointed poet of subtlety), the metapoetic delay opens a new dimension in the poem, in which the redefinition that the term *concetto* has undergone throughout the *Commedia* will finally be articulated in full. The central term in the three-element system of truth, concepts, and language, *concept* will have its semantic field shifted once and for all in the next tercet. From signifying mental representations of reality, it will come to anticipate the truth of incarnation. The term appears for the second time in the short span of nine lines, but with an alternative value:

> Quella circulazion che sì concetta
> pareva in te come lume reflesso,
> da li occhi miei alquanto circunspetta,
>   dentro da sé, del suo colore stesso,
> mi parve pinta de la nostra effige:
> per che 'l mio viso in lei tutto era messo.
>   (127–32)

That circling which, thus conceived, / appeared in you as light's reflection, / once my eyes had gazed on it a while, seemed / within itself and in its very color, / to be painted with our likeness, / so that my sight was all absorbed in it.

The theological point that these lines make refers to the conjunction of human and divine natures in the second person of the Trinity. After having surveyed the perimeter of the second circle of the triune God, the Pilgrim sees (and fixates upon) the human features of the Christ. They appear as if painted in it, in the same colour as the rest of the circle. The relation between the first two circles is again phrased as a reflection of light in light, and the technical word 'reflesso' is used again (as in line 118). What this tercet adds is the notion that the second circle is 'conceived' (or begotten) by the first one. As in *Paradiso* 2, the passage discussed at the opening of this section, the concept of poetry evokes here the conception of the Son. In *Paradiso* 2, the impossibility of conceptualizing the co-presence of two bodies in the same space had evoked the desire to see face to face the mystery of incarnation; coming full circle, the experience of the incarnated Christ follows upon the impossibility of conceptualizing the Divine and enucleating, that is, laying out, that concept through language. In both instances, the term 'concept' has a double valence: by rapidly shifting from designating mental images in the lexicon of poetics to indicating the conception of the Word in that of metaphysics, Dante's concept belongs to two different dictionaries and has two different meanings. His poetry chooses to locate itself in the field of tension they create.

Two final notes should be added to the points I have made thus far. First, if I have emphasized some passages in the final section of the *Commedia*, I know that they do not control the poetics of the poem. Even if in them Dante treats concepts in a new way, conceptual poetry still exists in the *Commedia*, of course, and it would be unwarranted to define Dante's redefinition of the role of concepts in it as indicating a wholesale conceptual bankruptcy. Throughout the *Commedia*, poetry is still put in charge of communicating ideas, and a host of passages in which the poem launches into explanations of 'things as they are' can be brought to prove the point (as the example of *Paradiso* 24 reviewed above amply suggests). However, it is also true that conceptual poetry is the poetry that Dante makes, not the one that he talks about when he stops and reflects on it. While one can easily prove, for instance, that much of the didactic impulse of *Convivio* is still in place in the *Commedia*, and that – broadly speaking – Dante does philosophize in the poem as much, if not more, than in the treatise, it is also true that in the *Commedia* he talks about his activity in different terms, stressing different aspects of the same keywords, opening them up to a wider array of meanings. The second point to be made is a related restriction of the scope of my argument, which attempts to dispel potential misunderstandings about the goals of this study: Dante's redefinition of the role of concepts in the *Commedia* and his ensuing final advocacy of trans-conceptual poetry was just as instrumental to a promotion of his poetry as was the concept-based theory of the pre-*Commedia* treatises. As such, it should not be understood as a better, more mature, or more effective strategy: it is just a different one. Saying as much would amount to 'praising' Dante for a higher understanding of his role as a poet – which is a typical teleological interpretive move. Rather, to witness the discrepancies that exist between two of Dante's self-portraits as a poet and to explore their implications is what the texts invite us to do. In the *Commedia* Dante has found yet another way of talking about poetry, to yet another audience, with yet another vocabulary. The question we should ask is: what does this tell us about the cultural context that prompted him? The next chapter will re-examine the question focusing on what Dante has to say about what makes poetry what it is.

2 Poetics

You used to be so amused
at Napoleon in rags
and the language that he used.
                        Bob Dylan

Since I intend to treat this problem more fully in my work *L'Origine de la vérité*, I have approached it less directly in a partially written book dealing with literary language. In this area it is easier to show that *language is never the mere clothing of a thought which otherwise possesses itself in full clarity*. The meaning of a book is given, in the first instance, not so much by its ideas as by a systematic and unexpected variation of the modes of language, of narrative, or of existing literary forms. This accent, this particular modulation of speech – if the expression is successful – is assimilated little by little by the reader, and it gives him access to a thought to which he was until then indifferent or even opposed.

    Communication in literature is not the simple appeal on the part of the writer to meanings which would be part of an a priori of the mind; rather, communication arouses these meanings in the mind through enticement and a kind of oblique action. The writer's thought does not control his language from without; the writer is himself a kind of new idiom, constructing itself, inventing ways of expression, and diversifying itself according to its own meaning. *Perhaps poetry is only that part of literature where this autonomy is ostentatiously displayed.* All great prose is also a re-creation of the signifying instrument, henceforth manipulated according to a new syntax. *Prosaic writing, on the other hand, limits itself to using, through accepted signs, the meanings already accepted in a given culture.* Great prose is the art of capturing a meaning

which until then had never been objectified and of rendering it accessible to everyone who speaks the same language.
M. Merleau-Ponty, prospectus for *The Prose of the World*

The focus of this chapter is Dante as a theoretician of poetry in the years before the *Commedia*. It follows the traces that Dante left of his reflections on poetics, that is, the ideas about how poetry should be written that he entertained at various stages of his career and was confident enough to entrust to writing. In the pre-*Commedia* works, his theory is laid out in parcels: a bit is entrusted to *Vita nuova* 25, some more is offered in the proemial treatise of *Convivio*; other elements may be found in *De vulgari eloquentia*. In what follows, I review the passages contained in these three pre-*Commedia* works, teasing out from them an embryo of *poetica* (or *poetria*) *Dantis*. I will reserve the analysis of the poetics of the *Commedia* for chapter 3, after I have introduced some texts that are essential to understanding the principles on which Dante operates in that poem. Four main themes, whose keywords are anticipated in the highlighted section of the Merleau-Ponty's excerpt quoted above, will occupy this chapter: first, the relationship between form and content, as Dante sets it up at various stages of his development as a writer; second, and related to the previous question, the relationship between prose and poetry, and the various ways in which they collaborate or interfere in Dante's two vernacular *prosimetra*; third, the impact that these distinctions have on the way in which Dante frames the issue of translation; fourth and last, the availability of an alternative theory of language and of style, which could serve as a counterweight, if not as an alternative, to the one Dante apparently endorsed.

One general caveat is in order here: in these pages, I will look at what Dante says he does in the metapoetic passages of his pre-*Commedia* works, as much as at what he does in the body of the same texts. I am interested in the theory he articulates (and the aporias it may contain) together with his actual procedures, in the reasons why he chooses to set up the issues of his poetic activity the way he does, and in the points in which that theory jars with his praxis. In my study of Dante's poetics, however, I will privilege one strain of his thought: the one he articulates explicitly. Not because I believe that this line of thought is the only one (Dante's thinking is seldom univocal) or even the dominant one, but because by looking at what eventually will become his recessive views on poetry, his final understanding of the task of the poet may become clearer as well, in both its implications and the traditional theoretical background with which it is called to interact.

In order to tease out of Dante's multi-faceted poetics the main lines of his thinking, in what follows I will take (provisionally and to a specific end) Dante at face value and focus only on one side of several questions. That is, I will treat what he says about his activity as a poet as fully endorsed by him, bracketing the shifting circumstances in which his statements are made (the different projects and aims he was pursuing in the different works). Doing so does not mean that I suppose that 'Dante really believed what he was writing' or, in a more refined formulation, that 'his (conservative) theory could actually account for his (often revolutionary) praxis,' to use Barański's interpretive framework. Instead, the opposite is rather true. My choice is mainly strategic; if I emphasize his theoretical statements, this is because they seem to be at odds with his practical choices. The discrepancies between what Dante says he does and what he does are not the locus for the emergence of a Freudian repressed in the form of a literary neurotic symptom or a *Witz*; they are, rather, the indicators of a shared grammar of thinking about literature. Taking seriously, even literally, the explicit poetics of the pre-*Commedia* works is a heuristic process. Examining what Dante has to say about his activity as a poet may help illuminate the basic cultural lexicon and syntax of Dante's audience. As we shall see in crossing over from the pre-*Commedia* works to the poem, if in his theory he did little to change this platform, in his praxis he deeply upset its foundations.

Dante's statements about the nature and purpose of poetry, as he lays them out in *Vita nuova*, *Convivio*, and *De vulgari eloquentia*, may appear as a set of uncomplicated, black-and-white, often traditional, principles. They are, however, useful. Even though they now appear unsurprising, Dante's statements on matters of poetics did, in the end and for his audience, bear his signature (whether they became a matter of public record or not). And even if he did not really fully stand behind them, and they did not represent more than an experimental phase in his career as a writer, Dante would eventually need to address the salient points in his theory of poetry when he revisited it in a new project.

2.1 The Making of Poetry: *Verba* and *Sententia* as *Discretive Mixta*

In his first discussion of the nature of poetry in *Vita nuova* 25, Dante sounded a radically modernist note, by suggesting that classical and new vernacular poets should enjoy the same privileges when it came to the use of rhetorical artifice:

> Con ciò sia cosa che *a li poete sia conceduta maggiore licenza di parlare che a li prosaici dittatori, e questi dicitori per rima non siano altro che poete volgari*, degno e ragionevole è che a loro sia maggiore licenzia largita di parlare che a li altri parlatori volgari: onde, se alcuna figura o colore rettorico è conceduto a li poete, conceduto è a li rimatori. (*Vita nuova* 25.7)

> *In Latin, greater license is conceded to the poet than to the prose writer, and since these Italian writers are simply poets writing in the vernacular*, we can conclude that it is fitting and reasonable that greater license be granted them than to other writers in the vernacular; therefore, if any image or coloring of words is conceded to the Latin poet, it should be conceded to the Italian poet.

The novelty of Dante's argument, putting on the same footing classical and modern versifiers, should not make us forget the fully traditional set of assumptions on which it rests. Both the ancient poets and the best among their modern followers, Dante specifies, have used these artifices only as an addition to the meaning of their poems. Indeed, the relationship that should exist between these artifices and the zero-degree of communication is the same that exists between body and clothing, and hence great care should be taken not to compose figurative (clothed) poetry without being able – when asked – to account for its (body) meaning in prose:

> Grande vergogna sarebbe a colui che rimasse cose *sotto vesta di figura o di colore rettorico*, e poscia, domandato, *non sapesse denudare le sue parole da cotale vesta*, in guisa che avessero verace intendimento. (25.10)

> Great embarrassment would come to one who, having written things *in the dress of an image or rhetorical coloring*, and then, having been asked, *would not be able to strip his words of such dress* in order to give them their true meaning.

We will come back to this passage and its larger context in due course, in order to evaluate its hermeneutic implications. For now we should concentrate on the metaphor through which Dante characterizes the relationship between 'meaning' (the 'intendimento' – a word that involves authorial intention as well as a reader's understanding) and 'poetic language.' For the author of *Vita nuova*, the true meaning of poems lies beneath the overlay of figures and rhetorical colours that the poet has imposed on them. A neat division and definition of competence ensues: poetry is designed to enrich the process of communication by adding a complex web of images to a thought. As the previous sentence in the paragraph had made clear, prose serves to reduce the rhetorical complexity of poetry and helps retrieve meaning, the thought content of the text:

> Dunque, se noi vedemo che li poete hanno parlato a le cose inanimate, sì come se avessero senso e ragione ... degno è lo dicitore per rima di fare lo somigliante, *ma non sanza ragione alcuna, ma con ragione la quale poi sia possibile d'aprire per prosa*. (25.8)

> So, if we discover that the Latin poets have spoken to inanimate objects as if they possessed sense and reason ... then it is fitting that the vernacular poet do the same, *not without some reason but rather with a motive that later can be revealed by prose*.

In this meta-poetic statement, Dante appears to play a rather conservative game, and does so in two ways. First, he casts the relationship between form and matter as one between body and clothing. Second, he appears to connect verse with the rhetorical garb of a text and prose with its content. The 'greater license' that is to be granted to the writers of poetry is measured exactly against the alternative, and more essential, 'naked' writing of prose makers. In the theory set forth in *Vita nuova*, ancient and modern poets have constructed their texts according to a simple and effective model: they have covered their ideas beneath a garment of rhetorical colours. Their poetry's worth should be measured, the text suggests, in terms of both the 'naked' ideas they embedded in their texts, and of the artifices of style they have adopted. The metaphors he picks are not neutral ones.

The absence of explicit contextual qualifiers in the passage just quoted should not deceive: Dante's statement here serves a specific purpose (to defend and promote poetry *over* prose) and is to be considered valid only for a specific area of the text (his treatment of the character of Amor). The poetics laid out in the passage does not apply to the whole book. While Dante accepts and espouses the principle that the poet's task includes producing a *fictio*, a 'prosaic' content that will then be rhetorically elaborated into 'poetry,' he also limits to the fictional side of his work the sphere in which prose may divest poetry and resolve its figures and actions into an intellectual narrative. After all, what prompted Dante's theoretical digression is only the personification of the God of love, which – unlike Beatrice – is little more than a figurine moving on a mental stage. And it is only on that figure – not on the character of Beatrice – that the *libello* suggests the poet should and may exercise his power of divestiture. In the strenuously achieved balance between prose and poetry in *Vita nuova*, narrative, analytical, and lyrical elements coexist by observing their respective limits. In Dante's first work as self-commentator, the principle according to which prose is the preferred tool to unlock the meaning of poetry leaves the core of the narrative intact. The content of the *Vita nuova* can be termed a *fictio* only to some extent, and the *libello* balances the claims of this meta-poetic section with repeated statements about the 'truthfulness' of its story. The same restrictions, however, do not seem to hold true for *Convivio*.

In his first years of exile Dante will return to the 'clothing' metaphor, but with greater import and impact than it had in *Vita nuova*, where it seems incidental and of limited instrumental purpose. In the theory of poetry advanced in *Convivio*, the same basic division of labour between prose and poetry is at work, but it appears to have an all-encompassing sphere of application, since the principle that philosophical truths are hidden under the pleasing surface of the poems is said to apply unconditionally. Dante again adopts the same metaphorical field of body and clothing. While setting up the reading guidelines for his self-commentary, he points out that the 'literal' exposition of the *canzoni* will always precede the 'allegorical' reading in his treatise.[1] After providing a fourfold argument demonstrating the structural, ontological, architectural, and logical necessity of advancing – as he does – from the literal to the allegorical explanation (*Convivio* 2.i.8–13), Dante writes:

> Sopra ciascuna canzone ragionerò prima la litterale sentenza e appresso di quella ragionerò la sua allegoria, cioè *la nascosa veritade*. (*Convivio* 2.i.15)

> I shall on each occasion discuss first the literal meaning concerning each canzone, and afterwards I shall discuss its allegory (that is, *the hidden truth*).

That the truth of the poetic text is 'hidden,' and that the commentary prose is designed to unveil it, is clearly stressed again in the course of the treatise. Moving from the literal to the allegorical reading of *Voi che 'ntendendo*, for instance, Dante repeats that it is time to step into the allegorical – and true – exposition ('la esposizione *allegorica e vera*,' as per 2.xii.1). From principles such as these, only two inferences seem likely to be drawn. First, that prose commentary is the ideal tool for uncovering the true meaning of the texts to which it is attached, as *Vita nuova* 25 had already suggested. Second, that poetry is perhaps not up to its task: it is inadequate to convey meaning without the aid of prose. In isolation, poetry may suffer from a lack of clarity: it may even be misleading. 'Truth is hidden' in poetry and the 'true explanation' of a text is to be found in prose.

In an attempt to mitigate the dichotomy between prose and poetry, we could start by questioning the relevance of the point just made in *Convivio*, or at least try to restrict its scope, as was the case in *Vita nuova*. If Dante appears for a moment to distrust poetry, one may argue, it is only because of the peculiar allegorical claims of his current work. Dante appears to offer prose as a supplement for poetry, but this might be the case only for the prose of *Convivio*, which strove to reduce the *allegorical* superstructure of its poems. According to this reasoning, prose appears to be only strategically privileged, and it appears to be superior to poetry merely because it is able to draw back the allegorical veil that Dante had placed on the intellectual content of his poetry. In short, prose can decipher poetry because on the level of *inventio* the texts Dante sets out to comment upon were allegorical in nature; or, at least, this is what the prose now makes them.

Most likely this is what Dante meant to do when he sketched out the elements of the poetry–prose relationship for his work. However, the language that he used was neither neutral nor inconsequential. The metaphor we have explored above prompted a coherent set of observations that Dante made in several *loci* of both *Convivio* and *De vulgari eloquentia* and cut deeper into the fabric of the text, beyond the level of *inventio*. The corollaries of the initial metaphor form a compact front of statements suggesting that there is something about prose that makes it the right tool for expounding the meaning of poetry. And there is also something about poetry – even at the fundamental level of *elocutio* – that makes it dependent upon prose. For instance, while including among the virtues of the new vernacular *di sì* its ability to express the highest and newest concepts 'convenevolmente, sufficientemente e acconciamente,' Dante contrasts the 'nudity' of prose with the 'accidental adornments' of poetry. The simile he introduces at the core of his defence casts the essence of poetry in far from positive terms. Paradoxically for a work in which poetry is presented as the master and prose as its servant, Dante claims that the great virtue of the Italian vernacular was hindered by the rhetorical garb of poetry:

> [La gran bontade del volgare di sí ... non si potea bene manifestare] ne le cose rimate, *per le accidentali adornezze* che quivi sono connesse, cioè la rima e lo ri[ti]mo e lo numero regolato: sì come non si può bene manifestare la bellezza d'una donna, quando li adornamenti dell'azzimare e de le vestimenta la fanno più ammirare che essa medesima. (*Convivio* 1.x.12)

> [The great goodness of the vernacular of *sí* ... could not be expressed perfectly] in verse, because of *the accidental adornments* that are tied to it, that is, rhyme and meter, just as the beauty of a woman cannot be perfectly expressed when the adornment of her preparation and apparel do more to make her admired than she does herself.

No argument calling into question the allegorical nature of the *canzoni* on which *Convivio* is focused can mitigate the force of the point Dante makes here.[2] The issue is not the effect of allegorical *inventio* on the poetic text, as was the case in *Vita nuova* 25; it is precisely what makes poetry what it is that works as an impeding factor in the way language carries out its work. In the argument of *Convivio* 1, the artificial beauty of the poems is not the allegorical veil or the diegetic fiction of Lady Philosophy; it is rhyme, rhythm, and regular syllabic scansion. In the continued simile adopted here, the distinctive markers of poetry are to the natural beauty of language what Dante will again call an 'accidentale adornamento':

> Onde, chi vuole ben giudicare d'una donna, guardi quella quando solo sua naturale bellezza si sta con lei, da tutto accidentale adornamento discompagnata. (*Convivio* 1.x.13)

> Therefore, if anyone wishes to judge a woman justly, let him look at her when her natural beauty alone attends her, unaccompanied by any accidental adornment.

In the theory of *Convivio*, prose commentary and poetic texts are juxtaposed in a relationship that is hardly to the advantage of the allegedly pre-eminent poetry. In the argument Dante advances in *Convivio* and *De vulgari eloquentia*, prose is not only free from the imaginative superstructures of allegorical poetry, but it is also free from the fettering constraints of style by which poetry is necessarily bound. And this, for the author of *Convivio*, who is engaged in an attempt to promote himself as a philosopher, is a good thing. Philosophy is the controlling agent and eventual justification for his poems: in Merleau-Ponty's terms, in *Convivio* Dante practises 'great prose,' but he theorizes 'prosaic writing.'

Not unexpectedly by now, we find the same situation in the Latin of *De vulgari eloquentia*. In the course of a different argument, but with practically the same language, Dante returns to the simile of the 'accidental accoutrement of a woman.' The consequences of his reasoning are the same as well. In the opening of book 2 of *De vulgari eloquentia*, while discussing in rather traditional terms the notion of *convenientia* between subject matter and style, Dante notes:

> Unde cum *sententia versificantium semper verbis discretive mixta remaneat, si non fuerit optima, optimo sociata vulgari non melior sed deterior apparebit, quemadmodum turpis mulier si auro vel serico vestiatur.* (*De vulgari eloquentia* 2.i.10)³

> So, *since poets' thought is mixed with their words but can always be distinguished from them,* when that thought is not of the best it will not seem better for being mixed with the best type of vernacular, but worse – *as would an ugly woman swathed in gold or silk.*

What is striking in these two passages is the parallel simile linking the 'content' of writing (*sententia*) with its 'form' (*verba*). The simile uses the same metaphorical model of body and clothing encountered earlier, a model in which a discrepancy between the outer and the inner image *can* exist. As we have seen, in *Convivio* the linguistic mechanism for the expression of concepts can be hindered by poetry's external adornment. Similarly, in *De vulgari eloquentia* Dante condemns any possible discrepancy between the *optime conceptiones* and that unity of language and style that the *optima loquela* has become in book 2 (i.8). In spite of the instrumentally different arguments to which they belong, the points made in *Convivio* and *De vulgari eloquentia* coincide. In the two works, Dante's argument constantly moves in the same value-laden metaphorical field and relies upon the same notion of a separation between *verba* and *sententia* – the stylistic clothing of meaning versus meaning itself. The *exornatio* mentioned in paragraph 9 is like the *azzimare* of *Convivio* 1.x.13. They both are metaphorically external and conceptually heterogeneous (*discretive mixta*) with respect to the 'true content' of the poetic text. They both act as a hindrance to the natural flow of meaning through the poetic text.

My reading of these two *loci* radically diverges from the widely accepted interpretation that Mengaldo advanced in his 1967 introduction to the Latin treatise and repeatedly defended in later statements on the matter.[4] Mengaldo argues that rather than reinforcing each other, the passage in *De vulgari eloquentia* reformulates and actually undercuts that of *Convivio*, replacing Dante's focus on traditional ornamentation with a newly discovered notion of stylistic decorum (*convenientia*). While it is true, as he maintains, that the principle of *convenientia* delimits and qualifies the generic category of *ornatus*, it is no less true that Dante has not let go of either the notion that poetry is constituted by extrinsic additions to prose meanings or of the metaphor of style as accoutrement. The active principle that subject matter and language remain *discretive mixta* is still valid. In *De vulgari eloquentia* Dante restrictively claims that *only* poets endowed with *ingenium* and *scientia* should use the illustrious vernacular, and then *only* when singing in the highest register (the *canzone*), and *only* about the highest kind of human experience; but the argument he develops still rests on the fundamental notion that the sensory and semantic spheres of poetic language are distinct and separable. Indeed, the argument can function only because of this separation:

> Et ubi dicitur quod quilibet suos versus exornare debet in quantum potest, verum esse testamur; sed nec bovem epiphiatum nec balteatum suem dicemus ornatum, immo potius deturpatum ridemus illum: *est enim exornatio alicuius convenientis additio*. (*De vulgari eloquentia* 2.i.9)

> And as for my remark that anyone should embellish his lines as much as he can, I declare that this is true; but would not call an ox well-adorned if it were dressed up to look like a horse, or a sow if it wore a sword-belt – rather, we would laugh at their disfiguring get-up, *for true adornment consists in the addition of something appropriate*.

Insofar as they are of inferior quality, Dante treats these poems in a different register, and they are now metaphorized as animals. Accordingly, their linguistic and stylistic accoutrements may become these animals' unsuitable harnessing. The metaphorical field has slightly shifted, but the essential and unmitigated split between surface and depth, form and content, style and meaning, has remained the same. The image of a harnessed ox or of a pig wearing an epic *balteum* are certainly more inappropriate than the clothing of a human body, but the form of the metaphorical relations remains the same. While making a point about poetry and style in which the role of *convenientia* is stressed, Dante reasserts the same split between *sententia* and *verba* with which he had already familiarized us in *Convivio*: *additio* is in no way a neutral term.

In sum, Mengaldo might be right in suggesting that *De vulgari eloquentia* complicates the perspective of *Convivio* by introducing the notion that not *any* kind of ornamentation fits *any* subject matter or *any* writer. Yet, in order to defend Dante in matters of *decorum*, he is forced to downplay Dante's initial, surprisingly strong, and logically foundational statement. That is, he is forced to disregard precisely the traditional features that are still present in Dante's argument and connect it with the position he held in *Convivio*. In both treatises, poetry 'adds' something that is 'accidental' and 'non concretive' to its content. In the theory of poetry Dante develops in the treatises, poetry always has two distinct components, and meaning is said never to be one with language. In the chemistry of Dante's poetics, when mixed together, words and meanings never form a solution – at best they are able to achieve a state of (more or less stable) emulsion.

2.1 Meaning in Poetry: The Task of Prose

As we know, *Convivio* starts off with a strong, if nuanced, declaration of continuity with *Vita nuova* and suggests a retrospective and radically selective reading of the *libello*.[5] Instrumental as they are, Dante's words at the onset of the later treatise attempt to build a coherent picture and present his earlier book as not incompatible with his new blend of allegorical poetry and scholastic prose:

> E se ne la presente opera ... più virilmente si trattasse che ne la Vita Nuova, non intendo però a quella in parte alcuna derogare, ma maggiormente giovare per questa quella; veggendo come ragionevolmente quella fervida e passionata, questa temperata e virile esser conviene. Ché altro si conviene e dire e operare ad una etade che ad altra. (*Convivio* 1.i.16–17)

> If in the present work ... the subject is treated more maturely than in the *Vita Nuova*, I do not intend by this in any way to disparage that book but

rather more greatly to support it with this one, seeing that it understandably suits that one to be fervid and passionate, and this one tempered and mature.

We have already seen and briefly examined the programmatic declaration at the core of these lines. When read together with a larger portion of their context, however, Dante's statements gain in weight and relevance. Framed in an argument on what is suitable to each age in a man's (and a writer's) life, they now appeal to a notion of *convenientia* that holds the place of nature's law. The mature writer looks back to the start of his career and presents his first steps as the first stages of a linear development. The apparent break between the earlier and the new *prosimetrum*, a discontinuity in inspiration that Dante himself cannot pretend to ignore, is confidently translated into a peaceful evolution. However, while the author is confident, the reader is less so: the key elements of *Vita nuova* that need to be discounted or radically rewritten for the two works to be aligned are so many that readers of both works have often resisted the author's hermeneutic pressure. As we are about to explore, there are good reasons for this to happen.

When Dante invited readers to see linear progression in his moving from *Vita nuova* to *Convivio*, he was certainly forcing their hand. However, one element of Dante's intellectual mindset and writing practice remains constant in both the youthful *libello* and the mature treatise – something that may have helped readers not to dismiss the cited paragraph as purely conciliatory rhetoric. Just as it was in *Vita nuova*, in *Convivio* prose is called upon to interpret past poetic texts. This time the explicit goal of prose is to prove that Dante's poetry had been about love only in a limited, merely literal sense – starting, at least, from the episode of the 'donna gentile' in the *libello*. On a deeper and truer level, or so Dante insists now, his poetry had always been serious, philosophical, and encyclopedic:

> E con ciò sia cosa *che la vera intenzione mia* fosse altra che quella che di fuori mostrano le canzoni predette, per allegorica esposizione quelle intendo mostrare, appresso la litterale istoria ragionata. (*Convivio* 1.i.17)

> Since *my true meaning* was other than what the previously mentioned canzoni outwardly reveal, I intend to explain these canzoni by means of an allegorical exposition, after having discussed the literal account.

Dante soon returns to the point, again stressing his authorial mandate to gloss his own poetic texts and predicating a split between apparent and recondite meaning in his poems:

> Intendo anche mostrare *la vera sentenza di quelle*, che per alcuno vedere non si può s'io non la conto, perché è nascosta sotto figura d'allegoria. (1.ii.17)

> I intend also to show *the true meaning of the canzoni*, which no one can perceive unless I reveal it, because it is hidden beneath the figure of allegory.

What is particularly interesting in these programmatic passages is the split Dante posits between 'apparent' and 'authentic' meaning (*intenzione, sentenza*) of the poems that he will use as a springboard for his arguments in *Convivio*. These poems have an outward surface (*di fuori sotto figura*) and an inside core (*sentenza*), the former covering and hiding the latter. His choice of giving up the results he had achieved in *Vita nuova* and drastically reorienting both the poetics and the plot of his first work has a price – one that will be most evident on the level of Dante's poetics. If he lends to the project of the vernacular treatise the force of the most powerful arguments he can muster, Dante also feigns oblivion to the potential disruptiveness of his own enterprise.

To be sure, the theory of poetry Dante produces in *Convivio* and that of style advanced in *De vulgari eloquentia* are designed to account for and promote his present (or at least most recent) poetic output. However, though never explicitly denied in the two treatises, Dante's identity as a poet is subordinated to the new role he casts for himself as a 'serious' intellectual, who appears to privilege prose as the vehicle of his more authentic intention. The *canzoni* which he now says hide a philosophical content under a fictional erotic veil are only, of course, the pretext to spin a web of arguments encyclopedic in aspiration. (Dante's ideal model at this stage is most likely Brunetto Latini, in particular his Old French encyclopedia, the *Tresor*.)[6] But aside from the choice of his *alter ego*, one element in his strategy is striking: Dante presents himself essentially as a writer of prose and in his enthusiastic philosophical writing he brackets one crucial corollary of the theory he sets forth. His exaltation of prose runs the risk of marginalizing poetry and condemning it to a minor role. The line of argument pursued in the treatises, seemingly paradoxical for a poet who still claims to be writing a commentary 'in the service' of his poetry, produces a theoretical imbalance between the two components of his *prosimetrum*. In the strain of argument we have followed thus far, Dante reveals a penchant for privileging prose at the expense of poetry – at least in his programmatic statements.[7]

The paradox embedded in Dante's treatment of the prose/poetry dichotomy is that in the new framework the specific qualities of poetry are destined to be treated, at least in theory, as dispensable. This feature of his new 'prosaics' is rooted, as we have suggested in chapter 1, in language. In addressing the virtues of the vernacular Dante confidently says that the more transparent language is, the better it is able to perform its function:

> [Ciascuna cosa è virtuosa in sua natura che fa quello a che ella è ordinata; e quanto meglio lo fa tanto è più virtuosa]. Così lo sermone, lo quale è ordinato a manifestare lo concetto umano, è virtuoso quando quello fa, e più virtuoso quello che più lo fa. (*Convivio* I.v.11)[8]

> Everything is virtuous in its nature which fulfills the purpose toward which it is directed; and the better it does this, the more virtuous it is. Thus language, which is constituted to express human thought, is virtuous when it does this, and the more completely it does this, the more virtuous it is.

This apparently innocent and almost commonsense observation, stemming from the definition of language as a tool to manifest concepts, hides a disruptive corollary, at least for a poet. If the goal of language is clarity, then prose is far superior to poetry in achieving it. In the avowed logic of *Convivio*, words (as signifiers) are the repository of beauty, whereas it is to their meanings (what is signified) that goodness is entrusted. In the context of a disjunctive argument, in which the beauty and goodness of any given language are opposed, each is assigned a sphere of influence. Dante eventually subsumes them under the wider category of intellectual pleasure, but in the passage excerpted above they maintain distinct identities. The same will be true in the summary with which Dante concludes his survey of the virtues of the vernacular, but with even stronger language:

> E però dico al presente che la bontade e bellezza di ciascuno sermone sono intra loro partite e diverse, che la bontade è ne la sentenza, e la bellezza è

ne l'ornamento de le parole; e l'una e l'altra è con diletto, avvegna che la bontade sia massimamente dilettosa. (*Convivio* 2.xi.4)

Therefore I say here that the goodness and the beauty of every discourse are separate and different from one another; for goodness lies in the meaning, and beauty in the adornment of the words; and both the one and the other give pleasure, although goodness is especially pleasing.

The last statement is a symptomatic afterthought: even if both beauty and goodness are sources of pleasure, it is from goodness that the author of the mature prose of *Convivio* deems that the greater pleasure may arise. This is the pleasure connected with the 'amoroso uso di sapienza' – the practice of philosophy – that is central for the prose project of *Convivio*.[9] It is a pleasure that might, in a particular case, use poetry to be elicited, but that surely does not need it. By predicating separation between meaning and adornment and assigning independent spheres of influence to each (*partite e diverse*), Dante the 'lover of wisdom' subordinates the contribution of poetry to that of prose. Poetry is, for the purposes of *Convivio*, an accessory. Of course, Dante will never be ready to do away with it altogether, but the language he adopts in the metapoetic sections of the treatise suggests a measure of discomfort, at least for the modern reader.

This conclusion is not merely a modern critical extrapolation from Dante's text. At the beginning of his work, Dante had candidly admitted that his poetry *was in need* of the prose commentary:

> La vivanda di questo convivio sarà di quattordici canzoni sì d'amor come di vertù materiate, *le quali sanza lo presente pane aveano d'alcuna oscuritate ombra*, sì che a molti loro bellezza più che loro bontade era in grado. (*Convivio* 1.i.14)

> The meat of this banquet will be prepared in fourteen ways: that is, in fourteen canzoni, whose subject is both love as well as virtue. *By lacking the present bread they possessed some degree of obscurity*, so that to many their beauty was more pleasing than their goodness.

Addressing nothing less than the question of why he ultimately wrote *Convivio*, Dante gives a simple answer: his texts have been misunderstood – at least by the *hoi polloi*. Readers had betrayed both local and general authorial intentions, and their interpretations needed to be corrected on two counts. First, readers had erred in attributing precise historical meaning to individual poems. They had fallen into the literal darkness of the text. Second, they had inadvertently contravened the new general requirement established by the philosophizing poet: they had enjoyed the extrinsic form rather than the intrinsic message of his poetry, while Dante's goal was goodness, not beauty. The author of the *Convivio* shows the need (and feels entitled) to correct the double hermeneutic error of his readers. Once again, the present declaration is not to be taken at face value. The causes the author of *Convivio* alleges for his work are of course instrumental to defending the general experiment with allegorical, at first, and eventually philosophical poetry that he is undertaking. They serve, that is, a specific practical purpose: 'justifying' the form of commentary that *Convivio* quite surprisingly adopts. Their force as programmatic statements, however, remains. They may be pretexts, but they still are allowed to be the keystone of the work's pact with its readership.

Readers, the argument of *Convivio* insists, are not the only ones to be blamed for the miscommunication: the poems themselves allegedly share some of the responsibility. If, in order to signify correctly, Dante's poetry needs to be supplemented with external aid, it follows that it must be lacking something: this is the 'ombra,' the slight degree of obscurity that the author imputes to them and which his later commentary will eliminate. If this were not the case, the whole project of adding a systematic prose commentary on his *canzoni* would make little sense.[10] By interpreting poetry – that is, by manifesting the 'conceived meaning' that the *canzoni* contained but apparently somehow failed to transmit on their own – the prose of the *Convivio* achieves a status paradoxically superior to the poetry in whose service it claims to have been deployed.

More than the alleged reasons for the composition of the commentary, however, it is the results that the commentary implies it will have on the poetry that may have worrisome consequences. In triumphantly declaring the value of the commentary he appends to his poetic texts, Dante insists that 'this bread' (the present explanation) 'will be the light that renders visible *every shade of their meaning*': 'Ma questo pane, cioè la presente disposizione, sarà la luce la quale *ogni colore di loro sentenza farà parvente* (*Convivio* 1.1.15). The conclusion of the argument appears irresistible. According to the author of the commentary, no residue of meaning will be left unexplained in his poetry: every particle of it will be illuminated. In short, according to the system of equivalence set up in the work, his entire text will be turned into prose. The argument is, again, essentially instrumental – aimed, as it is, to support the narrative of Dante's own intellectual progress – but the language of his poetics is far from neutral. In particular, it suggestively parallels that of his linguistics. As we have seen, in his treatment of Latin as a model-language (see chapter 1, but also, for the vernacular, the text of *Convivio* 1.v.8 cited above), Dante had touched on the same point. In its ideal state, language should become a transparent conveyor of concepts, a currency that is exchanged at a perfect one-to-one rate, leaving no residues of meaning 'untransacted.' Prose is now called upon to do the same. In sum, while they are subordinated to a promotion of poetry, Dante's arguments also reveal the limitations that he accepted in order to justify theoretically his poetic texts. Regardless of the strain they imposed on his reasoning, Dante accepted that his work as self-commentator in *Convivio* would frame his poetry in a cogently conservative set of principles.

What is more, Dante is apparently moving in a similar intellectual framework when he develops the central argument of *De vulgari eloquentia*. The same paradox perceptible in *Convivio*'s poetics, that of facing the necessity of dissolving his own poetry into the communicative prose of the commentary in order to make it authoritative, also potentially infiltrates the linguistics of the Latin treatise. Here too, Dante's search for a transparent language to communicate the state of things mirrored in the writer's concepts leads him to acknowledge that poetry can add only an obscuring veil to the truth that linguistic artefacts are to convey. Notwithstanding the attention he gives to poetry in book 2, Dante seems de facto unwilling to let go of the metaphorical field we have explored above and thus frames the poet's activity as one of extrinsic addition.[11] In *Convivio* the main corollary that ensued from this axiom was that an addition of further fictional and rhetorical layers to the meaning of a text only renders its decipherment more difficult. The same appears to be true for the theory of *De vulgari eloquentia*.

In his definition of poetry, Dante frames poetry in terms that are fully compatible with the reasoning of *Convivio*. If, as Dante states, poetry is nothing but *'fictio rhetorica musicaque poita'* (*De vulgari eloquentia* 2.iv.2), it follows that the compositional and creative activity of its author is merely *adding* figures and rhetorical colours to his subject matter. The exact value of Dante's word *fictio* has been widely debated. Though diverging radically from one another, the two current proposals do not resolve the problem raised by his choice of vocabulary. Poetry is either a 'composition *poita* (arranged) with the tools of rhetoric and music,' as Gioacchino Paparelli translates Dante's wording, stressing the elocutive, stylistic side of the definition, or a 'fiction composed with the tools of rhetoric and music,' as Mengaldo insists, stressing the inventive, content-related side of the definition.[12] Whether oriented towards content or form, Dante's notion of *fictio* subtends a discourse of *longue durée* on the role of the poet, one that extends as far back as *Vita nuova* 25, reaches several loci of *Convivio*, and culminates in the wording of *De vulgari eloquentia* that frames poetry as potentially hindering communication. In the metapoetic section of the *libello* as well as in the mid-career treatises, the specific role of the poet consists in his weaving a web either of fictions (on the level of *inventio*) or of rhetorical embellishments (on the level of *elocutio*) around an intellectual core. The question is not new: mirrored on a different level, it again posits a split between the surface and the deeper structure of poetry, its beauty and goodness, its sound and meaning. This is the same dichotomy we observed in the previous section of *Convivio*.

The keywords that make their appearance in the definition of poetry, that is, rhetoric and music, have in fact a parallel existence in *Convivio*. In glossing the literal sense of the *tornata* (envoy) of *Voi che 'ntendendo*, and basically paraphrasing it, Dante notes that even if the 'goodness' of his text has escaped many, its 'beauty' could still recommend its reading. Of the three components of the poem's beauty that he lists – that is, composition, order, and rhythm – two fall under the same categories isolated in the definition of poetry in *De vulgari eloquentia*:

> Che non voglio in ciò altro dire, secondo che è detto di sopra, se non: O uomini, che vedere non potete la sentenza di questa canzone, non la rifiutate però; ma ponete mente la sua bellezza, che è grande sì per [la] construzione, la quale si pertiene alli gramatici, sì per l'ordine del sermone, che si pertiene alli rettorici, sì per lo numero delle sue parti, che si pertiene alli musici. Le quali cose in essa si possono belle vedere, per chi ben guarda. (*Convivio* 2.xi.9)

> For I mean nothing by this, as has been said above, save: You men who cannot perceive the meaning of this *canzone*, do not therefore reject it; rather consider its beauty, which is great by virtue of its composition, which is the concern of the grammarians, by virtue of the order of its discourse, which is the concern of the rhetoricians, and by the virtue of the rhythm of its parts, which is the concern of the musicians. These things can be perceived within it as beautiful by anyone who looks closely.

To grammar, rhetoric, and music is entrusted this poem's beauty, which is extrinsic to the *sentenza*, the meaning that has remained hidden beneath the surface of the text and that the commentary is now unearthing. In what Barański calls the 'new balance' between prose and poetry that Dante is trying to achieve in *Convivio* (and, we may add at this point, in *De vulgari eloquentia* as well), poetry is strategically associated with complexity. And complexity, in the philosophical framework of the treatises, calls for the intervention of prose.[13]

In the passages examined above, Dante associates the surface of his texts with the past and their real meaning (their *sentenza*, his *intenzione*) with its present manifestation. The task as self-appointed commentator is to reveal now what he had hidden beneath their poetic clothing. If the stance Dante takes here completely overturns both the letter and spirit of his first work, this does not seem to constitute a problem for the author of *Convivio*. He appears ready to renounce whatever authority *Vita nuova* could grant him as an inspired and spiritual poet of love in order to prove the feasibility of his new project, namely, the ability to extract intellectual truths from his poetry and communicate those truths in the rational vehicle of vernacular prose. Engaged as he is in advancing through prose the immodest proposal that his own poetry is the highest intellectual achievement ever to be drafted in the illustrious vernacular, Dante brackets the potential paradoxes of his theory. The extreme consequences of the reasoning about language he had developed in *Convivio* and *De vulgari eloquentia*, however, have a force of their own. Once he has started to separate subject matter from poetic form and engaged in metaphorical reasoning that reinforced this idea, his argument tends to discount poetry in favour of prose. If poetry's goal is to transmit a content that is non-concretive with its form, and the goal of language is to convey concepts independently or even in spite of the form in which it does so, poetry becomes unnecessary for this project.

Within the framework of the vernacular treatise, the conclusion of the argument is that prose is destined to dissolve poetry into its philosophical meaning, reduce its polysemy, and – in spite of failing to have the same 'sweetness' and 'beauty' that poetry retains – finally exhaust it. Thus, paradoxically, the chronological supplementary nature of prose to poetry is also balanced by intimations that poetry can only partially convey meaning and that 'only' prose is likely to transmit it in full. To be sure, in the argument running through the *Convivio*, poetry still maintains exclusive control of the sensual sphere of communication, thanks both to the 'sweetness' that prose is never able to replicate and to poetry's higher linguistic 'regularity.'[14] Yet, when Dante comes to hermeneutics, to the instruments he sees as appropriate to retrieve meaning from poetry, he privileges the expository prose commentary he is now writing over the actual poetic texts he has already produced. Poetry may be in charge of originating meaning, but prose controls it, and it is only in prose that meaning finally resides. Let me state this again: the framework I am extracting from the meta-poetic areas of *Convivio* is for Dante both provisional and pretextual. The theoretical statements on poetry analysed above were instrumental to a specific project: Dante's fashioning of himself as a writer of poetry worthy of being read by those who sought wisdom. In his work of self-promotion in the philosophical camp, Dante accepted specific philosophical postulates, and chose a specific lexicon. As it was strategic, his choice was also temporary. The same statements explored above were soon to be reviewed and discarded, as Dante moved away from the allegorizations of the love poems contained in *Convivio* 2 and 3 to engage, with *Le dolci rime*, in the writing of immediately 'philosophical poetry,' a move which preludes most directly the poetry of the *Commedia*.[15] Just as, in the *Commedia*, he was eventually able to recover both the plot of *Vita nuova* and the historical foundation of poetry, discarding the ('mental' or 'psychological') allegorical option offered by his prose works, so too he will abandon in an inchoate state the experiment of his allegorical and philosophical *prosimetrum* he embarked upon with *Convivio* and the poetics that sustained it. If this is true, however, it is also true that, when he was engaged in writing the treatise, neither the features of *Vita nuova* that – from the vantage point of the *Commedia* – he will treasure nor the option in favour of self-sufficient poetry that will be the mark of the poem, received much space. At a certain point in his meditation on poetry, Dante appears to have thought that the ideas outlined above could work as the backbone of a justification of poetry. The fact that they could not and eventually needed to be revised or, in some cases, rejected should not be held against them: their currency may be local, limited to what traditionally has been seen as Dante's dalliance with (radical) philosophy, but inside those limits they do have some weight. Downplaying their importance may prevent us from acknowledging their return in the *Commedia*, as the disturbing foil for the new tacit theory and aggressive praxis of the poem.

We have seen that Dante's apparently more assertive advocacy of prose in *Convivio* is compatible, but should not be conflated, with the latently disturbing elements embedded in the poetics of *De vulgari eloquentia*. In the vernacular treatise, where the aim of the work was, at least in part, to advance a model of vernacular prose writing, the stress unambiguously fell on the superiority of prose over poetry for the philosophical task at hand. In *De vulgari eloquentia*, the situation is slightly different and Dante's approach more nuanced. Poetry is the object of Dante's promotion, and for it he prescribes an exacting and restrictive regimen of stylistic attention throughout the treatise. Similar restrictions should be put in place when we consider the thin thread uniting *Convivio* and *Vita nuova* on this point. In pointing out and underlining the common metaphorical field that links Dante's two *prosimetra*, we should be careful not to conflate these works completely. As suggested above, there are radical differences between the explicit poetics to which *Vita nuova* and *Convivio* respectively subscribe, contradictions that Dante will be hard pressed to elide in order to present a coherent public intellectual profile. The most radical and irreducible divergence between these works is the different status that Dante grants to their divergent narratives.[16]

In his first major enterprise, Dante offers for interpretation a series of poems that have had their origin in a fully historical series of events; the same cannot be said of the poems commented on in *Convivio*. Even if the two exegetical models appear side by side in the work, the poems of the *Vita nuova* seem to require the pseudo-biographical sketches, inspired by the Provençal *vidas*, more than the scholastic *divisioni*.[17] In *Convivio*, on the contrary, Dante's argument appears to move in the opposite direction, and he privileges the exposition of truths hidden within the letter of his poems over the narrative account of the letter itself. The two distinct kinds of hermeneutic prose (historical and analytical) appear again (and again in conjunction with one another), but the ultimate act of reading that Dante foresees is the one that goes beyond the fictional pseudo-historical narrative to reach what he claims is the 'true meaning' of the text (see, below, the text of *Convivio* 1.i.18). This distinction, though subtle, is crucial. In *Vita nuova*, the prose conveys the new, but in no way ultimate, meaning of the poems by framing them with a narrative structure that stabilizes their reference. The historical dimension, on the contrary, is progressively removed from the project of *Convivio*.[18]

In passing from the *libello* to an experiment with philosophical poetry, Dante makes the plot less substantial. It is not a question of historical accuracy: that kind of historicity is for both stories beside the point.

Rather, what matters is the difference in the quality of their respective plots which sets Dante's two *prosimetra* apart. In *Convivio*, the urban setting of *Vita nuova* is replaced by a mental setting. There are a host of witnesses who might be called to testify to what happened in *Vita nuova*, since several episodes (e.g., funerals and mourning sessions, the *gabbo*) take place on a public stage. But there are no witnesses to the plot of *Convivio* because there could have been none. The ultimate reference of the poetic texts commented upon in *Convivio* is to be found outside history, whereas in *Vita nuova* the 'meaning' of the poetry resides in the story – the facts that the prose claimed lay behind the poems, framed the work, and are entrusted to the *ragioni*. In *Convivio*, in sum, the meaning of the poems coincides with their being the formulation, beneath a thin veil of fictional narrative, of Dante's new intellectual position.

This difference is of some consequence for our eventual role as readers of the *Commedia*. *Convivio* is an experiment with a philosophical mode of writing that takes poetry as its vehicle and, in so doing, dehistoricizes it; the narrative explications provided in *Vita nuova* connect the poems to history. The prose of the treatise appeals to a traditional notion of poetry as a fictional veil for an intellectual content it calls truth; and this appeal distinguishes this work from *Vita nuova*, which endorses it in just one case, as we have seen. For the project of *Convivio*, the literal sense of the poems is to be resolved by the interpreting prose and dissolved as a pure 'poetic' *fictio* (in *Convivio* 2 and 3) or rhetorical *argumentatio* (in *Convivio* 4). For *Vita nuova*, prose was to support poetry by appealing to events that took place in time and space. The position of *Vita nuova* is, thus, eccentric with respect to the coherent poetic practices of both *De vulgari* and *Convivio*. It is set apart from the other works because it cannot be treated, strictly speaking, as a 'fictional' text, one that *demands* an allegorical reading in a philological vein.

Vita nuova resists this kind of interpretation, even though Dante attempts to accomplish precisely that through his later reconsideration (and recasting) of the *libello*'s last section in *Convivio* 2 and 3. In spite of the author's attempt to allegorize the episode of the poet-philosopher's infatuation for the 'donna gentile' as a sign of his love for Lady Philosophy, *Vita nuova* remains a radically historical work. In its narrative, Beatrice certainly is linked analogically to the sphere of the Divine, and thus transcends the level of what may be chronicled; yet she also resists being resolved into an allegorical projection of a philosophical tenet. If Dante claims for her a higher meaning, it is in her acting as a fully historical instrument of divine intervention into a precise set of temporal and spatial coordinates, not as a signpost for a lofty cultural ideal. Two features of *Convivio* are, on the other hand, symptomatic of Dante's adoption of a philosophical mode of writing, a choice that produced his provisional discounting of the historical dimension of his poems. First, as we shall see in the next chapter, the work contains a series of passages in which the narrative exposition of the *canzoni* is presented as merely instrumental to the discovery of the 'true meaning' through allegory. Second, with a more radical gesture, Dante even abandons both narrative and allegorical exposition in *Convivio* 4, admitting that the third *canzone* does not support any allegory and needs only a commentary on its literal meaning. As Barolini notes, this poem, the first for which allegory is explicitly deemed superfluous, is also the sole truly 'moral' *canzone* of *Convivio*, the only one in which no shred of narrative is needed.[19]

Dante's vernacular *prosimetra*, in sum, may originate in the same habit of self-commentary, but they are incompatible on a deeper level. Dante may well claim that '[he does] not intend by this in any way to disparage that book but rather more greatly to support it with this one'; yet the way he deals with the prose-poetry dichotomy and the models he selects for his prose are the source and the sign of their contrast. Noting the eccentricity of the *Vita nuova* on this particular point is not without relevance. In his first work, Dante provided his poems with a prose *explication de texte* that was intended to resolve their potential ambiguity, by anchoring them to the solid referential nature of the narrative from which the prose claimed the poems had originated. The *libello* was 'figural' rather than 'fictional': it did not rely upon a system of correspondences aimed at the dissolution of the literal sense, and prose had a more limited and more strictly ancillary role than in the *Convivio*. *Convivio* reversed this course, and it is not by chance that the *Commedia* will silently outflank the treatise on this point, reappropriating both the plot of *Vita nuova*, in its fully historical dimension, and the model of textual interpretation that the *libello* allowed. So too it is not by chance that the *Commedia* seldom, if ever, advocates the reductionist allegorical model envisioned in *Convivio*. The *Commedia* draws from *Vita nuova* a figural mode of signifying, in which interpretation is never allowed to dissolve the historical concreteness of characters and events.

One implication of a point I have made above needs to be briefly explored before we move into the examination of an essential corollary of the prosaic poetics advocated in the treatises. As I will argue in more detail in chapter 3, in *Vita nuova* Dante *permitted* a figural reading of his text but did not *advocate* it. He did not, in other words, overtly promote it as part of his poetics. Discussing the allegorical status of *Vita nuova*, Hollander explains Dante's reticence on this point as a sign of his invitation for his readers to 'solve the riddle' of the text (1980, 56–7). In avoiding head-on confrontation with its audience, the metapoetic section of *Vita nuova* is eerily similar to the *Epistle to Cangrande*: both texts are reticent about the major novelty they contain. As Barański has convincingly argued for the *Epistle* – though his argument could be extended to the meta-poetic section of the *libello* as well – rhetorically these texts are extremely conservative because they attempt to find a common meta-language with their audience. For the *Epistle* it is significant, as Hollander has suggested and as noted by adversaries of Dantean paternity, that it glosses over the crucial theological meaning of Dante's invocation at the beginning of *Paradiso* and that, in general, it presents an utterly traditionalist theory of genres. For the *libello*, it is chapter 25, the only one devoted to an explicit treatment of the principles that should govern the writing of poetry, that bears the weight of a poetics only limitedly able to account for the poetic practice of the book. In both cases, Dante's choice of joining conservative theory with surprising poetic practice is not so much the sign of a theoretical weakness of the author, but rather a strategic mediation.[20]

2.3 *Convenientia* across Secular and Biblical Writings

In spite of the principles that he declared he was following, Dante never gave up poetry. Rather, he abandoned the philosophical groundwork laid down in *Convivio* and *De vulgari eloquentia* and started off on a new path, one he had already traversed in *Vita nuova*. As we have seen while addressing issues of language and are again about to see in matters of style, Dante reoriented his inquiry on several interrelated points. In poetics, the notion that *verba* and *sententia* are *discretive mixta* is one of them. The traditional brand of poetics that he had practised so far made room for only two possible and very traditional goals for his poems. As defined in his pre-*Commedia* works, poetry can be either directed to the teaching of a truth (*bontade* hidden under the *inventio* veil of allegory) or intended as the pleasure-triggering element (*diletto* elicited by refined rhetorical *elocutio*) in the communication of that same truth. If they allow the poet momentarily to resist the pressure of a vociferous philosophically oriented culture and establish a dialogue – or, at least, open a channel of communication – with philosophically oriented readers, both these goals of poetic activity end up accepting and reinforcing a reductive framing of the question. In order to be tolerated alongside the exercise of dialectical rationality, Dante's pre-*Commedia* poetry accepts, at least in theory, a role subordinate to philosophical prose and limits its field of action to the sphere of imperfect, sensory, and transitory pleasure. But there is a problem. These principles actually promote a profoundly hedonistic theory of art that leaves poetry open to be indicted as mere *divertissement*. In this theoretical frame, if no intellectual content may be entrusted to poetry qua poetry, and the only addition to meaning that poetry can provide is pleasure, then there ultimately is no compelling reason for producing poetry at all. Any theory of poetry that hinges on the essential split and relative independence of beauty and meaning appears to lead to a dead end.

In his *Introduzione* to *De vulgari eloquentia* (pp. xl–xliv), Mengaldo directs our attention to a text, Bene da Firenze's *Candelabrum*, that might have been important for Dante's change of course. In this essentially traditional manual of rhetorical instruction, Mengaldo notes, scriptural authors are taken as the paradigm of a new kind of literary decorum (*convenientia*). The passages to which Mengaldo alludes come at the beginning of Bene's treatment of *dignitas orationis* (the ability to speak with elegance). The metaphor Bene chooses to characterize the relationship of matter and form is, unlike Dante's, one of interpenetration and intrinsic correspondence. Rather than garments and bodies, Bene connects elegance to the bond of body and soul. Human beings, he argues at the opening of book 2, have attained their elegance from the perfect combination of the elements, by virtue of the spirit that brings together body and soul ('carnem et animam virtute spiritus uniente,' 2.i.5). The metaphor is hardly inert. Indeed, for Bene it structures the more strict stylistics of oratory. In his definition, elegance of speech is the life that connects the bodily element of *voces* with the spiritual element of *intellectus*:

> Fabricam orationis homo efficit elegantem, ut voces, propriis intellectibus animate, virtute modorum significandi quasi quodam spiritu recte vivere videantur. (11–12)

> We are able to create an elegant edifice of speech when the words, brought to life by their appropriate meanings, appear to be enlivened by virtue of their modes of signifying – their spirit, so to speak.

Still moving within the central metaphorical field of body and soul, Bene attributes a special status to Holy Writ. This is the only product of human stylistic activity in which the potential of the initial metaphor is developed in full. It is only in Scripture, Bene writes, that one may find a double, and thus perfect, elegance:

> Sed quedam dignitas est verborum, et illa depingit orationem extrinsecus et colorat, et quedam dignitas medullam tantum sententiarum attingit, que ornatum intrisecus operatur. Ubi ergo utraque intervenit exornatio, ibi est omnimoda gratie plenitudo. (15)[21]

> But just as there is an elegance of the words, which paints and colours speech from the outside, so there is also an elegance that reaches the marrow of the meanings, and that one creates an inherent adornment. When both kinds of adornment, thus, come into play, you have the fullness of grace.

The use Mengaldo makes of some of these passages, treating them as antecedents for what he considers Dante's progress beyond the mechanical notion of ornamentation in *De vulgari eloquentia*, has one significant merit, but it is not without problems. While Mengaldo deserves recognition for pointing us in the direction in which Dante *will move* soon enough, he perhaps optimistically believes that Dante *has moved* already in *De vulgari eloquentia* in the same direction as Bene.

As far as one can see, in Dante's pre-*Commedia* works there is no trace of the double grace that Bene predicates of biblical texts: that is, rather, a principle by which, as we shall suggest in due course, Dante will abide in the *Commedia*. But before we reach that text we may want to look at another potential source of influence for the same notion, a source which, unlike Bene's *Candelabrum*, Dante will eventually cite in his works. A short detour into Augustine's meditation on classical and Christian rhetoric may help us to see that Dante could rely on other and, perhaps, weightier authorities than Bene when he re-evaluated some central notions in his poetics. In the third and fourth book of the *De doctrina christiana*, Augustine devotes ample space to defining the characters and aims of Christian rhetoric. The first notable feature of his treatment is the avoidance of a widely circulating argument (basically of Stoic origin) that opposed the absence of any rhetorical preoccupation in the Christian discourse to the artificial and highly formalistic rhetoric through which the classical high culture and knowledge were traditionally transmitted.[22] His argument takes a new turn. Rather than condemning and refusing rhetoric in itself, Augustine strives to prove that the language of the Scriptures was not lacking a rhetoric of its own. If the biblical authors practised a rhetoric differing in nature, principles, and aims from that of their non-Christian counterparts, so too the Church that based its teaching on these scriptures was not to renounce rhetoric altogether. It was, rather, to model its method of instruction and techniques of persuasion on a different set of examples. For Augustine, it was not a question of the presence or absence of rhetorical concerns from the Christian discourse, but one of two conflicting rhetorical systems that should be judged by their respective merits and then chosen between. *De doctrina christiana* devotes ample space, especially in book 4, to the solution of precisely this problem.

Moving into the exposition of a Christian paradigm for expression (*eloquentia*) after the contents to be taught – the doctrine (*scientia*) – had been laid out in the previous books, Augustine articulates his argument in two logically successive steps.[23] First, he declares the neutrality of the *ars rhetorica*, and then promotes a specific variety of it. Only after establishing that rhetoric can be used either for good or for wicked aims (in itself a rhetorical *topos* that finds its clearest expression in Quintilian's *Institutio* 2.16.5) does he proceed to detail a canon of Christian writers who had been able to combine their eloquence with the veracity of their doctrine, and then to lay out the foundations of a rhetorical appreciation of Scripture itself. The most extended section dedicated to the recovery of Scripture to the sphere of rhetorical and stylistic perfection, the second step in Augustine's treatment of rhetoric, is *De doctrina christianu* 4.vi.9–10. In two absorbing paragraphs Augustine delineates the magisterial role the Scriptures' stylistics should play in the cultural life of the Church. Scriptural authors, he maintains, have deployed all the typical features of classical rhetorical discourse. Their writings might even serve as a substitute textbook for the instruction of younger Christian intellectuals, providing them with a rhetorical expertise in no way inferior to that developed in a classical curriculum of *imitandi auctores*.

In addition to its equivalence with traditional works, however, Christian Scripture possesses a peculiar and superior rhetoric. Augustine very carefully introduces this element of novelty in his discourse, pre-empting – through a surprising use of the notion of *decorum* – the sceptical reservations that conservative and classicizing rhetorical theorists might have advanced. Against the objections that they may raise, he resorts to the fundamentally classicizing and conservative principle that there must be a *convenientia* between the speaker and his speech:

> Et audeo dicere omnes qui recte intellegunt quod illi loquuntur, simul intellegere non eos aliter loqui debuisse. Sicut enim est quaedam eloquentia quae magis aetatem iuvenilem decet, est quae senilem, nec iam dicenda est eloquentia si personae non congruit eloquentis, ita est quaedam quae viros summa auctoritate dignissimos planeque divinos decet. (4.vi.9)

> All who understand rightly what they [the Christian authors] say understand at the same time that it should not have been said in any other way. Just as there is a kind of eloquence for youth and another kind for age, that should not be called eloquence which is not appropriate to the person speaking. Thus there is a kind of eloquence fitting for men most worthy of the highest authority and clearly inspired by God.

The reasoning, couched in apparently traditional terms, hides beneath its brilliance and cogency a revolutionary statement. As a rule, classical precepts about *convenientia* had stressed the need to adjust one's rhetoric to *the circumstance of the reception of the speech* (time and place, social status of the audience, Aristotelian *ethos* of the hearers). They dealt only rarely and in passing with the necessity to accord the speech with *the circumstance of its production* (the social status of the speaker, his age, the office he might hold). This was, rather, the concern in the Greek tradition of the logographer – and the vaunt of the successful ones among them – for whom the distinction between the speaker and the writer of the speech turned the act of composing an oration into an extended exercise in 'speech in character' (*sermocinatio*).

By reversing the field of application of the traditional concept of *convenientia*, Augustine shifts his emphasis onto the moral characterization of the speaker.[24] He also prepares the ground for the definition of the new Christian rhetoric as 'alia rhetorica' that *De doctrina christiana* will give a few lines later. Once the outward stylistic appearance of biblical (and, in general, Christian) texts is linked via the notion of seemliness for, and correspondence to, the moral character of the speakers, the otherness of biblical and Christian rhetoric is not only justified but also rendered necessary by the very principles of the classical rhetoric it subtly comes to displace. The moral standing of Christian orators and writers, insofar as it differs from that of their counterparts, justifies and promotes the 'otherness' of biblical rhetoric for one fundamental reason. Christian intellectuals possess an intrinsic, polemically assumed, superiority with respect to non-Christians because their culture is theologically justified in subverting the classical ideal of stylistic *convenientia* between subject matter and level of style. Every aspect of Christian knowledge – rhetorical expertise included – is distinguished from, and rendered superior to, its counterpart – classical rhetoric included – for it is intrinsically related to the Christological paradox of collapsing high-low oppositions in the 'scandal' of the incarnation. The 'humiliation' of a God becoming man comes to subvert the traditional notion of stylistic *decorum* linked to the correspondence between high style and high content.[25]

There is, however, a second reason that Augustine offers to suggest the superiority of the new paradigm of literary culture he is advancing in *De doctrina christiana*. Whereas Christian rhetoric is associated with a dependence on the salvific message that the Scriptures transmit, Augustine connects the classical tradition with ideas of pride, display, and empty ostentation of technical virtuosity (see 4.vii.14). Christianity's rhetorical alterity is defined by the coming together of content and form. In the closing paragraph of chapter vii Augustine adds a final meditation on the goal of Christian rhetoric. Concluding his sampling of biblical stylistic excellence from Paul and the Prophet Amos, he notes:

> Et plura quidem, quae pertineant ad praecepta eloquentiae, in hoc ipso loco quem pro exemplo posuimus possunt reperiri. Sed bonum auditorem non tam, si diligenter discutiatur, instruit quam, si ardenter pronuntietur, accendit. Neque enim haec humana industria composita, sed divina mente sunt fusa et sapienter et eloquenter, *non intenta in eloquentiam sapientiam* sed a sapientia non recedente eloquentia. (4.vii.21)

> And more things which pertain to the precepts of eloquence may be found in this same passage which we have used as an example. But a good listener warms to it not so much by diligently analyzing it as by pronouncing it energetically. For these words were not devised by human industry, but were poured forth from the divine mind both wisely and eloquently, not in such a way that wisdom was *entirely focused on eloquence*, but in such a way that eloquence did not abandon wisdom.[26]

The force of biblical eloquence is located beyond human technical expertise and the all-too-human fixation on producing an artistic utterance. Divine inspiration (evoked in the clause 'divina mente fusa') rhetorically balances and conceptually replaces human artistry ('humana industria composita'). Concerns with the 'how' of writing are pushed into the background of this peculiar, innate, and self-confident (because self-effacing) eloquence of the biblical writers. The paragraph closes on the same note:

> Quapropter et eloquentes quidem, non solum sapientes, canonicos nostros auctores doctoresque fateamur, tali eloquentia qualis personis eiusmodi congruebat. (ibid.)

> Therefore let us say that our canonical authors and teachers were not only wise but eloquent in that kind of eloquence which is appropriate for such persons.

In Augustine's argument, the perfect and natural correspondence of speaker, subject matter, and mode of expression attained by Christian writers is measured against the foil of old, classical rhetoric. But it also becomes the keystone of his differential definition of a new paradigm of writing. In Augustine's theory of inspired, biblical writing, the very possibility of a divergence between the truth of the message and either its form or its sender has apparently disappeared. These are, one should note, the same splits that the theoretical set-up of Dante's treatises would not mend. Biblical literature and biblically inspired Christian writings are, at least in theory, immune from such potential drawbacks as we have seen dawning in Dante's pre-*Commedia* theorizations. They escape these problems, however, because they undeniably enjoy a special status. They represent a special kind of writing, one that Augustine, in his intellectual biography, will have to get to appreciate before he could advocate their stylistic merit on ethical grounds and invite their imitation.

Augustine's conversion to Christianity involved, alongside matters of an intellectual and ethical nature, a reconsideration of the stylistic value of the founding Christian texts. As he acknowledged both in the *Confessions* and elsewhere, one of the reasons that had long kept him away from the Christian faith was the indigestible style of the Christian sacred texts. A teacher of rhetoric who had based his training and formed his taste on the examples of classical Ciceronian and classicizing Quintilianean rhetoric, it was quite natural that Augustine should have met the Scriptures with open disgust and hostility. And in fact, in a famous passage in which he details the reasons for his initial aversion, he labels them 'indigna quam tullianae dignitati compararem' (unworthy in comparison to the dignity of Cicero; *Confessiones* 3.v.9).²⁷ Mobilizing a moral vocabulary and array of concepts that he will deploy in the later treatise, in the *Confessions* Augustine retrospectively attributes to his own prideful and stubborn disposition his inability to accost the Scriptures the right way. His final conversion to Christianity was not only moral: it was, to a certain degree, stylistic as well. Once he had shed the pride of his classicizing bias and fixation on an autonomous pursuit of style, Augustine gained the ability to regard biblical texts as rhetorically 'different' from, not 'inferior' to their classical counterparts. The notion of 'alia rhetorica' we have explored above was forged precisely in this ethical and aesthetic crucible.

In matters of style and rhetorical theory, Dante has left no explicit declaration accompanying his transition from unmarked indifference to pointed appreciation of the biblical model as we find in Augustine. All we are left to work with are, rather, the subtler, but no less significant traces of Dante's reconsideration and implicit correction of his earlier stance. By focusing on the question of the translation of poetic biblical texts, the next section will attempt to follow precisely these traces. It will show that Dante's evolving sensibility to biblical writing paralleled, in some respects, Augustine's experience, and suggest that Dante's eventual adoption of a biblical model for the *Commedia* was a choice that matured in his dialogue with Augustine's ideas and texts.

2.4 On Translating Meaning: Biblical Poetry and the Sweetness of the Psalms

Let us return to *Convivio*'s theorizations and see what Dante had to say about biblical writing in the treatise. In the previous sections, we have isolated several themes in Dante's thinking about his task as a poet in the pre-*Commedia* years that are linked by a recurring dichotomy. The opposition of content and form, which generates and parallels that between prose and poetry and spawns the flourishing of body-clothing metaphors explored above, has emerged as the underlying principle guiding his reflection. The core oppositional pair finds a further, sensitive area of application: Dante's notes on translation. Silently at times, and at times explicitly, the issue of translation is a constant in Dante's reflection on poetry, starting from the stance that he takes in *Convivio* 1, when he claims that no satisfactory translation of poetry is ever possible.

In *Convivio* 1.vii.15, Dante defends his choice to use the vernacular for his commentary, stating that a Latin commentary would have transgressed the limits of the poems' intentions. A Latin commentary, he argues, was going to be both too much and too little for his vernacular poems. On the one hand, a Latin commentary would only have been able to explain the meaning of Dante's *canzoni* to the learned – a fraction of the potential audience for his lyric texts. On the other hand, as the acknowledged official language of European culture, Latin would have brought the meaning of Dante's texts to too vast an audience – to 'Germans, English, and others,' who were not going to appreciate their beauty. His *canzoni*, metaphorically speaking, did not command their servant, the prose commentary, to perform either task:

> E qui averebbe passato lo loro comandamento; ché contra loro volere, largo parlando dico, sarebbe essere esposta la loro sentenza colà dov'elle non la potessero colla loro bellezza portare. (*Convivio* 1.vii.12–13)

> And here it would have exceeded their command; for it would have been against their will (broadly speaking, I say) for their meaning to have been explained where they could not convey it together with their beauty.

To the metaphorical argument Dante immediately adds a general statement about poetry. No poetic text, he maintains, can be translated without losing its distinctive quality, namely, sweetness: 'nulla cosa per legame musaico armonizzata si può della sua loquela in altra trasmutare sanza rompere tutta sua dolcezza ed armonia' (nothing harmonized according to the rules of poetry can be translated from its native tongue into another without destroying all its sweetness and harmony, 14). The rather inconsequential connection of the argument (moving from the prose of the commentary to the poetry of the lyric texts) is an indication that Dante is replying to a potential, albeit unexpressed, objection. If his goal is to grant the largest possible access to his poetry, why had he not translated his *canzoni* into Latin? Incidentally, if his poems were to be in Latin, adding a Latin commentary to a Latin text would be a natural option. Dante's insistence that no poetry can be translated without a loss of sweetness answers the implicit question: he did not translate his poems into Latin because a translation would dissolve their distinctive quality – it would make them cease to be poetry.

This consideration alone prevents him from pursuing self-translation in addition to self-commentary.

Dante's move is striking: his refusal even to consider the possibility of translating his own poetry amounts to a resistance against accepting the logical conclusions of his own postulates. His insistence on preserving the poetic quality of his texts constitutes the first intimation that his assumptions on matters of style may have become too narrow for him, and that he will soon need a way out of the self-imposed strictures of his poetics. Not yet, however. At this point of his career, Dante still prefers to keep his postulates in place and accept instead a corollary with wide-ranging consequences. Translation is so deadly for poetry that it has decreed the death of Homer, lost in the first *translatio* of power and knowledge from Greece to Rome:

> E però sappia ciascuno che nulla cosa per legame musaico armonizzata si può de la sua loquela in altra trasmutare, sanza rompere tutta sua dolcezza e armonia e questa è la cagione per che Omero non si mutò di greco in Latino, come l'altre scritture che avemo da loro. (*Convivio* 1.vii.14–15)

> Therefore everyone should know that nothing harmonized according to the rules of poetry can be translated from its native tongue into another without destroying all its sweetness and harmony. This is the reason why Homer has not been translated from Greek into Latin as have been other writings we have of theirs.

The passage may appear in tune with contemporary concerns, but the context to which it pertains should cast some doubt on its ultimate meaning. A mute mirage for the Latin West, the loss of Homer acts for Dante as sign of a foundational loss: however, in the same breath as it bears witness to Homer's inaccessibility, the prose of *Convivio* also surprisingly isolates him in this condition. If Homer is untranslatable, as Dante proceeds to argue, the opposite is true 'for the other writings' that Latin inherited (or rather, took over) from Greek; if sweetness is lost in translation, the semantic force of any non-poetic text is not. The point is not a minor one, and Dante does not make it in passing. Translation from poetry and transference of meaning are actually what the whole project of the prose treatises is concerned with. It may suffice to apply the same (perhaps deadly) coherence that Dante himself displayed when developing the core principles of his linguistics, and his seemingly (post)modern argument in favour of non-translatability is soon reduced to an untenable conclusion. According to the brand of rationalistic philosophy Dante practises there, the 'conceived meaning' of any utterance remains unaffected when transferred from a specific linguistic code to a new one. The process of cultural translation may well affect the poetic surface of linguistic utterances, compromising their sensual effects, but it never touches their meaning. This is the reason why we do not have a 'translated Homer,' while we do have a body of translated Greek prose: for the pre-*Commedia* Dante, translation of any non-poetic utterance is possible. As we shall see momentarily, translation also appears to leave no residue.

Thus, again, why does Dante resist the option of self-translation in *Convivio*? And why does he defend the original monolingualism of his vernacular poetry? The answer may be found in the example of the one attempt at translation, which he thinks went terribly wrong. As we have just read, according to the account Dante gives of the translation currents flowing through the Latin West, whereas Greek prose texts have been successfully translated and their meaning carried from Athens to Rome, biblical poetry suffered a deadly blow when it was transported from the original language to a new one. The specific nature of poetry – its frailty, if you will – is the reason why biblical poetry lost all its 'poetic' sweetness. Since poetry's *genus proximum* is language and its specific difference is that it is 'harmonized,' the necessary translation of the Psalms turned them into un-poetic language. Extending the taxonomy of disastrously translated texts beyond Homer's untranslated poetry, Dante notes:

> E questa è la cagione per che li versi del Salterio sono sanza dolcezza di musica e d'armonia; ché essi furono trasmutati d'ebreo in greco e di greco in latino, e ne la prima transmutazione tutta quella dolcezza venne meno. (*Convivio* 1.vii.15)

> And this is the reason why the verses of the Psalter lack the sweetness of music and harmony; for they were translated from Hebrew into Greek and from Greek into Latin, and in the first translation all their sweetness was lost.

The present account of the un-poetic quality of biblical writing reflects Dante's ambiguous handling of the question of translation. If his philosophy of language may allow Dante to argue that poetry – qua poetry – is not translatable, the same principles governing his linguistics compel him to conclude that the substance of language always is. Even when *Convivio* explicitly indicts Latin translations of the Psalter for having destroyed the sweetness of the original biblical poetry, it also directly implies that translation of meaning is *always* possible. In translation, sweetness alone is lost. And this loss, as we have had occasion to observe, is not crucial for the theory Dante develops in the treatises. The specific example Dante gives of a poetry that has ceased to be such may account for the utter lack of interest he shows in biblical Latin in *De vulgari eloquentia*. In that work, no biblical text is included in Dante's canon of *idonei auctores*: Virgil, Ovid, Statius, and Lucan provide the poet-to-be with the examples of the highest style in poetry, while Livy, Pliny, Frontinus (or Fronto), and Paulus Orosius cover the side of prose.[28] The Latin poets are labelled significantly 'regulatos poetas'; they have used a language (and have been guided by an explicit poetics) that Dante recommends for his readers' imitation:

> Differunt tamen a magnis poetis, hoc est a regularibus, quia magni sermone et arte regulari poetati sunt, hii vero casu, ut dictum est. Idcirco accidit ut, quantum illos proximius imitemur, tantum rectius poetemur. Unde nos doctrine operi intendentes doctrinatas eorum poetrias emulari oportet. (*De vulgari eloquentia* 2.iv.3)

> Yet they differ from the great poets, that is, those who obey the rules, since those great ones wrote their poetry in a language, and with a technique, governed by rules, whereas these write casually. Thus, it comes about that, the more closely we try to imitate the great poets, the more correctly we write poetry. So, since I am trying to write a theoretical work about poetry, it behoves me to emulate their learned works of poetic doctrine.

In its exemplarity, the 'regulated poetry' of the classics is neither subject to time nor the object of a possible translation: *Convivio* remarks that Latin comedies and tragedies 'non si possono trasmutare.' Both their language and their poetics concur in endowing the Latin texts with linguistic stability and stylistic normative value. On the contrary, by having undergone a triple *translatio*, by having lost their sweetness at the time of their first metamorphosis, and by having become prose, biblical Latin texts – even David's songs – have become stylistically inert. Dante's silence about biblical writing in his treatise is telling: it is a cultural blind spot, one caused by the theory of style that he espoused in both treatises.

The same general notion that biblical Latin has lost its poetic quality is also responsible for Dante's practice of translating into his vernacular all passages from the psalms he quotes in *Convivio*. It appears that, when he invokes the authority of the Bible in an argument, the outward appearance of the texts conveying this authority is irrelevant to the point he makes. The author of *Convivio* freely quotes the 'meaning' of these texts, reducing them to prose – *his* vernacular prose.[29] Nowhere in *Convivio* does Dante give any indication that he considers his translating from biblical Latin at all problematic. Having lost its sweetness, the Latin of the Bible is a stylistic *res nullius*.[30] Things change, radically, as the author of *Convivio* and *De vulgari eloquentia* becomes the author of the *Commedia*. Here the poetic quality of the Psalms is not only reasserted, but it also becomes the centre of Dante's attention.

Coming from a reading of *Convivio*, we may in fact be surprised by the words Dante attaches as a gloss to Nimrod's garbled speech in *Inferno* 31. In a few lines, Virgil will make clear that the words of the giant are to be taken as incomprehensible – the perfect and absolutely unique example of Wittgenstein's theoretically impossible 'private language' – with their meaning irretrievably lost in God's just punishment of the proud. The first feature of these words that the text of the poem targets, however, is their phonetic quality: Nimrod's words are labelled 'harsh.'[31] Dante chooses a significant way to make this point; he intimates the harshness of Nimrod's words by contrasting the speech he relates with the sweetness of a different text:

'Raphèl, maì amècche zabì almi'
cominciò a gridar la fiera bocca,
cui non si convenia più dolci salmi.
(*Inferno* 31.67–9)

'Raphèl maì amècche zabì almi,' / the savage mouth, for which no sweeter / psalms were fit, began to shout.

Of course, Dante's choice of the adjective 'dolci' has a contextual explanation: the words of the giant anticipate the linguistic harshness that dominates the third and lowest zone of hell. It is only proper that they be contrasted with the sweetness of other linguistic products. Yet, it is striking that Dante chose to contrast them with the sweetness of biblical poetry. The juxtaposition with Nimrod's words implies that the Psalms are, at least implicitly, and at least by contrast, poetically sweet. Perhaps only instrumentally, and yet unquestionably, Dante grants that Psalms are – or at least may be – poetic again. According to the theory laid out in *Convivio*, the only stage in their history of multiple translations at which Dante's assessment may have been appropriate for the Psalms would be their 'original' Hebrew. In their first linguistic form, those poems were actually sweet. Is then Dante alluding to their 'original' form when he comments upon Nimrod's voice? It may be so. But it may also be true that when he claims that the Psalms are indeed sweet, Dante is not talking about the un-translated Hebrew Bible (to which he had no access); he is talking about the only Bible he and his readers ever knew and, most importantly, were used to hearing: the Latin version of the Vulgate. There is a chance, in other words, that Dante is here exploring the other side of the question of translation and accepting the fact that, notwithstanding all the intervening translations, the words of the Psalmist still may sound sweet.

It is certainly too soon to talk about a new theory of poetic translatability, but if we read further and pay attention to Dante's practice of citation from the Psalms in the *Commedia*, we find evidence that actually supports this possibility. Whereas in the prose of the vernacular treatise Dante had felt free to give his own renditions of the un-poetic texts, the *Commedia* does not shy away from quoting the Latin in which they are now readable, starting from the first word the protagonist utters in the poem: 'Miserere' in *Inferno* 1.65 (echoing the incipit of Ps. 50). In the beginning, Dante will not expound on the quality of the texts he will hear the blessed sing in Purgatory and Paradise, but it will become increasingly clear that sweetness is the principal connotation of the language of David's songs – even in their new linguistic form. The first psalm Dante includes in the poem by quoting its incipit in the original Latin is number 113: *In exitu Israel de Aegypto*, which opens *Purgatorio* 2 (4–6). The souls who are ferried to the shores of Purgatory sing it in unison. Once again, Dante does not comment upon the quality of their song. In a calculated contrast with the explicitly 'sweet' love song that the newly arrived soul of Casella will sing for Dante, the psalm is a neutral song – one that marks the detachment from the wasteland of carnal life. The *Commedia* explicitly notes the sensorial quality of Casella's performance of *Amor che ne la mente mi ragiona* (the *canzone* of *Convivio* 3): 'cominciò sì dolcemente, / che la dolcezza ancor dentro mi suona' ('so sweetly, / that I still hear that sweetness sound in me,' vv. 112–14).

Accordingly (and contrastingly), the psalm sung by the newly arrived souls is not presented as pleasing to the ear. The moral duty of purgation, as the stern intervention of Cato will soon remind characters and readers alike, should leave no room, nor time, for the enjoyment of art through the senses. Their attachment to the sensorial world is exactly what these souls should leave behind in their journey towards freedom. Dante's silence might have moral grounds.[32]

As the Pilgrim moves up through the ledges of the mountain, however, the text will not refrain from glossing the poetry of the Latin Psalms as sweet. In *Purgatorio* 23, for instance, the souls of the gluttons sing a line from another psalm (Ps. 50), of which Dante provides a slightly modified quotation: *Labia mea Domine (aperies)*. The tercet in its entirety reads:

> Ed ecco pianger e cantar s'udìe
> '*Labïa mëa, Domine*' per modo
> tal, che diletto e doglia parturìe.
> (*Purgatorio* 23.10–12)

When with weeping we heard voices sing / '*Labïa mea, Domine*' in tones / that brought at once delight and grief.

The last line contains the first intimation that the singing of a psalm can be a source of aesthetic delight as well as instruction for the hearer. Couched in an ambivalent image, the pleasure-pain dyad represents the first instance of a larger phenomenon affecting the rest of the canto, namely, the necessarily oxymoronic form of any account of what purgation is about. As Forese, the protagonist of the episode, will remark, his purgatorial 'suffering' is also a 'joy.' First, on line 72, the character corrects his first assessment of his *pena*, redefining it as *sollazzo* ('I speak of pain but I should speak of solace'); then, in a bolder gesture, he enunciates the principle that purgation is the perfect (and perfectly poetic) coincidence of opposites – its metaphor being 'the sweet wormwood of torments' ('lo dolce assenzo d'i martìri,' v. 86). The paradoxical nature of the purgatorial process is mirrored in the liturgical songs that accompany it. The penitents' sufferings are a joy; the songs they sing mix pleasure and pain.[33] The bitter medicine of the mountain, including its musical ministration, is also sweet.

It is finally in *Purgatorio* 30.83–4 that the hints disseminated in the previous passages become an explicit statement about the sweetness of biblical poetry. The context is fairly straightforward: Beatrice has just started her harangue against Dante, and her powerful opening argument has been inspired by God's Justice rather than Mercy.[34] Beatrice, 'haughty mother,' is the bearer of a 'stern pity.' Dante should not be there, she remarks – how did he dare to reach the summit of the mountain where perfect earthly happiness is attained? Her questioning forces Dante to introspection: he lowers his gaze only to withdraw it when he sees his reflection in the stream of Lethe. Potentially, her harsh words have the effect of congealing Dante's soul in the memory of his past sins. To balance that effect, Dante introduces the song of mercy (Psalm 30) in the voice of the angels:

> Ella si tacque; e li angeli cantaro
> di subito 'In te, Domine, speravi';
> ma oltre 'pedes meos' non passaro.
> (Purgatorio 30.82–4)

> Then she fell silent and at once / the angles sang: 'In te, Domine, speravi,' / but did not sing past 'pedes meos.'

As the angels invite Beatrice to have mercy on him, Dante finally weeps. What melts 'the ice that had restrained *his* heart' is that he hears the angels intercede on his behalf 'ne le *dolci* tempre' (in their sweet harmonies).[35] Perhaps belatedly, but finally unambiguously, Dante's ever-present biblical poetry is acknowledged as sweet, even in its Latin translation.

Seen in retrospect, the psalm the angels sing for Dante comes to balance the quality of Casella's song in *Purgatorio* 2. When Dante's friend sang *Amor che ne la mente mi ragiona*, the sweetness of the song was such that it traversed the temporal and moral hiatus between poet and character. Its quality reverberated from the encounter on the shores of Purgatory to the workshop of the poem. When the angels sing the Psalm of David's (and Dante's) repentance, the sweetness of their song provokes the first phase of Dante's confession. As the end of his confession is reached, and he is ready to be immersed in the waters of Lethe, the psalm is sung again. This time, in explicit contrast with Casella's song, its sweetness surpasses memory and understanding:

> Quando fui presso a la beata riva,
> 'Asperges me' sì dolcemente udissi,
> che nol so rimembrar, non ch'io lo scriva.
> (Purgatorio 31.97–9)

> When I had come close to the blessed shore / I heard *'Asperges me'* so sweetly sung / that I cannot recall nor write it down.

The examples just examined suggest that Dante's outlook on the poetic quality of the translated Bible has changed in the time between the treatises and the poem. Dante's new appreciation of the poetic quality inherent in biblical writing mirrors Augustine's argument we have surveyed above. The Augustinian connection, however, extends beyond a mere coincidence in conclusions: Dante shares the same premises as Augustine as well. Just as in Dante linguistics and poetics go hand in hand, so too does Augustine's high regard for biblical poetics rest on linguistic grounds, in particular on an argument of historical linguistics. In discussing the double nature of Scripture, which he sees at the same time as divinely inspired and mediated by human authors, Augustine makes a remark strikingly similar to the essence of Dante's argument in *De vulgari eloquentia* (1.vii and viii.1–3), but with a different set of connotations. Both Augustine and Dante trace back to Babel – Nimrod's impious challenge to God's authority – the division and scattering of human languages. They both locate the origin of the need for translation in the punishment of human pride. Augustine, however, sees the need for God's word to be translated into different idioms as a less traumatic episode in the history of Mankind than Dante will:

> Ex quo [the sin of *superbia* punished at Babel] factum est ut etiam scriptura divina, qua tantis morbis humanarum voluntatium subvenitur, ab una lingua profecta, qua opportune potuit per orbem terrarum disseminari, per varias interpretum linguas longe lateque diffusa innotesceret gentibus ad salutem. (*De doctrina christiana* 2.v.6)

> Thus it happened that even the Sacred Scripture, by which so many maladies of the human will are cured, *having departed from one language, by which it could be conveniently disseminated through all the world*, it was scattered far and wide in the various languages of translators so that it might be known for the salvation of peoples.[36]

Babel, the incident that brought about the linguistic fall, retains its centrality as an age-defining moment in Augustine's treatise as it did in Dante's. Yet, the necessity of translation is presented in less dire terms than one might have expected. Augustine underplays the original linguistic trauma. The carefully balanced notion of Scripture's mixed character that he constructs in his work rescues the text of the Bible from the loss of 'sweetness' for which Dante, as we have seen, will not hesitate to condemn it in *Convivio*. Augustine's ecumenical spirit also eschews the related idea that language is in need of a *reparatio*, as *De vulgari eloquentia* instead suggests at 1.ix.11 in order to justify the invention of rational and fully human grammatical languages.[37]

Unlike Dante, Augustine does not postulate the need to remake a rational language in order to repair the damage done at Babel. For him, linguistic differentiation and the ensuing translation of Scripture are not necessarily an evil – nor will they be for Dante author of the *Commedia*. The answer to the multiplication of languages is dissemination through different idioms, rather than coercion into one artificial language of culture. Augustine's position is in perfect accord with his general understanding of Scripture as an essentially mediating artefact. By bridging the domains of human and divine language, God's word is from the start the result of a process of translation: the encryption of God's meaning into a human protocol for information sharing. The specifics of this or that code (linguistic differentiation) add very little to the basic hermeneutic process that is designed to retrieve that meaning. For Augustine, the inevitable process of translation that follows Babel can be configured as a 'loss' *only* because it is related to the third rebellion of mankind against its Creator.

To be sure, it was an act of pride consummated at Babel that brought about God's third exemplary chastisement – the confusion of idioms – after the banishment from Eden and the Flood did not curb Man's overreaching pride. The third 'original' sin of Mankind is not, however, as threatening to the process of communication as Dante presents it. Unlike Dante, Augustine sees Babel as a purely moral problem, not as a linguistic or stylistic one:

Ista signa igitur non potuerunt communia esse omnibus gentibus peccato quodam dissensionis humanae, cum ad se quisque principatum rapit. Cuius superbiae signum est erecta illa turris in caelum, ubi homines impii non solum animos sed etiam voces dissonas habere meruerunt. (*De doctrina christiana* 2.iv.5)

These signs could not be common to all peoples because of the sin of human dissension which arises when one people seizes the leadership for itself. A sign of this pride is that tower erected in the heavens where impious men deserved that not only their minds but also their voices should be dissonant.

The traumatic loss of unity does not coincide, for Augustine, with a loss in the power of human language to convey God's meaning. Any power that language had before the breakdown of linguistic unity is maintained in the new state of linguistic dispersion. God's plan of self-mediation through Scripture (hence, through human language) did not change because of Man's sinning at Babel and the ensuing breakdown of a prelapsarian monolithic language. Man's linguistic original sin might have made the task of the interpreters a little more complicated. It did not, however, distort God's message or obscure it beyond repair.

Linguistic differentiation had the sole effect of requiring from biblical scholars the knowledge of more than one idiom – an expertise that allowed them to retrace the chain of translations from Hebrew to Greek to Latin – and the ability to correct the material errors of previous translators.[38] It did not erect any insurmountable linguistic barrier between them or condemn biblical poetry to a loss of sweetness. The opposite is perhaps even truer. It is significant that Augustine, discussing biblical figurality and style, brings in an example from Solomon's song (Cant. 4:2) and introduces the Latin word for 'sweet' to comment upon it: *Et tamen nescio quomodo suavius intueor sanctos, cum eos quasi dentes ecclesiae video* ('Nevertheless, in a strange way, I contemplate the saints *more pleasantly* when I envisage them as the teeth of the church,' *De doctrina christiana* 2.vi.7). Unlike the 'prosified' Bible that Dante imports into his minor works, Augustine's Bible is free from the accusation of being unpoetic. As a poetic artefact not lacking its own distinctive rhetoric and style, it may even become an active model for the poetry of the *Commedia*. The new role that biblical poetics and hermeneutics will play in Dante's poem will be the focus of the next chapter.

3 Hermeneutics

Lo ben che fa contenta questa corte,
Alfa e O è di quanta scrittura
mi legge Amore o lievemente o forte
            (*Paradiso* 26.16–18)

At the end of this analysis, two notions of sense emerge as applicable to a text. The first notion, engendered by extending the semiological analysis of the phonetic and lexical level to the level of discourse, indicates only the interplay of internal correspondences; that is, a play of structures. This notion of sense governs the explication of a given text. The second notion of sense, engendered by the semantic analysis of the sentence, the smallest unit of discourse, attracts sense into the gravitational field of reference; that is, towards what lies outside language. This second notion of sense governs the interpretation of a given text. In truth, to interpret a text does not mean to look for an intention *hidden behind* it, but rather to follow the movement of sense towards reference – that is, towards the kind of world, or better of being-in-the-world, *open in front* of the text. To interpret means to unfold the new mediations that the discourse sets up between Man and the world. Are these two notions of sense mutually exclusive? Quite the contrary: not only are they not mutually exclusive, they actually reinforce one another. What good could bring an explication that would not lead to an interpretation? To a new way of seeing things under the aegis of the text? Similarly, what force would an interpretation have that had not patiently circled around the deep semantics of a text, the level that only a serious structural explication may approach?

Paul Ricoeur, 'Sign and Sense,'
Encyclopedia Universalis (1968), 1014

In Ricoeur's analysis of the twofold nature of sense, its production and retrieval appear so involved with one another that he needs to treat them in one breath. In the passage quoted above, which is drawn from an extended meditation on semantics, the two notions of sense he isolates correspond to two differently inflected approaches to the hermeneutic of a text. On the one hand, when more attention is paid to the internal mechanisms by which sense is produced in a text, what is engendered is its explication. In this state of affairs, sense is the meaning that can be located inside the text – what is being talked about. Better yet, sense is 'the intention hidden behind it.' On the other hand, when more attention is paid to the extra-linguistic reference of language, what is being practised is interpretation. In this framework, sense is the meaning of the world out there – the things to which we point in speaking – and interpretation amounts to an ethical call to practise new configurations of our relation to the world. As the final sentence makes clear, the difference between the two hermeneutic approaches mirrors the coexisting components of a sign's *Sinn* and *Bedeutung*, sense and reference (adding, perhaps, only an ethical twist – collaboration being the hermeneutic equivalent of coexistence). Just as it is impossible to rescind, in semantics, the nexus of sense and reference, so too the alternative between explication and interpretation of a text is to be understood as a matter of emphasis. In the encounter of reader and text, both attitudes should always be present: the real issue is, in what proportion.

The following pages will look at the different emphases that at different stages in his career Dante put on explication and interpretation of his own and his peers' poetic texts. In his work as self-commentator, Dante opted at times for an explicative attitude, insisting on the intention hidden behind the surface of his texts and qualifying this intention as his own; at other times, he suggested that interpretation, the outward gaze of the interpreter following the outward gaze of the text, could and should complement, and perhaps even supersede, explication. As is the case in Ricoeur, so also in Dante hermeneutics and poetics – the inscribing of meaning or its triggering – are two sides of the same coin. Understanding a text means for Dante different things at different times. *Convivio* declares that it operates in the first mode: there the author adopts, albeit for contingent reasons and perhaps for the sake of a larger argument, a poetics in which he features as the sole producer of meaning. Reading primarily means explaining; that is, reconstructing a textual world in which authorial intention allegedly dominates. In *Vita nuova* and, more forcefully, in the *Commedia*, Dante opts for the second mode: a different poetics dominates the texts, one in which authorial control yields some ground to inspiration as a source of meaning. In these works, understanding a text means engaging in interpretation; that is, interacting with a discourse so as not to leave untouched our relation to the world, including ourselves.

In focusing on the set of interdependent principles for reading poetry that Dante envisioned in and for his texts, this chapter also begins to address in a new light the central question of Dante's poetics in the *Commedia*. To follow Dante's progress in hermeneutics means, in fact, to reconstruct a further element constantly accompanying his evolving poetics. In an attempt to reconstruct Dante's evolving ideas on how to interpret poetry, the focus will be on a peculiar aspect of his theory and praxis of self-exegesis, one that has so far been overshadowed, in the critical discourse, by wider and more widespread treatments of the problematic theory of allegory offered in his works. Instead of asking what is the nature of Dante's texts, and then inferring from the answer the reading strategies that they demand, the following pages investigate the possibility that Dante inscribed different hermeneutic principles at various stages in his work. Rather than asking whether *Vita nuova*, *Convivio*, and *Commedia* are conceived as relying on the allegory of the poets or on the allegory of the theologians, and then proposing a reading method modelled on the nature of the texts, they ask whether Dante recommends an author- or a reader-centred hermeneutics, and then investigate what kind of writing principles are implied in the reading strategies which Dante has established. In turn, the answer to this question dictates a new text-based inference about the allegorical status of both the poem and the texts that preceded it.

In order to reconstruct the method for interpreting poetic texts that Dante inscribed in his works, my argument once again proceeds in chronological order and moves from the consensus of the earlier texts to the radical revolution of the poem. In *Convivio* and (partly) *Vita nuova* – and, implicitly, in *De vulgari eloquentia* – Dante's quest for authority hinges on a strategy of self-promotion that casts the author as privileged reader, perfectly in control of the ultimate meaning of his texts. Tracking the evolution of Dante's notion of hermeneutics from the context of the minor works to a specific episode in the *Commedia*, my argument then proposes to reconsider *Purgatorio* 21 and 22 in this light. It suggests that, by providing in Statius the positive example of an 'active' reading in the poem, one in which the meaning a reader discovers in a text is more fruitful and true than the one its author encoded into it, Dante takes a position on matters of textual interpretation that represents a radical novelty in his thought. Statius's surprising claim that the reading of two passages from Virgil's *Aeneid* 3 and *Eclogues* 4 had the effect of converting him to both a more balanced use of his wealth and to Christianity clearly signals the new direction Dante took.

Featuring the encounter of three poets, the opening act of Statius's long performance in *Purgatorio* provides the poem with a textual space in which to address in a technical vein the principles controlling the production and fruition of poetic texts. The episode also revolves around complementary questions of textual interpretation of a similarly technical nature. In particular, it sets against one another two reading strategies, a literalist and a constructivist one, respectively embodied by Virgil and Statius. The *Commedia* contrasts these two characters both for the results that their hermeneutics can achieve and for the bipolar morality that they construct: Virgil is just as condemned to eternal exile in hell as he is a literalist reader, whereas Statius is just as saved a soul as he is a constructivist one. In the *Commedia*, the hermeneutic model that lay at the heart of Dante's minor works is objectified and projected onto the character of Virgil; the dynamics of the poem suggest that it is also overcome and renounced in favour of the one embodied by Statius.

Finally, my argument proceeds to isolate a possible antecedent for Dante's new hermeneutic model. In spite of its apparent radical modernity, traces of the notion of literature it constructs are not alien to the culture of Dante's time. Dante's new 'Statian' hermeneutics had ancient roots and was not a complete novelty for his contemporaries. They could find the basic tenet of the model Dante imports into the *Commedia* in Augustine's *De doctrina christiana*. Tackling a different problem, but reaching similar conclusions, Augustine had already developed a system of hermeneutics for the Scriptures that allowed – with some restrictions – the interpretation of biblical texts to go beyond the intention of their immediate author. By appropriating Augustine's model for biblical hermeneutics and by having Statius apply it to Virgil's text, Dante revolutionizes both the rules of hermeneutic engagement he designs for (his) texts and the paradigm he proposes for their composition.[1]

3.1 The Burden of Interpretation: Authorial Intention in Dante's 'Minor' Works

Dante's engagement with the question of how to interpret texts appears soon in his reflection about poetry. Already in the metapoetic chapter 25 of *Vita nuova,* one can find in embryonic form all the elements that will ground his hermeneutic praxis in the later prose works. While proposing a close equivalence between classical poets and vernacular 'rhymers,' with respect to the rhetorical and stylistic figures that they are allowed to use, Dante adds a revelatory caveat:

> E acciò che non ne pigli alcuna baldanza persona grossa, dico che né li poete parlavano così sanza ragione, né quelli che rimano deono parlare così non avendo alcuno ragionamento in loro di quello che dicono; *però che grande vergogna sarebbe a colui che rimasse cose sotto vesta di figura o di colore rettorico, e poscia, domandato, non sapesse denudare le sue parole da cotale vesta, in guisa che avessero verace intendimento.* E questo mio primo amico e io ne sapemo bene di quelli che così rimano stoltamente. (*Vita nuova* 25.10)

> And in order that some thick-witted person not become too daring from what I have said, let me add that just as the Latin poets did not write as they did without a reason, so vernacular poets should not write in the same way without having some reason for writing as they do; *for great embarrassment would come to one who, having written things in the dress of an image or rhetorical coloring, and then, having been asked, would not be able to strip his words of such dress in order to give them their true meaning.* And my first friend and I are well acquainted with some who compose so witlessly.

We already had a chance to discuss this passage in chapter 1, in particular its metaphoric substratum; we should now focus on the role Dante assigns to authors as the sole agents in the production of meaning in their texts. The vantage point adopted here is quite new. What critics usually stress in this passage is the radical novelty of Dante's stance when he claims for vernacular poetry the same rhetorical freedom and the same rhetorical status as the one produced by ancient *auctores*. The traditional critical emphasis is not unjustified. Dante's gesture appears even more courageous when one thinks of how he based, after all, his authority on an extremely limited corpus of texts and on a tradition of poetry that was admittedly very recent.[2] To be sure, the main novelty in Dante's statement is his claim to what we may call, risking some anachronism, a poetic 'freedom in emulation' equivalent to the one the ancient models enjoyed. This courageous move is not, however, the only interesting element. Rather than our focusing on the innovations, some old and essentially traditional features in Dante's statement deserve a more careful evaluation: in particular, one by-product of his central argument on the hermeneutic authority of the author.

In an extremely revealing afterthought, Dante addresses the question of how to judge the vernacular poets 'who, having written things in the dress of an image or rhetorical coloring, ... would not be able to strip [their] words of such dress in order to give them their true meaning.' In sketching out the limits of an authorized figurativeness, Dante remarks that it would be shameful for a poet to compose a text and then be unable to control its meaning. The derogatory closing statement that Dante and Cavalcanti know of many poets who fall into this disparaged category is not an anticipation of the Shakespearean cry for 'more matter with less art'; that is, it does not simply call for the production of a poetry rich in intellectual content. Instead, it is the sign that Dante conceives the relationship between the author and the truthful *intendimento* (*intentio*, meaning) of his work as one of strict dependence. According to the Dante of chapter 25 of *Vita nuova*, in poetry meaning depends on the active intervention of the author. In a metaphor that, as we have seen, will be central to both *Convivio* and *De vulgari eloquentia*, Dante argues that, as a body precedes its clothing, so 'meaning' precedes its being covered by the poet with figures and fancy rhetorical colours. It may appear that Dante makes the point only in passing, and hence any insistence on its alleged importance may seem excessive. After all, one may argue, Dante draws both the notion of poetry and the language he employs from the common stock of ancient and medieval rhetorical theories of the *ornatus*. On the contrary, the passage is of the utmost relevance, because it is used to justify the existence of the *prosimetrum* itself. If the author is the primary agent responsible for the meaning of the poetic text, who better than he to produce a body of exegetical writing that derives from, and bears upon, that text?

Dante's daring operation of self-commentary finds its central authorizing principle in the model of controlled poetics and authorial hermeneutics sketched out in the closing sentence of chapter 25. According to this model, to read means to undress a text's meaning and free it from its rhetorical fetters. In the process of writing and reading, all the activity is on the side of writing: it is the author who can best decode his poetry because it is he who encoded its meaning in the rhetorical garb of the text. The author of *Vita nuova* believes, in short, in an 'active poetics.' Dante also makes clear what the recommended tool is to undress (technically: to open) his poetic texts. As later in *Convivio*, the instrument designed to maintain authorial control over poetry and guide the reader towards meaning is prose. A few sentences before the passage quoted above, we read:

> Dunque, se noi vedemo che li poete hanno parlato a le cose inanimate, sì come se avessero senso e ragione ... degno è lo dicitore per rima di fare lo somigliante, *ma non sanza ragione alcuna, ma con ragione la quale poi sia possibile d'aprire per prosa*. (*Vita nuova* 25.8)

> So, if we discover that the Latin poets have spoken to inanimate objects as if they possessed sense and reason ... then it is fitting that the vernacular poet do the same, *not without some reason but rather with a motive that later can be revealed by prose.*

Glossing this passage, Domenico De Robertis rightly pointed out that Dante's use of the word 'prose' is not to be read as alluding merely to the 'interpretation of poetry's use of metaphors, but also as representing a 'poetics' for the book itself.'[3] Indeed, the authorial voice in the *libello* repeatedly declares that it is only now – the narrative frame and the prose *divisiones* having been added – that the poems are fully clear.

Hints at Dante's authorial poetics are not limited to the metapoetic section of the *Vita nuova*. From the start of his self-commentary, Dante clearly spells out that the ultimate meaning of his collected texts can be retrieved only now, and only through the narrative prose of the new work. He glosses the first poem that, in the framework of the *libello*, he deems relevant in his career, the sonnet *A ciascun alma presa*, with an account of the 'dream vision' that prompted it:

> *Lo verace giudicio* del detto sogno non fue veduto allora per alcuno, ma ora è manifestissimo a li più semplici. (*Vita nuova* 3.15)[4]

> The *true interpretation* of the dream I described was not perceived by anyone then, but it is very clear to even the least sophisticated.

He reiterates the argument at least twice in the course of the work, repeatedly implying the possibility of a split between the *intendimento* of the author and what the text *prima facie* displays:

> Ne la seconda [parte di *O voi che per la via d'Amor passate*] narro là ove

Amore m'avea posto, *con altro intendimento* che l'estreme parti del sonetto non mostrano. (7.7)

In the second part, I tell of the position in which Love had placed me, *with a meaning other than that* expressed in the beginning and ending of the sonnet.

Similarly, in commenting on the fourth section of *Morte villana*, Dante admits:

Ne la quarta mi volgo a parlare a indiffinita persona, avvegna che *quanto a lo mio intendimento* sia diffinita. (7.12)

In the fourth [part], I turn to speaking to an apparently indefinite person, *yet very definite in my mind*.

Statements such as these suggest that the model for reading and composing poetry that Dante defends in his first prose work preserves some traces of a traditional model, in which 'the authority of the author' is paramount, and his intention has a foundational value.

The passages I have isolated are, of course, not representative of the whole work: the way *Vita nuova* signifies is a complex issue, and, as we have repeatedly seen, there quite regularly appears to be a gulf between the shreds of (mainly traditional) theory it contains and its (often revolutionary) praxis. On their basis, one should not conclude that these declarations are the sign of Dante's commitment to the model of an author-oriented hermeneutic for the whole book: the implicit model epitomized in the passage quoted above is to be read under a double set of restrictions. First, in its divergence from Dante's praxis, the hermeneutic-poetic model is but a 'minority' element in the complex canvas of the work; second, in its consonance with traditional outlooks on poetics, it may have its raison d'être in Dante's desire to have his work accepted, if not fully understood, by his technically qualified audience.

The restrictions that are easily implemented for *Vita nuova* seem, however, to apply only in part for Dante's next *prosimetrum*. In the philosophical prose of *Convivio*, meaning is more unambiguously contingent upon the degree of mediation that Dante is able and willing to grant to his readership. In the prose commentary on his now more mature poetry, Dante reiterates the point we have isolated in the metapoetic section of *Vita nuova*:

> *E con ciò sia cosa che la vera intenzione mia fosse altra che quella che di fuori mostrano le canzoni predette,* per allegorica esposizione quelle intendo mostrare, appresso la litterale istoria ragionata; sì che l'una ragione e l'altra darà sapore a coloro che a questa cena sono convitati. (*Convivio* 1.i.18)

> *Since my true meaning was other than what the previously mentioned canzoni outwardly reveal,* I intend to explain these canzoni by means of an allegorical exposition, after having discussed the literal account, so that both arguments will be savored by those who have been invited to this supper.

This programmatic statement, which will soon be reinforced by similar ones, leaves little room for doubt. In spite of the blatantly contradictory account of the final resolution of the plot of *Vita nuova* that he gives in *Convivio*, and in spite of his shifting from narrative to expository prose, it appears that Dante finds and stresses a further element of continuity linking his old and new *prosimetra*. In both works he appears to call on the commentary to play the same role. To be sure, the contradiction between the established reign of the figural Beatrice at the end of the *libello* and the victorious intrusion of the allegorical *donna gentile* in *Convivio* remains unresolved and almost unaddressed by the author.[5] Both *prosimetra*, however, advance the same principles for interpreting poetic texts. According to Dante's prose, both the poems in *Vita nuova* and his *canzoni* in *Convivio* have meanings that are ultimately caused by their author and that no other interpretive agency can expound better than the author himself.

The treatise will further develop the point Dante makes in its introductory section. While acknowledging that his *Convivio* had been written under the *aegis* of Boethius and Augustine, Dante reiterates the assertion that the true meaning ('vera sentenza') of his *canzoni* can be uncovered only thanks to the commentary he is now adding to them. The statement is rather extreme:

> Intendo anche mostrare la vera sentenza di quelle, *che per alcuno vedere non si può s'io non la conto,* perché è nascosta sotto figura d'allegoria. (ibid. 1.ii.17)

> I intend also to show *the true meaning of the canzoni, which no one can perceive unless I reveal it,* because it is hidden beneath the figure of allegory.

The message the poems are to deliver is again dependent upon the mediation of their author: he is called upon to lift the veil of the allegorical fabric of his texts, and he is the only one up to the task. Again, in the statement the rhetorical stress falls upon the interpretive agency of the first-person singular.

The implicit parallel that *Convivio* draws with the experience of Augustine as autobiographical writer reinforces the importance of Dante's self-expository attitude. Organized along the dichotomy between 'timore d'infamia' (associated with Boethius) and 'desiderio di dottrina dare' (associated with Augustine), Dante had just stated that 'a fear of infamy moves me, and a desire to give instruction moves me, which in truth others are unable to give' ('Movemi timore d'infamia, e movemi desiderio di dottrina dare la quale altri veramente dare non può,' ibid. 1.ii.16). Apparently, the author of *Convivio* projects his situation onto his model: Augustine's privileged access to his own autobiography justifies Dante's own claim to privileged access to the meaning of his poems. The example of the *Confessions* helps defuse Dante's anxiety about controlling and supplementing the meaning of his poetry.

The complete heteronomy of the poetic signifier, together with its total dependence on the authority of the poet to achieve any fullness of meaning, is presented in such extreme terms that it even appears to Dante as a 'defect' inherent to his poetry. It is not only because of the circumstance of his exile that Dante is prompted to write his commentary on the *canzoni*. The prose commentary is designed to overcome also a 'defect' of the poetic texts:

> E però che lo mio pane è purgato da una parte, convienlomi purgare da l'altra, per fuggire questa riprensione; *ché lo mio scritto, che quasi commento dir si può, è ordinato a levar lo difetto de le canzoni sopra dette*, ed esso per sé fia forse in parte alcuna un poco duro. (*Convivio* 1.iii. 2)

> Now that my bread has been cleansed on the one side, it is necessary for me to cleanse it on the other to escape a censure of this kind, *for my writing, which can almost be called a commentary, is intended to remove the defect of the canzoni mentioned above*, and this may itself prove to be perhaps a little difficult in part.

The metaphoric hardness of the bread accompanying the *canzoni* (resolved from metaphor: the difficulty of the commentary) is a reflection of the similar hardness and obscurity marring the poetic texts to which it is attached. Dante acknowledges – and it is a notable concession – that the prose work is ultimately prompted by a shortcoming of his poems. This defect consists essentially in their inability to convey meaning in a sufficiently clear and straightforward manner. Once again, just as was the case in *Vita nuova* 25, the authorial – and hence allegedly authoritative – prose commentary appears necessary to rescue poetry from its gravest natural danger: rhetorical opacity. In the *libello* opacity was leading to a potentially dangerous polysemy; in the treatise it threatens communication itself.

If the present account of the model of Dante's pre-*Commedia* hermeneutics is correct, the example of a new, salvific reading offered by Statius in *Purgatorio* 22 must come as a surprise. The systematic displacement of authority and authorial intention that one witnesses in Statius's reading of Virgil's works is far removed from the centrality that both the literalist Dante of the 'minor works' and now, in the poem's plot, the character of Virgil attributed to them. The idea that the author of a text is also its best reader, which was the driving force and ultimate foundation of both *Vita nuova* (in theory) and *Convivio* (in practice), has disappeared. It has been replaced by a hermeneutic model in which the active intervention of the reader shows a higher and more effective power of penetrating the poetic text than that of its author. Now the poem's meaning originates not in the mind of the author but elsewhere. It is engendered when reader and text are joined by the act of reading: when the reader is ready to look past the shadow of authorial intentions and the text is designed to be traversed by readers without detaining them.

3.2 *Per te poeta fui, per te cristiano*: Texts and Authors Framing Statius's Christianity

After seven centuries of almost uninterrupted critical success, it is difficult to convey today the daring freedom that Dante took when he decided to make of the Latin poet Statius a saved Christian.[6] The poem has in a way naturalized itself, and any judgment that the poet passed on both his contemporaries and forerunners – including Statius's presence in purgatory – no longer surprises readers of the *Commedia*.[7] Yet Dante's choice to make him a Christian is a problem. In the poem, Statius's salvation comes as an unexpected tear in its moral-theological fabric. His sudden appearance fully justifies, on the one hand, Virgil's surprised reaction, and on the other hand throws the habitual image of Statius we might have formed by reading his *oeuvre* off-balance. Attempts have been made to locate hints of a late antique or early medieval tradition that could have turned Statius into a Christian.[8] Still, in the sometimes confusing (and often contradictory) image of the literary figures of the pagan past that Dante could have inherited from the culture of his time, nothing of conclusive weight has yet been found. And it probably never will be. Since part of the meaning of the episode lies in the surprise that Dante built into it, 'over-naturalizing' his strategy may, in the end, be a disservice to his text. To be sure, our knowledge is necessarily limited by the chronological and cultural remoteness of Dante's text, and thus any argument *e silentio* can be deceptive. However, at the present stage of research, it seems probable that it is only thanks to Dante that Statius's soul is featured among the saved. What is more, it is only thanks to Dante that potential traces of Christianity can now be read back into his texts.[9]

When did Dante decide to cast Statius in this unorthodox role, and why? While the latter question requires some elaboration, the former is not difficult to answer. Dante already knew that he was going to 'save' Statius for something special in his poem when he was composing *Inferno* 4. The presence of the poet's soul in *Purgatorio* 21 is as conspicuous as his absence from the 'bella scola' of poetry in the episode of the *nobile castello* staged in limbo. There the strangeness of Statius's absence is just as problematic as his appearance later. While sketching out the canon of the poets who had accompanied him from the very beginning of his career as a committed writer, Dante bypasses an author whose authority he had already used to advantage in *Convivio* and *De vulgari eloquentia*.[10] Commentators usually remove the difficulty of not finding Statius where they expect him to be by force of a gloss, pointing ahead to the presence in purgatory of the sixth member of the 'scola,' and thus completing Dante's portrait of his classical poetic past. The critical move of artificially restoring Statius to the context of *Inferno* 4 has one advantage. While it might endanger the specificity of the character's treatment in the *Commedia* and reduce the peculiarity of his position in Dante's carefully structured universe, it still helps to rule out from the start any attempt to date Dante's 'serious' reading of Statius's poem to a stage later than the composition of *Inferno* or to attribute Dante's knowledge of the Theban *materia* to intermediary sources. In other words, it shows that Statius's relatively late appearance in purgatory is not due to a lack of information on Dante's part, as might be true for some of the other classical names that the *Commedia* drops in *Purgatorio* 22 to complete its panoramic account of what Dante had come to regard as the classics.[11]

If the soul of the Latin poet appears only with the earthquake that announces his deliverance from purgation and his readiness to move beyond the second realm, the text of his *Thebaid* has already made its presence strongly felt in the poem. As others have shown, Dante's lower hell derived specifically from Statius's first epic its distinctive 'Theban' register, and basically all that Dante knows about Achilles' pre-war dalliance on Scyros derives from Statius's unfinished *Achilleid*.[12] The context of *Inferno* 4 is thus pertinent to *Purgatorio* 21–2, but a simple footnote referring forward from one to the other is not sufficient to exhaust the relevance of Dante's gesture. Actually, the text of the *Commedia* invites reference from one canto to the other, but it does so only in the opposite direction: from *Purgatorio* 21–2 to *Inferno* 4. The supplementary catalogue of Limbo-dwellers Virgil includes in his response to Statius's in *Purgatorio* 22.100–14, and the reappearance of a memorable half-line 'tra cotanto senno' transposed from *Inferno* 4.102 to *Purgatorio* 22.23, cannot be used to justify the Latin poet's absence from hell. Both signals are meant to draw retrospective attention to Dante's decision of excluding Statius from the souls of the *megalopsychoi* in limbo, but Statius's inclusion among the Christians and his deferral to the context of purgatory remains unprepared, wilful, and in need of interpretation.

Why did Dante decide to defer Statius's appearance to the late cantos of *Purgatorio*? A signal of his possible motives can be found in the recurrence of a distinct and unique rhyme scheme across two cantos of the second *cantica*. The three rhyme-words *fiamma/mamma/dramma* (flame, mommy, ounce) appear for the first time in the long speech Statius gives at the end of *Purgatorio* 21, and in which he praises the *Aeneid* before knowing that he is actually addressing Virgil's shadow. The same rhyme-words recur nine cantos later, in Dante's unspoken farewell to his first guide.[13] By way of this repetition of a charged lexicon, Dante's poem organizes the triad of poets in a proportional relation that turns the character of Statius into an intradiegetic 'double' for Dante's projected poetic self. Statius's reading of Virgil's text mimics Dante's own reading of that text: the elaborate episode that brings the two Latin poets face to face works as an objectified version of Dante's encounter with Virgil's work.[14] This argument is not fully new. Robert Hollander has advanced the idea that Statius is the character through whose agency in the poem Dante negotiates his ambiguous relationship with Virgil's texts. Hollander's reading of the episode may, however, be developed further. As we will see, Statius certainly represented a double of Dante in the poem, but so too did Virgil. The character of Virgil will have a role to play in the episode that is parallel to the character of Statius, though marked by an opposite set of connotations. In the cantos analysed in detail below, he too will embody a model of reading poetic texts. Unlike Statius, however, Virgil will be the bearer of a failing hermeneutics. As a misguided reader of texts and contexts, Virgil is depicted as practising Dante's own pre-*Commedia* reading strategies. The long interaction among the three poets is, in short, a narrative laboratory in which Dante's poem defines its hermeneutics in contrast with its author's previous habits.

That the whole episode is concerned with textual interpretation is made fairly clear from the start. Every turn in the plot is presented as a consequence of an act of reading, beginning with Statius's own self-presentation and the courteous exchange in the close of canto 21. In both cases, it is as writers and readers of texts that Statius and Virgil define their relationship. The first to do so is the younger poet. While inscribing into his autobiographical account a literary genealogy, Statius singles out the role played by the *Aeneid* and its author:

> 'Al mio ardor fuor seme le faville,
> che mi scaldar, de la divina fiamma
> onde sono allumati più di mille;
>   'de l'Eneïda dico, la qual mamma
> fummi, e fummi nutrice, poetando:
> sanz'essa non fermai peso di dramma.'
>   (*Purgatorio* 21.94–9)

'The sparks that kindled the fire in me / came from the holy flame / from which more than a thousand have been lit – / I mean the *Aeneid*. When I wrote poetry / it was my *mamma* and my nurse. / Without it, I would not have weighed a dram.'

In his extended *vita*, Statius presents his primary intertextual model in a loaded *lumen de lumine* metaphor, in which the imagery of love intersects with that of intellectual activity.[15] He also sets up the light imagery that will recur in a short while to describe Virgil's role as both an unknowing prophet of Christ's birth and a no-less-unknowing teacher of morality (respectively *Purgatorio* 22.64–72 and 37–45). The three rhyme-words define the relationship of Statius's poetry to Virgil's epic in terms of filiation, illumination, and measure. In a gender-inverted definitive resolution of that 'family romance' of which Harold Bloom spoke in his *Anxiety of Influence*, the *Aeneid*, as 'mother-text,' has nursed a 'daughter poem,' the *Thebaid*, whose author can wholeheartedly recognize the lineage to which he belongs: the relationship could hardly be more positive.[16] Statius is even ready to embark on a rhetorically motivated theological paradox:

> 'E per esser vivuto di là quando
> visse Virgilio, assentirei un sole
> più che non deggio al mio uscir di bando.'
>   (100–2)

'To have lived on earth when Virgil lived / I would have stayed one year's sun longer than I owed / before I came forth from my exile.'

When the Pilgrim involuntarily discloses the identity of his guide, Statius falls on his knees and tries to embrace Virgil. But the embrace does not take place. Virgil points out the moral inappropriateness of the gesture, and Statius pulls back (vv. 130–2). The brief scene is more than a simple vignette illustrating the great courtesy of the poets. Such a scene, contrastively resolved by a successful embrace, has in fact already taken place in *Purgatorio* 6, acted by Sordello and Virgil, fellow countrymen and co-practitioners of poetry.[17] For the new context not to become a mere repetition, one should pay attention to the deliberate avoidance of the embrace and the motives that lie behind it. The closing of the canto may help to reconstruct them.

Dante has Statius admit in the final tercet that a fully human affection has lead him to forget the 'vanity' of his own and Virgil's souls in the afterlife and has caused him to use poor judgment:

> 'Or puoi la quantitate
> comprender de l'amor ch'a te mi scalda,
> quand'io dismento nostra vanitate,
> trattando l'ombre come cosa salda.'
>   (133–6)

'Now you can understand / the measure of the love for you that warms me / when I forget our emptiness / and treat our shadows as bodied things.'

Inscribed in the text, the renounced embrace is a sign that invites the readers to reckon with a secondary insubstantiality, one that is deeper than the aerial nature of the bodies given to all the souls. The love of the saved poet for his condemned predecessor is so warm, Dante suggests in the final tercet, that it not only leads Statius to treat the shade of his model 'as a solid thing,' but it has led him to make an additional, though temporary, unsubstantiated inference as well. The double 'vanity' that affects Virgil and Statius is that they are both incorporeal shades and characters (re)constructed from a set of texts. Statius's mistake coincides with his second implied inference: desiring to embrace Virgil, he had established an erroneously direct causal relationship between Virgil, the author, and his texts.

Conflating the works of Virgil with their author, their effect with their instrumental cause, Statius makes a mistake that he promptly acknowledges and corrects on the level of the plot and of the critical theory that accompanies it.[18] Virgil's reaction to the attempted deferential embrace is merely to point out the fundamental equality of all the souls in the afterlife: 'Frate, / non far ché tu se' ombra e ombra vedi' ('Brother, there's no need – / you are a shade, a shade is what you see,' *Purgatorio* 21.131–2).[19] Statius's response appears to be better articulated. He acknowledges his mistake on the level of the immaterial physics governing the souls, but he does not stop at that: he also sees and corrects the hermeneutic mistake that prompted him to try to embrace Virgil. From this point on, Statius will be most careful to distinguish the relative value of the author and that of his texts, so much so that in the next canto a number of his answers to Virgil will be addressing this first misapprehension.[20] They will focus precisely on the illegitimacy – and, subtly, the moral inappropriateness – of drawing inferences about authors from their texts, and vice versa.

In *Purgatorio* 22, Virgil appears as constitutionally unable to overcome the hermeneutic limit suggested in the scene of the unconsummated embrace. When he mistakes Statius's sin for avarice, it is on account of his reading 'literally' the moral architecture of purgatory. Similarly, he believes that he can 'read' Statius by 'reading' literally his work, when he wonders how the author of the *Thebaid* could have been a Christian when his poetry displayed a traditional, fully pagan invocation to the Muses (vv. 58–60). In this light, it becomes clear why, in Dante's treatment, Virgil appears as the shadowy, inadequate, and always-unconscious instrumental cause of his own works. Dante again leaves with Statius the responsibility for making this point, but he surely appears to share it. Statius phrases the argument in a dense simile, in which Virgil's blindness in front of his texts is balanced by the light they cast, and his insufficiency as instrumental cause is redeemed by their effects:

> 'Facesti come quei che va di notte,
> che porta il lume dietro e sé non giova,
> ma dopo sé fa le persone dotte ...'
> (*Purgatorio* 22.67–9)

> 'You were as one who goes by night, carrying / the light behind him – it is no help to him, / but instructs all those who follow ...'

In Statius's imagery two distinct authorities converge – Augustine's account of his initial self-taught approach to pagan literary and philosophical works at the end of *Confessiones* 4, and Cicero's discussion of friendship (and private property) in the first book of *De officiis*, a passage in which three lines from Ennius are quoted in a confirmatory fashion.[21] The interplay of the two sources produces the stratification of the possible interpretations of the passage, according to the readership each source constructs. Augustine's text is concerned with his studies in the pagan curriculum and describes his progress as that of a man moving away from the divine source of light:

> Dorsum enim habebam ad lumen et ad ea quae inluminantur faciem, unde ipsa facies mea, qua inluminata cernebam, non inluminabatur. (*Confessiones* 4.xvi.30)[22]

> I had my back to the light and held my gaze toward the things that were lit. My eyes, with which I could see the things in the light, were in the darkness.

Statius's homage to Virgil crossbreeds the Augustinian metaphoric situation with Cicero's cursory discussion of the things that can, by nature, be shared:

> Omnium autem communia hominum videntur ea, quae sunt generis eius, quod ab Ennio positum in una re transferri in permultas potest:
>   Homo, qui erranti comiter monstrat viam,
>   Quasi lumen de suo lumine accendat, facit.
>   Nihilo minus ipsi lucet, cum illi accenderit.
>   (*De officiis* 1.xvi.51)[23]

> Human beings should hold in common all the things that belong to a particular class. About them Ennius writes that if found in one thing, they can be transferred to many others: when one points out the way to erring fellow travelers, / he acts as if he were to let them light their lamp from

his own lamp. / His light does not decrease when it shines for others as well.

Ennius's poetic authority casts the act of sharing knowledge in terms that deeply resonate with Dante's moralized metaphoric setting. Statius describes Virgil's poetic influence as an act of physical no less than moral enlightenment: through his works, Virgil 'guided' Statius. By way of example, he showed the morally correct direction in which one should move (thus 'pointing out the way'). He also produced a flame by which others were able to draw new light. Not unlike Augustine's misguided self, however, Virgil had his back to the light and was ultimately unable to benefit from it.

Statius's dissection and recombination of sources may have important hermeneutic consequences. If, instead of choosing between the two 'sources' for Dante's narrative metaphor, we were to accept the presence of a double allusion, the poignancy of Statius's strategically classicizing language may be greater than it appears. On the verge of misquoting Virgil to expose an unintended Christian meaning in his text, Dante has Statius construct a simile with an ambiguous pedigree. Virgil may read it as Ennian and referring to the social duties of friendship, whereas for a more enlightened, Augustinian reader the image of the *lampadoforo* foreshadows a discourse about the Christian God. Once perceived through the lens of Augustine, the new simile helps to conceptualize the essential paradox of a soul who is searching for divine truth while erring in a region populated by un-divine signs. Augustine's efforts to make his way through what he calls 'the liberal arts' were destined to be frustrated; and yet, at the same time, they were necessary, instrumental in producing his advancement towards God.

The interplay of sources seemingly produces a conciliatory effect: it fosters the idea that Virgil was instrumental for Statius's (and Dante's) conversion. However, the simile may hide its poison in a subtext it indirectly evokes – once again of Augustinian origin. When we read Statius's simile as confrontational rather than conciliatory, another intertext becomes pertinent. In order to refute Virgil's literalist reading of his own texts – or, at least, to show its gravest shortcomings – Statius's simile evokes Augustine's invective in his *De symbolo ad catechumenos* 4.4 (*PL* 40, 664) against the literalist Jews. Augustine's texts redeployed the same image we have encountered above: *O Iudei, ad hoc ferentes in manibus lucernam Legis, ut aliis viam demonstraretis, et vobis tenebras ingeratis* ('You, the Jews, have so far carried in your hands the lamp of the Law in such a way that you show the way to others and bring only darkness to yourself'; my translation). If this is the text that Statius's simile is designed to recall to readers, the words Dante has him speak are poetically cruel. Patterned upon the Apostolic construct of the Jewish interpretation of the Old Testament as exemplarily anti-spiritual, Dante's construction of Virgil's literalism is part of his poetic supersessionism.[24]

3.3 Reading beyond the Author: Two Stumbling Blocks in *Purgatorio* 22

Once framed in this light, *Purgatorio* 22 reveals its constant preoccupation with establishing the guiding principles for the hermeneutics of poetic texts. The meeting of the Latin poets on the terrace of avarice is glossed by a distancing commentary: it is the poetic word mediated by Virgil, not the poet himself, that deserves the merit for the conversions recounted in *Purgatorio* 22. Conversely, the peculiar hermeneutics Statius practises on Virgil's texts is used to prove the complementary point: Virgil's failure is not that of his works. Statius's ironic rendering of the two Virgilian fragments in *Purgatorio* 22 makes clear that, by attributing to Statius a systematic strategy of mistranslation of his model, Dante eliminates any reflex of authorial intention from the hermeneutic frame he advances in his own text. Both the surprising rendering of *Aeneid* 3.56–7 (*quid non mortalia pectora cogis / auri sacra fames*) in *Purgatorio* 22.40–1,[25] and the subsequent untenable Christological reading of *Eclogues* 4.6–7 (*iam redit et Virgo, redeunt Saturnia regna, / iam nova progenies caelo demittitur alto*) on lines 71–3 of the same canto show the same strategic mishandling of Virgil's words.[26] Dante's misrendering of Virgil's lines turns them into a text capable of producing a conversion to morality and Christianity to which its author did not have access. Through the mediation of the character of Statius, Dante stages a productive misuse of a primary source. He advances a model for reading poetic texts that can produce conversion and – through conversion – ultimately lead to salvation. The post-Virgilian epic poet is, thus, made the bearer of a Christian hermeneutics which anticipates Dante's own sense of his poem's final goal.

We shall come back to this point – the second step in Dante's construction of an active hermeneutics for his texts – in the next section of this chapter, when the fundamental, mediating text of Augustine will have been introduced through Dante's reference to it in his *Monarchia*. For now, the reading of the Virgilian passages in *Purgatorio* 22 should serve as a reminder of the profoundly ambiguous relationship Dante establishes with the text of Virgil. The importance of these passages and of the misreading they occasion coincides with the novelty their interpretive method represents in Dante's career. The hermeneutic method that underlies them is, by all signs, a discovery of the poem, but it is intended to reflect back onto the minor works. Played out against the homogeneous background of *Vita nuova*, *Convivio*, and *De vulgari eloquentia*, the hermeneutic approach Dante develops in the canto of Statius is an indication of how radically the *Commedia* diverges from the works that preceded it. Unlike Virgil-the-character and the Dante of the minor works, the author of the *Commedia* does not seem to believe in the identity of authorship and interpretive authority.

On the level of the plot, the surprising double misquotation of Virgil's text is designed to resolve two doubts that the Pilgrim's first guide expresses about the situation in which he meets the soul of the saved Latin poet. On the level of hermeneutic theory, they embody, more importantly, a correction of the two radical mistakes that Virgil makes in 'reading' Statius. In a prefatory *terzina* that frames both of the answers he will give to Virgil's queries, Statius identifies the hermeneutic nature of Virgil's perplexities:

> 'Veramente più volte appaion cose
> che danno a dubitar falsa matera
> per le vere ragion che son nascose.'
> *(Purgatorio* 22.28–30)

> 'But, in truth, things often are misleading / when their true causes remain hidden, / thus leading us to false conclusions.'

Commenting upon the opacity of reality as if it were made of texts, Statius lays out the theory of hermeneutics that he will develop in the rest of the episode. Reality is not transparent. It calls for an interpretation that might be able to bring reasoning back from the 'false grounds for doubt' to the 'true hidden reasons.'[27] Armed with this premise, he will move to address Virgil's questions and correct his mistakes.

The first essential mistake Virgil makes concerns the ledge on which he meets Statius. Virgil assumes that the mere fact that Statius's soul was located among the avaricious also meant, necessarily, that avarice was the disposition he had to correct:

> 'Ma dimmi, e come amico mi perdona
> se troppo sicurtà m'allarga il freno,
> e come amico omai meco ragiona:

come poté trovar dento al tuo seno
loco avarizia, tra cotanto senno,
di quanto per tua cura fosti pieno?'
                    (19–24)

'But tell me – and as a friend forgive me / if with too much assurance I relax the reins, / and as a friend speak with me now – / how could avarice find room / amidst such wisdom in your breast, / the wisdom that you nourished with such care?'

The younger Latin poet first replies with a smile (*un poco a riso*), a charitable reaction to Virgil's misapprehension. Then he clearly states that his fault was not avarice; rather, it lay on the opposite side of the Aristotelian moral spectrum:

'Or sappi che avarizia fu partita
troppo da me, e questa dismisura
migliaia di lunari hanno punita.'
                    (34–6)[28]

'Know then that avarice was much too far / removed from me and that this lack of measure / lunar months in thousands now have punished.'

The difficulty Virgil experiences while reading the signs of the immediate purgatorial reality is mirrored in a parallel difficulty of reading signs in texts of a different order. Following the tercet just quoted, Dante inserts the first surprising case of Virgilian (mis)translation to which I referred above:

'E se non fosse ch'io drizzai mia cura,
quand'io intesi là dove tu chiame,
crucciato quasi a l'umana natura:
  'Perché non reggi tu, o sacra fame
de l'oro l'appetito de' mortali?',
voltando sentirei le giostre grame.'
                    (37–42)

'And had I not reformed my inclination / when I came to understand the lines in which, / as if enraged at human nature, you cried out: / "Why cannot you, o holy hunger / for gold, restrain the appetite of mortals?"'[29]

Both the ledge of avarice and the text of the *Aeneid* are made to support a double interpretation, and the very same topographical and textual place can be the *locus* for accommodating radically opposed meanings. By reading as a complementary invitation to restraint what in the *Aeneid* was intended undoubtedly as a cry against avarice, Statius shows that the ultimate 'meaning' of a statement (that is, both its semantics and its relevance) resides more in the reading method than in the letter of the text or in its original context. To Virgil's univocal authorial literalism, Statius juxtaposes a hermeneutic model based on a plurivocal, collaborative, and actively transitive interpretation – the phrase *'io intesi'* retains the active valence of 'I interpreted your words.' The simple fact that Statius's 'erroneous' interpretation of Virgil's text saved his soul, while Virgil's privileged authorial access to those same words did not grant him any better place than limbo in the afterlife, is sufficient proof of how Dante wants his readers to judge Statius's reading. Dante's new 'comic' hermeneutics may seem radically revolutionary; yet, he makes clear what model he envisions in his Christian poem. In the strict axiology of the chronotopic system built in the *Commedia*, if the 'intentionalist' reading of a text does not get a character beyond the first circle of hell and a different reading places another one's soul in the second realm, it is not hard to decide which hermeneutic practice readers are meant to pick.

Subjected to Statius's active reading, the text of the pagan *Aeneid* proves to be marked by the same degree of complexity, the same richness of meaning, and the same ability to accommodate multiple – even opposed – interpretations that the reality of the Christian world beyond permits. Just as on the ledge of avarice we find both squanderers and hoarders, so also in the very same line of Virgil's poem we find both an invitation to moderation in spending and a deprecation of greed. The context from which Virgil's line originated made clear – and Dante could not have avoided knowing it – that the exclamation 'quid non mortalia pectora cogis / auri sacra fames' was originally intended as a curse against the effects that an 'execrable hunger for gold' may have when it is allowed to run free. The very personal and idiosyncratic rendering that one receives from Statius turns it, against its author's intention, into a precept about generosity held in proper reserve.

Some readers have interpreted the oddity of Dante's choice as a sign either that he was reading a corrupted text of the *Aeneid*, or that he simply did not understand the Latin he was translating. Both arguments probably miss the point of Dante's operation. They strive to make the meaning of his text conform to the meaning that Virgil clearly intended, or to assume that conformity to the original's intention was Dante's goal. On the contrary, the author of the *Commedia* is fully responsible for his misrepresentation of Virgil's text – and fully conscious of it. After all, it was clear that the episode of Polydorus, from which the misquoted lines are drawn, was for Dante an example of greed. He had already employed it in *Inferno* 13 (together with Ovid's account of Driope's transformation into a tree from *Metamorphoses* 4.367–74), as a building block for the *contrapasso* of the suicides.[30] He had also inserted it as one of the deterring examples in the canto immediately preceding this one (*Purgatorio* 20.149–50). There is no doubt that he knew what it was designed to mean. More recently, a different line of interpretation has been developed – one which has focused on Dante's intentional mis-rendering of Virgil.[31] Building upon this contemporary tradition, I propose to treat Statius's 'free' translation as above all Dante's lesson in reading – his recommending for Virgil's text a new and better hermeneutics than the one traditionally reserved for classical works. Dante knew perfectly well what Virgil had meant in composing the lines he quotes; by mistranslating them he just shows that there is a better reading than the one the author may have ever imagined. Surprisingly enough, this morally 'superior' interpretation is semiologically creative rather than philologically respectful: a reading is not good because it recovers the literal meaning of a text, fixating on the passive reproduction of authorial intention; a reading is good because it improves the reader and his chances of achieving salvation.

In the second movement of the Statius episode, the same dynamics explored above return, this time more narrowly focused on a literary product. Virgil expresses the second of his doubts about Statius's condition, wondering how it was possible for the author of the *Thebaid* to be a Christian when his text displayed an all-too-traditional pagan Pantheon:

>'Per quello che Cliò teco lì tasta,
>non par che ti facesse ancor fedele
>la fede, sanza qual ben far non basta'
>   (58–60)

>'It does not seem from what you wrote with Clio's help, / that you had found as yet the faith, / that faith without which good works fail.'

As we may expect, Statius replies by insisting on the ambiguity of signs

– both the ones he displayed in life and those now intrinsic to his condition in purgatory:

> 'E pria ch'io conducessi i Greci a' fiumi
> di Tebe poetando, ebb'io battesmo;
> ma per paura chiuso cristian fu'mi,
>   lungamente mostrando paganesmo;
> e questa tepidezza il quarto cerchio
> cerchiar mi fé più che 'l quarto centesmo.'
>   (*Purgatorio* 22.88–93)

'I was baptized before, in my verses, / I had led the Greeks to the rivers of Thebes, / but, from fear, I stayed a secret Christian, / long pretending I was still a pagan. / More than four centuries, because I was lukewarm, I circled the fourth terrace.'

What one should note in the poet's reply is the care with which he points out the hiatus that exists between the religious beliefs he upheld and what his text and his behaviour showed externally. His reply returns to the problem of treating shades as solid things, the meaning intended by authors as the ultimate meaning of texts. According to Statius, the distance between a text and its author cannot be bridged either by a simple act of superimposition or by a direct inference. While he, as a Christian, has been able to move beyond a notion of coincidence between author and text, Virgil makes the mistake all over again. To show by way of a familiar example how illegitimate is his predecessor's critical operation of superimposing texts and authors, Statius returns incidentally to the second Virgilian fragment. To Virgil's textual misinterpretation, in short, he responds with a creative reading of Virgil's own text.

By reading a prophecy of Christ's birth into Virgil's prophecy of the return of the golden age through the birth of a child, Statius proves once again a better reader of Virgil's text than its author. To the obscurity in which Virgil moves, Statius contrasts the light of his texts:

> 'Facesti come quei che va di notte,
> che porta il lume dietro e sé non giova,
> ma dopo sé fa le persone dotte,
>   quando dicesti: "Secol si rinnova;
> torna giustizia e primo tempo umano,
> e progenïe scende da ciel nova."'
>   (67–72)

'You were as one who goes by night, carrying / the light behind him – it is no help to him, / but instructs all those who follow – / when you said "The centuries turn new again. / Justice returns with the first age of man, / and new progeny descends from heaven."'

We have seen how allusive the first tercet in Statius's reply could be; we must now explore the second misappropriation of Virgil's text that Statius performs for the sake of its astonished author. This misreading is perhaps even more violent and goes deeper than the previous one. Just like Dante's Statius, so also the author of the *Commedia* was perfectly aware that the late antique and medieval interpretations identifying the son of the consul Pollio (if he is the *puer* in question) with the Saviour and the Virgo (Astraea/Justice) with the Virgin Mary were, from a literalist point of view, untenable.[32] They were clearly forcing on Virgil's text a religious palingenetic meaning that was not intended in its original context. We know that Dante knew that the literal referent of Virgil's Virgo in the Eclogue was Astraea, not the Virgin, and that, consequently, the author of that text could by no means be counted among the prophets of Christ. If the insistence on Virgil's eternal confinement in hell that we find in the *Commedia* were not enough to rule out the possibility of counting him among the believers in 'Cristo venturo,' another text by Dante, his *Monarchia*, makes clear the position Dante takes on the issue. In the context of a historical reading of Virgil's Eclogue, Dante glosses the passage according to the author's intention and the Roman cultural tradition in which it was written: '*Virgo' nanque vocabatur iustitia, quam etiam Astream vocabant* ('Justice was called *The Virgin* and also *Astraea*,' 1.xi.1).

Both for Dante's Statius and for the author of the *Commedia*, those readers who tried to make the author of the fourth Eclogue responsible for the presence of a Christological and prophetic intention in his text had no case. This did not mean, however, either for Statius or for Dante, that the text of the Eclogue could not support precisely that interpretation. Even if Statius does not endorse the allegorical interpretation based on the equivalence of Virgo and the Virgin Mary, he still is able to extract a salvific meaning from the text. However literal his reading of Virgil's Virgo as Justice may be, it suffices to make him a Christian. Once again, the outcome of the reading Dante attributes to Statius is a salvation that stands in stark contrast to Virgil's eternal exile. The younger Latin poet is saved on account of a conversion triggered by his hermeneutics. On the contrary, Virgil's reading, however 'authorially' privileged it might seem, proves an inadequate key to open the text.

As noted above, Statius is the first soul fully free from sinful dispositions that the Pilgrim meets in the poem. In the poem's narrative and moral system, his special status isolates and legitimizes the extremely modern hermeneutics which he is made to embody. In particular, his sudden appearance contrasts with Virgil's continuous presence. While the first act of the episode dedicated to Statius is an occasion for the text of the *Commedia* to temper its endorsement of the first guide, it is also a sign that readers should not miss any chance to question Virgil's competence and authority. Virgil's limitations extend not only to matters of faith – for which he is ready to call upon other and higher authorities (such as Beatrice in *Purgatorio* 17.48) – but also, perhaps more surprisingly, to questions of poetics. The 'poetic' revision that Virgil undergoes in the present episode is crucial to our understanding of the poem's mechanisms, because it may be the sign of one of Dante's 'self-revisions.' If the hermeneutic model that Dante advances through Statius in the *Commedia* is new, and represents one of the major discoveries of the poem, the older and displaced kind of interpretation sounds uncannily familiar to Dante's readers. As we have seen, the latter was the guiding idea of poetry omnipresent in Dante's minor works, while the former is – as a reading of *Purgatorio* 24.52–4 will show in the next section – the consequence of the new meaning Dante gives to the notion of inspiration in the *Commedia*.

When projected against the background of the key statements about hermeneutics that populate the works predating the poem, the hermeneutic position Dante takes through Statius in the *Commedia* appears as a small-scale revolution with large repercussions. The fully coherent series of pronouncements on issues of interpretation and authorial intention that we have found at the core of *Vita nuova* and *Convivio* is radically incompatible with the new position Dante takes in the poem and dramatizes in *Purgatorio* 22. From a critical point of view, it is as if the mistakes that, incessantly and mercilessly, Dante has Virgil commit were brought to coincide on this point with positions that Dante himself had taken in a not-so-distant past. By projecting them on Virgil, the author of the *Commedia* uses the fully conscious and ironic revision of his own 'intentionalist' and literalist theories as the springboard for advancing a new, successful, and salvific model of reading and writing poetic texts.[33] Using his first guide as a 'poeta dello schermo,' Dante carefully distances himself from, and radically revises (a revision of), his earlier self.[34]

3.4 Augustine's *Regula Caritatis* and the Interpretation of the *Commedia*

The hermeneutic model Dante designs for Statius appears as a surprising novelty to readers who come to the *Commedia* from a study of his minor works. It was not, however, unprecedented in itself. Dante could find an antecedent for his active reading strategy in Augustine's *De doctrina christiana*, a treatise in which the authority of the biblical author is constantly counterbalanced by the authority of the reader. In Augustine, the possibility of generating a double reading that could accord with what he called 'the rule of charity' depended on the double authority and double authorship of Christian Scripture. In turn, the hermeneutics Augustine proposed relied on his treatment of the nature of Scripture. While striving to define the limits and the resultant strategies for the interpretation of Holy Writ, Augustine directly addresses the problem of the double authority (and double nature) of Christian Scripture several times in the treatise. In his view, Scripture is at the same time the product of a human activity – a linguistic artefact possessing what E.R. Curtius will call 'a rhetoric of its own' (1953, 73) – and the vehicle for God's word to Man – a provisional object, ultimately pointing to a metaphysical reality beyond itself. Strictly dependent on this twofold model, the work Augustine plans to carry out in *De doctrina* consists of laying out the technical rules for interpretation of the sacred text. In order to be successful Augustine needs to hold in balance the human and divine side of biblical writing.

One can measure how necessary this equilibrium was – and how difficult to obtain – from the objections Augustine's reasoning addresses at the beginning of his treatise. His work confronts hostility from two opposite fronts. On the one side, Augustine needs to defend his plan to provide readers with a set of fully human hermeneutic rules; he reacts, therefore, against the so-called charismatic readers who were advocating a direct, mystical access to the ultimate meaning of the Bible.[35] His insistence on the necessary role of mediation that God chose to assign to man, both in inspiring the writing of Scripture and in guiding its translation, is designed to respond to this need. According to Augustine, God chose to speak to man, condescending to the limited human faculties and making His ineffability 'speakable.' It follows that the movement of condescension towards man and through man that brought about the existence of the Bible as a material text could also be retraced in the opposite direction by human means. Though inspired – and hence not merely human – Scripture participates in the *dispensatio temporalis* ('worldly economy'), because it is a historical and linguistic object. Its partial 'worldliness' acts as the foundation for the exegetical rules provided in the treatise and justifies their use. On the other side, *De doctrina christiana* needs to respond to a complementary argument (potentially Manichean), namely, that God's condescension was the equivalent of a descent into the negative sphere of the corporeal and the temporal. According to a radical line of argument, the participation of Scripture in worldliness could only end up obscuring the message and thus reflecting the unbridgeable chasm between God and World.[36]

In *De doctrina christiana* Augustine anticipates this argument (essentially the same one that Nietzsche will eventually formulate as the 'all-too-human' nature of positive religions) by arguing that God's adoption of a human language and rhetoric does not imply a complete entanglement in the limitedness of that language and that rhetoric. Though possessing a rhetoric of its own and being the product of the activity of immediate human authors, Scripture does not suffer any loss in its ability to point to what lies beyond its language and rhetoric.[37] For Augustine, Scripture has a human author and speaks in a necessarily human language to a human audience; it ultimately has, however, a different author who uses the human agent as an instrumental cause to convey His message. The double authorship guarantees the ambiguous status of the Bible: it belongs 'to this world' and yet its salvific potential is not compromised by its worldliness. In Augustine's treatise, Scripture is treated as the instrument of God's self-mediation for and through man. By playing the role of intermediary, the sacred text is part of that *dispensatio temporalis* to which all of human life pertains.[38]

Augustine rephrases the argument more than once in his work, most notably in the *Prooemium*, devoted to a pre-emptive discussion of the potential objections raised by the charismatic readers of the Bible. His stress constantly falls on the role of mediation that the Scriptures are called upon to play. They are the means through which the Christian reaches truth, a truth that is located – as ends are with respect to means – beyond them. Though not merely human, given their quality as inspired texts, the Scriptures essentially bear the signs, in their language and in their form, of human limitations. In his discussion of the nature of signs at the beginning of book 2, Augustine suggests that a taxonomy of speakers may be formed and that the different ways in which animals, men, angels, and eventually God communicate could be a worthy subject of study. He soon dismisses it, however, as inessential to his purpose of treating the conventional, that is, linguistic, signs that we find in Scripture. For him there appears to be no intrinsic difference between communication among human beings and God's (and the angels') speech addressed to man. In order to speak to human beings, Augustine argues, God employs an earthly language. Scripture, the repository of the signs God addresses to mankind, is written in a human language and its semantics are fully human:

> Horum signorum genus [the *signa data*], quantum ad homines attinet, considerare atque tractare statuimus, *quia et signa divinitus data, quae scripturis sanctis continentur, per homines nobis indicata sunt qui ea conscripserunt.* (*De doctrina christiana* 2.ii.3)
>
> We propose to consider and to discuss this class of signs in so far as men are concerned with it, *for even signs given by God and contained in the Holy Scriptures are of this type also, since they were presented to us by the men who wrote them.*

The first implication of this idea is that scriptural exegetes need to reckon with the fallen nature of human language, but are not hindered by it. In general, a Christological (proportional) paradigm seems to be at work in Augustine's thought. Just as the redemption of mankind is made possible by Christ's *exinanitio* (emptying out – what Dante will call His 'humiliation' in *Paradiso* 7.120), so also God's message of redemption is transmitted to mankind through mankind itself. Neither the incarnation of Christ nor the writing of the Bible implies a descent into the sphere of absolute negativity. On the contrary, God's condescension is to be read as a sign of human dignity.[39] The Scriptures participate in this world, but their participation in the earthly sphere does not imply any divestiture of their authority; it simply justifies Augustine's own attempt to indicate to the exegetes some techniques for retracing the path of God's condescension in the sacred text. As we are about to see, Augustine will indeed address biblical rhetoric with partly traditional rhetorical tools and elucidate the text's meaning with fully human means.

A further element holds Augustine's view of the sacred text in equilibrium. By partaking of the *dispensatio temporalis*, Scripture simply does not represent the *ultimate* end of a Christian's progress towards the knowledge of God. Although it is valuable, even priceless, it is neither the only nor the perfect means to salvation. Scripture is the product of a compromise and it serves a purpose; it is not an end in itself. This notion balances the stress Augustine placed on the role played by the human component in the production of biblical writings. Augustine states the point most effectively at the close of book 1:

> Homo itaque fide et spe et caritate subnixus eaque inconcusse retinens non indiget scripturis nisi ad alios instruendos. Itaque multi per haec tria etiam in solitudine sine codicibus vivunt. Unde in illis arbitror iam impletum esse quod dictum est: 'Sive prophetiae evacuabuntur, sive linguae cessabunt, sive scientia evacuabitur' [1 Cor. 13:10]. (1.xxxix.43)

> Thus a man supported by faith, hope and charity, with an unshaken hold upon them, does not need the Scriptures except for the instruction of others. And many live by these three things in solitude without books. Whence in these persons I think the saying is already exemplified, 'whether prophecies shall be made void or tongues shall cease, or knowledge shall be destroyed.'

The hermeneutic project of *De doctrina christiana* hinges on this notion: the Scriptures are necessary only insofar as a Christian needs instruction in and for this world. As they are intrinsically 'moral' objects, they are intended as a guide for the process through time: they fall under the rubric of ethics. Any reading of the Scriptures should take into account their double nature: they are historical (that is, they come into time) and they are mediated human rhetoric. It also needs, however, to acknowledge the existence – beyond their primary human authority – of a higher authority and – beyond their instrumentality – of an ultimate goal. Containing a message that points beyond itself, Scripture can be described metaphorically as a vehicle for man's return to God – literally an *instrumentum*.[40] Augustine organizes his treatise around the notion that a dichotomy exists between *utenda* and *fruenda*, and the Scriptures appear to fall into the first category.[41] They are God-inspired, to be sure, and play an essential role in shaping a Christian path towards salvation, but Augustine conceives of them as a means towards the acquisition of the highest truth – not as themselves the truth.

When *De doctrina christiana* addresses the motives that drive a reader to study the Bible, Augustine's language clearly reflects on the status the treatise attributes to its object. The hermeneutics required to penetrate the Scriptures must take into account their instrumental nature. While their meaning is ethical, their way of signifying is rhetorical; and the reader should be able to move from one level to the other:

> Quam [namely, the *scripturam divinam*] legentis nihil aliud appetunt quam cogitationes voluntatemque illorum, a quibus conscripta est, invenire *et per illas voluntatem Dei*, secundum quam tales homines locutos credimus. (2.v.6)[42]

> (Who reads the Scriptures) desires to find in it nothing more than the thoughts and desires of those who wrote it *and through these the will of God*, according to which we believe those writers spoke.

The idea that the authorship of the sacred text is constitutionally double is not merely part of the argument about the instrumental nature of Scripture outlined above, it also serves as the keystone of Augustine's hermeneutics. From this notion stems also the *regula caritatis*, the hermeneutic principle according to which the essential message (and the final criterion for the interpretation) of God's Word is the construction in the reader of the double love for God and neighbour.[43] Augustine's point of departure is a commonplace in the Latin rhetorical tradition, the so-called argument 'de scripto et voluntate' (on the letter and the meaning of a text).[44] In Christian discourse, the classical argument treating the interpretation of any legal text as a necessary step in their enforcement intersected with the Apostle's dichotomy between the letter and spirit of the Law, as formulated in 2 Cor. 3:6, 'Littera occidit, spiritus autem vivificat' ('The letter kills, but the spirit gives life,' quoted by Augustine in *De doctrina christiana* 3.v.9), and the subsequent split between the hermeneutic traditions of Christianity and Judaism.[45]

The intersection of the Roman legal and Christian apologetic tradition produced a discourse of *longue durée* dominated by the call to interpretation, onto which Augustine's authoritative treatise was soon grafted. Augustine's argument is nuanced and detailed. He introduces at first the notion of a 'transverse' reading of the Bible:

> Quam sit utilius viam non deserere, demonstrandum est, ne consuetudine deviandi etiam in transversum aut perversum ire cogatur. (*De doctrina christiana* 1.xxxvi.41)

> A reader is to be corrected and shown that it is more useful not to leave the road, lest the habit of deviating force him to take a crossroad or a perverse way.

Differing from a *perverse* reading, *transverse* readings are able to reach the ultimate goal towards which the text is oriented, in spite of their stretching beyond the author's immediate and literal intention. The final aim of every interpretation of the sacred text should be the construction of charity; the instrumental path one takes to reach charity seems to matter less. Once distilled from his beloved hodoeporics metaphor, Augustine's point is simple. Whoever interprets the text without building charity has not yet properly understood the intention of the text. On the other hand, whoever interprets beyond the writer's intention can be said to be wrong, but if his hermeneutic builds charity he is wrong in an innocent way – he does not lie:

> Quisquis igitur scripturas divinas vel quamlibet earum partem intellexisse sibi videtur ita ut eo intellectu non aedificet istam geminam caritatem Dei et proximi, nondum intellexit. *Quisquis vero talem inde sententiam duxerit ut huic aedificande caritati sit utilis, nec tamen hoc dixerit quod ille quem legit eo loco sensisse probabitur, non perniciose fallitur nec omnino mentitur.* (ibid. 1.xxxvi.40)

> Whoever, therefore, thinks that he understands the divine Scriptures or any part of them so that it does not build the double love of God and of our neighbor does not understand it at all. *Whoever finds a lesson there useful to the building of charity, even though he has not said what the author may be shown to have intended in that place, has not been deceived, nor is he lying in any way.*

On the notion of the *regula caritatis* as the final touchstone for interpretation Augustine again insists in the passage immediately following. Here, he admits that some correction might be in order when an interpretation goes beyond or against the intention of the immediate author, but he immediately reiterates his trust in an active hermeneutics:

> Sed quisquis in scripturis aliud sentit quam ille qui scripsit, illis non mentientibus fallitur, sed tamen, ut dicere coeperam, *si sententia fallitur, qua aedificet caritatem, quae finis praecepti est, ita fallitur ac si quisquam, errore deserens viam, eo tamen per agrum pergat quo etiam via illa perducit.* (ibid. 41)

> But anyone who understands in the Scriptures something other than that intended by the one who wrote them is deceived, although they do not lie. However, as I began to explain, *if he is deceived in an interpretation which builds up charity, which is the end of the commandments, he is deceived in the same way as a man who leaves a road by mistake but passes through a field to the same place toward which the road itself leads.*

Notably, for Augustine, a reading beyond the apparent intention of the writer can be a good one *only* because of the authorship model he sets up for the Bible. A 'transverse' reading (i.e., an interpretation deviant in its course but ultimately successful in its results) is possible *only* because the decisive agency of the text is the Holy Spirit, who, in order to reach man, works through a human intermediary:

> Id tamen eo conante qui divina scrutatur eloquia, *ut ad voluntatem perveniatur auctoris, per quem scripturam illam sanctus operatus est Spiritus*, sive hoc assequatur sive aliam sententiam de illis verbis, quae fidei rectae non refragatur, exsculpat, testimonium habens a quocumque alio loco divinorum eloquiorum. (3.xxvii.38)

> For he who examines the divine eloquence, *desiring to discover the intention of the author through whom the Holy Spirit created the Scripture*, whether he attains this end or finds another meaning in the words not contrary to right faith, is free from blame if he has evidence from some other place in the divine books.

Augustine also acknowledges that the ultimate author of Scripture does not coincide with their immediate human author, and the final meaning of God's word can sometimes be neither controlled nor even perceived by the immediate author:

> *Ille quippe auctor in eisdem verbis, quae intellegere volumus, et ipsam sententiam forsitan vidit et certe Dei spiritus, qui per eum haec operatus est, etiam ipsam occursuram lectori vel auditori sine dubitatione praevidit.* Nam quid in divinis eloquiis largius et uberius potuit divinitus provideri, quam ut eadem verba pluribus intellegantur modis, quos alia non minus divina contestantia faciant adprobari? (ibid. 39)

> *For the author himself may have seen the same meaning in the words we seek to understand. And certainly the Spirit of God, who worked through that author, undoubtedly foresaw that this meaning would occur to the reader or listener. Rather, He provided that it might occur to him, since that meaning is dependent upon truth.* For what could God have more generously and abundantly provided in the divine writing than that the same words might be understood in various ways which other no less divine witnesses approve?

In sum, a reading that stretches beyond the *voluntas* of the immediate author is not automatically wrong. When it conforms to the rule of charity, it is a legitimate reading that perhaps (*forsitan*) the human author was able to perceive, and surely (*certe … sine dubitatione*) the Holy Spirit foresaw. The presence of the higher authority of the Holy Spirit backs up the intention and the authority of the human author. Readers may thus interpret the text spiritually: they are allowed to move beyond the (literal) meaning intended by the intermediary author. In Augustine's discourse, to the double authority (immediate and ultimate) of the sacred text there also corresponds a double hermeneutic strategy. The reader should aim in the first place to reconstruct the *voluntas auctoris*, but he should also be ready to go beyond it, gaining access to a different and higher cause for the text. As we have seen, Statius appears to be interpreting Virgil's text exactly along these lines.

The stance Dante takes through the character of Statius on the issue of a potential double authorship of, and active hermeneutics for, poetic texts is certainly more radical than what Augustine might have been willing to grant in the case of a secular author. One may rightly object that the aim of the *De doctrina christiana* was, after all, to lay out the foundations for a hermeneutics of Scripture – and for it alone. Dante instead appropriates Augustine's tools only to apply them first to the writings of a pagan author – an unacceptable, radically mistaken object – and then, as we shall see, to his own text – a surprising and dangerous move. In *De doctrina christiana*, the immediate authors of the Scriptures are inspired writers. However inadequate one might consider their language, their authority had a high and steady source. One could not possibly say the same of the author of the texts to which Statius attributes his conversion, and, as the previous section has shown, Dante did not want it to be said of his Virgil. One should not, therefore, call upon Augustine to certify Dante's having Statius read Virgil's *Aeneid* or his Fourth Eclogue 'spiritually,' or to justify Dante's desire to have his readers do the same with his text.

For all its cogency, however, this argument does not undermine the possibility of seeing an Augustinian model loom large beneath *Purgatorio* 22. Rather, it reinforces this possibility, insofar as it justifies the step that Dante takes beyond Augustine by extending a spiritual reading to an arguably uninspired text, while always remaining on a solid, fully Augustinian ground. The forceful argument advanced in *De doctrina christiana* – on the difference between the Scriptures' God-inspired authors and the pagan, misguided poet – does not imply the total irreconcilability of their texts when it comes to the *use* that a Christian reader might make of them. There does not seem to be any essential, ontological difference between the instrumentality of biblical texts and that of Virgil's texts when it comes to their role as vehicles of divine truth. In *Purgatorio* 22, Dante suggests that even texts that have their origin outside the sphere of the sacred can be properly reused when they are read so as to conform to Augustine's rule of charity, building in their readers *gemina caritas*. The mere fact that Statius was drawn to the love of God and the love of his neighbour by his active reading of Virgil's text would be enough reason to 'save' the texts of the pagans. The contrast between, on the one side, divine inspiration and, on the other, authorial blindness can also be seen as the reason why Dante chose to stretch Augustine's formula of a double authorial intention – and, in order to save his teacher's texts, to discount and discard Virgil's intention altogether. *Purgatorio* 22 is so radical in stressing Statius's active hermeneutics that it brackets (and potentially altogether eliminates) Virgil's mediating agency and authorial authority. The salvific texts that Dante has Statius read in the course of his life and now, in their purgatorial afterlife, gloss for the benefit of their author did not have an author who could claim he was divinely inspired. In Dante's poem, the power to lead to salvation that belongs to pagan texts depends only on the active reading of their interpreters, who are able – as Statius was – to see their conformity to a higher intention. In the Christian Scriptures, the ultimate meaning of a text can be located beyond the authority of the inspired author because there is an ultimate author, God, dictating its meaning. Conversely – and this is a huge step, but a necessary one nonetheless – the truth of uninspired authors can be located only in their texts and in the inspired reading of their interpreters.

But there is perhaps more. In claiming legitimacy for Statius's use on Virgil of a hermeneutic model originally designed for texts of a different nature, Dante could count on the authority of Augustine himself. In stretching Augustine's argument Dante knew that he was not betraying the fundamental drive that his work contained to recover for a morally useful end the 'scriptures' of the classical past (as the *Epistle to Cangrande* will call them).[46] On the contrary, it was precisely on Augustine's authority that Dante could found the relationship of continuity with classical literature he established in his poem. In so doing, he was surely developing the project of recovering the classical past beyond the limits that Augustine himself had set in some of his works. Yet, he also knew that he could rely in his daring operation on some key elements that he had found in Augustine's mediating work on the instruction of the Christian. In Augustine's treatise, Dante had an example – hardly an irrelevant one – of a semiologically constructive and morally fruitful reading of religiously questionable texts. In his exemplar, he could find a qualified defence of pagan learning and detailed instructions on its correct use. Dante's claim that a pre-Christian text could be used to produce a Christian meaning was, in essence, parallel to Augustine's own metaphorization of classical lore as 'gold of the Egyptians.'

A work of mediation between two opposing cultural urges, *De doctrina christiana* was, in fact, based on a strategic recovery of classical textual culture, on which a new Christian cultural paradigm could be built. The controlling metaphor Augustine chose for this process of re-use was the despoliation of Egypt. The Christian intellectual, Augustine maintains, should feel entrusted to appropriate the classical curriculum of instruction since God granted the same permission, typologically, to the Hebrew people fleeing from their captivity in Egypt. In Augustine's long-lasting and influential cultural allegory, the 'gold of the Egyptians' of Exodus 3:21–2 and 12:35–6 is called upon to represent the heritage that a Christian intellectual can and should claim from the classical past, in terms of both positive knowledge and instructional techniques. In *De doctrina christiana*, at the end of book 2, Augustine writes:

> Sicut enim Aegyptii non tantum idola habebant et onera gravia, quae populus Israhel detestaretur et fugeret, sed etiam vasa atque ornamenta de auro et argento et vestem, quae ille populus exiens de Aegypto sibi potius tamquam ad usum meliorem clanculo vindicavit non auctoritate propria sed praecepto Dei, ipsis Aegyptiis nescienter commodantibus ea quibus non bene utebantur, sic doctrinae omnes gentilium non solum simulata et superstitiosa figmenta gravesque sarcinas supervacanei laboris habent, quae unusquisque nostrum duce Christo de societate gentilium exiens debet abominari atque devitare, sed etiam liberales disciplinas usui veritatis aptiores et quaedam morum praecepta utilissima continent. (*De doctrina christiana* 2.xl.60)

> Just as the Egyptians had not only idols and grave burdens which the people of Israel detested and avoided, so also they had vases and ornaments of gold and silver and clothing which the Israelites took with them secretly when they fled, as if to put them to a better use. They did not do this on their own authority but at God's commandment, while the Egyptians unwittingly supplied them with things which they themselves did

not use well. In the same way all the teachings of the pagans contain not only simulated and superstitious imaginings and grave burdens of unnecessary labor, which each one of us leaving the society of pagans under the leadership of Christ ought to abominate and avoid, but also liberal disciplines more suited to the uses of truth, and some most useful precepts concerning morals.

Augustine's use of this typological reading is particularly telling. It is the product of a cultural embarrassment of sorts. In the Christian discourse, the despoliation of the Egyptians must be read figurally, because it cannot be a mere event in history. To justify what appears as a simple theft, there must be both a mandate from God and a meaning for God's order that transcends the literal, historical truth of Egypt's (retributive, almost retaliatory) despoliation at the hands of the chosen people. By interpreting the biblical episode typologically, Augustine is able to settle a double account. On the one hand, in a classic case of supersession, he severs the new Christian learning from its Jewish roots, relegating the formerly chosen people to the sphere of the 'carnal' (the Jews, after all, did actually take from Egypt the physical signs of wealth and power). On the other hand, he settles his account with the Latin classical tradition, transferring its learning to Christian culture, and basing this transfer on God's injunction to put to a better use the badly deployed instruments of traditional pagan culture. From the beginning, Augustine's typological reading was of fundamental importance for the wider negotiation of the disparate strains of influence that contributed to the eventual cultural identity of the Latin Church. Its exemplary power legitimized the forming culture to incorporate and subsume the otherness of its antecedents and antagonists. Once it reached Dante, however, the cultural metaphor began to work in the opposite direction, and turned into the keystone of a novel classicism. Just as Dante's Statius appears in the *Commedia* as a reader who practises Augustinian hermeneutics on a non-sacred text, so too Dante's poem proposes to recover that text (and the cultural heritage it is made to stand for) and put it to a better ethical use.

When we realize that Dante patterns the peculiar art of interpretation he attributes to Statius on the model of Christian scriptural hermeneutics that Augustine had advanced before him, one further aspect of Dante's poetics emerges in a new light. If the author-centred poetics of the minor works had promoted and produced an author-centred hermeneutics, the reader-centred hermeneutics now proposed in his text has crucial effects on the poetics of his poem. By structuring a long and complex episode around the encounter of the Latin epic poets, Dante has his readers appreciate the difference between the alternative interpretive models embodied by Statius and Virgil. But he does not stop at that; he also suggests that his own text may (and, perhaps, should) be read according to Statius's model. The shift in hermeneutic principles from the minor works that Dante's readers witness when they come to the episode of Statius has an essential effect: not unlike the work of the pagan author, once it is interpreted in a Christian light, Dante's *Commedia* occupies a middle ground between rhetorical (classical) and inspired (scriptural) artefacts. On the one hand, by being the product of a human writer, the poem invites its readers to deploy an active hermeneutics that relegates the author to a position similar to that of the biblical writer, who is always subjected to the higher authority of the Holy Spirit. On the other hand, the text of the poem may become the object of such a process of interpretation only because its author made it the vehicle of a spiritual truth, for which a different and higher author is ultimately responsible. The openness to interpretation that ensues is the most evident sign of the text's divine inspiration. As the next chapter will show, Dante bases the authority of his poem on the possibility (and, perhaps, the necessity) of employing a readerly hermeneutic on the Bible, the *scriptura paganorum*, and his own *Commedia*.

3.5 Augustine's Hermeneutics and the Poetics of the Spirit

The influence Augustine's hermeneutics has exerted on the *Commedia* is not limited to the Statius episode. A particular juncture in *Paradiso* 26 provides additional evidence of how crucial Augustine's thought proved to be for the author of the *Commedia*. Dante formulates his idea of what makes biblical writing unique in a language that is deeply indebted to Augustine's treatment. As we are about to see, Dante agrees with Augustine on the crucial notion that love for God and one's neighbour is both the aim of all biblical interpretation and the *conditio sine qua non* for any correct reading of it. Phrased as the first response the Pilgrim offers during his examination on charity, the third and fundamental theological virtue, Dante's answer gives his definition of biblical writing in purely Augustinian terms. What is more, in the passage he addresses precisely the issue of how the Scriptures signify.[47]

In the critically tormented passage that follows, Dante constructs a similarly circular relationship between *caritas* and Scripture, Love and writing:

> Lo ben che fa contenta questa corte,
> Alfa e O è di quanta scrittura
> mi legge Amore o lievemente o forte.
> (*Paradiso* 26.16–18)

'The good that satisfies this court / is alpha and omega of whatever scripture / Love teaches me in loud or gentler tones.'[48]

Traditional commentaries on the passage share several basic elements. While the general sense of the tercet is clear, there is a technical difficulty in assigning precise syntactic roles to *Amore* and *scrittura*. Dante clearly says that all his love is directed towards God, the *summum bonum* whom the heavenly court perpetually enjoys. The difficulty resides in the lines immediately following, and it is triggered by the metaphor of God as the beginning and end of all Scripture. In these lines, either *Amore* is the subject, and he does all the reading of (or, better yet, the lecturing on) the *scrittura*, or *scrittura* is itself what 'reads out and signifies' *Amore*. Love is, in short, either the cause or the effect of the reading of the Scriptures.[49]

The problem with the traditional argument is that the either/or frame critics impose on Dante's tercet should probably be recast as an Augustinian both/and. The syntactic ambiguity of situation in which Love produces a reading of the Scripture and one in which Love is the product of a reading of the Scripture mimics what one may call the virtuous circularity of Augustine's hermeneutics. In the first two books of *De doctrina christiana*, Augustine had developed an argument that hinged on the notion that the *regula caritatis* is two things at the same time. 'Love' is the specific content one should retrieve from the reading of the Scriptures, and it is the framework necessary to engender a constructive and productive reading of God's word. The way the treatise is structured is indicative of this approach. Augustine first presents the object of instruction and only then the methods of extracting that object from the texts. For him the ultimate truth of Christianity is love; correspondingly, the final rule for reading Scripture is also love. The vehicle and object of the message coincide. Love for God and neighbour, the *gemina caritas*, is the condition for interpreting the Scriptures *and* it is the result of their reading – simultaneously the controlling principle and the product of a Christian hermeneutics. Dante's syntactic ambiguity, perhaps, is designed to be accepted as such.[50]

To be sure, the relevance of the passage goes beyond the presence of a literal ambiguity and the ensuing possibility to produce, in practice, two diverging readings of the same poetic utterance. What matters is, rather, the unambiguous way in which Dante follows Augustine in advancing a technical *petitio principii* for the openness of biblical hermeneutics. Augustinian influence on Dante's treatment of Love as means and meaning of all biblical hermeneutics does not stop at the level of content: the tercet is cast in a fully Augustinian language. Not only does Dante treat the correlation of Love and Scripture, he also addresses the question of a double register in God's way of communicating with man through the Scriptures. Once an Augustinian frame is brought into the discussion, the adverbs *lievemente* and *forte* can hardly be read as referring to the 'higher or lower volume' of Love's voice in lecturing. Neither can they refer to the 'deep or superficial quality' of Love's calling, as the *secolare commento* has sometimes proposed. As Benvenuto da Imola was the first to point out, the adverbs relate to the dichotomy between ease and difficulty in the interpretation of the Scriptures. The vocabulary and the notion are mediated by Augustine's assessment of obscurity in the biblical text. For Augustine obscurities are not only always balanced by other clear and straightforward formulations elsewhere in the canonical writings; they are also providentially preordained and functional to preserving the hermeneutic challenge and appeal of the text. They are willed by God.

De doctrina christiana returns more than once to the issue, but the clearest formulation is to be found perhaps in the context of a discussion of biblical rhetoric. After having attributed 'sweetness' to the rhetorical use of similes in the Scriptures, Augustine notes that the alternation of immediately comprehensible and difficult passages in the Bible is designed to elicit a salubrious appetite in readers: metaphorically speaking, the open passages sate the reader's hunger for meaning, while the difficult ones defy satiety. The Holy Spirit, who is the ultimate author of the biblical text, has endowed it with this most distinctive rhetorical feature:

> Magnifice igitur et salubriter Spiritus sanctus ita scripturas sanctas modificavit, ut locis apertioribus fami occureret, obscurioribus autem fastidia detergeret. *Nihil enim fere de illis obscuritatibus eruitur, quod non planissime dictum alibi reperiatur.* (*De doctrina christiana* 2.vi.8)

> Thus the Holy Spirit has magnificently and wholesomely modulated the Holy Scriptures so that the more open places present themselves to hunger and the more obscure places may deter a disdainful attitude. *Hardly*

anything may be found in these obscure places which is not found plainly said elsewhere.

For Augustine, the Bible balances these two modes of writing in a providential and mixed text. The collaborative dichotomy between the passages in which God's word is designed to be obscure (Dante's *forte*) and those in which it is designed to be clear (Dante's *lieve*) appears to be replicated in Dante's examination on Love. The same mixture of soft and hard passages which collaborate to produce *caritas*, the hermeneutic equivalent of the poetic *trobar leu* and *trobar clus*, also governs the wording of the poem.

Dante's use of the terms in other areas of his work confirms that *lievemente* and *forte* indeed have a strong hermeneutic valence in *Paradiso* 26. For instance, the adverb *lieve* (and *lievemente*) appears quite often in discussions of hermeneutics: already in *Vita nuova* 19.21 the term is used as a cursive signal for the hermeneutic accessibility of the poetic text, *Donne ch'avete intelletto d'amore*, but only once has its explanation reached the poem's envoy: 'questa ultima parte è lieve a intendere.' Again suggesting immediate comprehension of the text at hand, in *Doglia mi reca* the adverb appears in its technical sense of 'easier to understand,' and it is even the object of an internal gloss: 'più lieve, sí che men grave s'intenda' (simpler [...], so that its meaning is less hard to grasp, v. 56). The same oppositional couple *lieve* and *grave* is echoed in *Paradiso* 24.37, when Beatrice asks Peter to test Dante on faith, touching on both easy and difficult articles: 'tenta costui di punti lievi e gravi' (test this man as you see fit on points, / both minor and essential). The perfect synonym of *lieve*, the term *leggiero* appears in *Convivio* 2.ii.6 at a key juncture of Dante's argument in favour of self-commentary. His lyric poems, Dante argues, need to be dissected into their constituent parts so that their meaning will be easier to grasp: 'sí che leggiero sarà poi lo suo intendimento a vedere' (so that afterwards it will be easy to perceive its meaning). Again in the technical sense of being able to interpret easily what lies beneath the thin veil of allegory, the term also appears at *Purgatorio* 8.21: 'che certo 'l trapassar dentro è leggero' (that piercing it [the veil] is surely easy).

Correspondingly, the adjective *forte* conveys the opposite notion of hermeneutic challenge and interpretive difficulty in two passages from *Convivio*: in 2.xi.7 Dante comments upon lines 55–7 of *Voi che 'ntendendo*, noting that few will understand the real meaning of the *canzone*, since the poetic text conveys it in a harsh and difficult way: 'saranno radi ...

/ color che tua ragione intendan bene, / tanto la parli faticosa e forte' (They will be few indeed / Who'll rightly understand your sense, / So difficult and complex is your speech).

Similarly, and again referring to the philosophical density of *Le dolci rime* in 4.xxi.6, Dante adds: 'Io parlo sì che par forte ad intendere' (I speak in a way that seems difficult to understand). Other passages in the *Commedia* reiterate the notion of interpretive hardness. *Purgatorio* 29.42, in the invocation opening the description of the seven candelabra, points out the inherent challenge of turning into poetry concepts which are difficult to grasp: 'forti cose a pensar mettere in versi' (to put in verse things hard for thought). *Purgatorio* 33.50 characterizes Beatrice's first prophecy of the *DXV* as a difficult enigma: 'questo enigma forte,' which history will soon solve. Finally, in *Paradiso* 7.49, Beatrice's explanation of the double meaning of Christ's crucifixion – a crime for the Jews, a just retribution for God – should have cleared all doubts in Dante's mind: 'non ti dee oramai parer più forte' (No longer, from now on, should it seem puzzling). In sum, the two terms that conclude Dante's definition of love appear so often in a fixed constellation with the related notions of understanding and interpretation that nothing seems to prevent us from reading them in a technical sense in *Paradiso* 26 as well. Actually, the larger context seems to conspire with the local Augustinian allusion and rule out any other sense.[51]

But what are the implications of Dante's and Augustine's shared notion that Love is both the ideal means of interpretation for biblical writings and the end of that interpretation? The previous discussion of biblical hermeneutics has provided an answer in ethical terms: a good reading is a reading that produces love for God and one's neighbour. The following pages address the other side of the question, by focusing on the author rather than the reader in the text. In particular, they explore the role that for Dante the Holy Spirit is called upon to play both in the explanation and in the inspiration of the text. Just as the hermeneutic act binds together reader and text in the act of reading, so too the poetic act of composition connects the text with its ultimate author. Dante's hermeneutics have been shown to be Augustinian; so too his poetics can be shown to have developed under the formative influence of Augustine. Let us resume for a moment the hermeneutic perspective and focus once again on the act of interpretation. For Augustine and for Dante, the openness to interpretation that the biblical text affords never coincides with infinite proliferation of meaning.

Rather, in both writers it is always balanced by a controlling set of limitations.[52] In a crucial passage in *De doctrina christiana* 2.viii.9 (taken up again at viii.13) Augustine assigns to the seven gifts of the Holy Spirit a clear role in biblical hermeneutics: they act as a precondition for interpretation. Dante seems to have been receptive to Augustine's idea as early as *Purgatorio* 29, in his first poetic framing of the biblical canon. By having seven candelabra precede the mystical pageant of biblical books in Eden, Dante figurally patterned his allegorical vision on Augustine's discussion of biblical hermeneutics. The procession has the same structure as Augustine's theoretical treatment: in *De doctrina christiana*, the seven gifts of the Holy Spirit are discussed immediately before the canon of the Bible is detailed: they function as a precondition for reading the text. Just like Augustine, Dante lists his canon of inspired authors only after suggesting, through a symbolic detail in the mystical procession, the correct (inspired) way of interpreting them.[53]

The role Augustine predicates of the Holy Spirit is in no way limited to His being part of the checks and balances necessary to keep the interpretation of the sacred text within bounds. As we have observed, Augustine also insists on the *authorial* role the third person of the Trinity plays in inspiring the writing of Scriptures. The notion is foundational for his overall argument on biblical hermeneutics: by guiding the human authors, the Holy Spirit is responsible for the ultimate meaning of the text. Dante's writings preserve clear traces of this Augustinian notion. In addition to their common argument *a parte subjecti*, Dante too subscribes to Augustine's idea that the Scriptures intrinsically have a double authorship and a double nature. In *Paradiso* 25.1–2, he offers the controlling metaphor for his poem's poetics: it is a *poema sacro*, that is, the product of collaboration between *cielo e terra* similar to what for Augustine produced Scripture itself: 'This sacred poem, / to which both Heaven and earth have set their hand.' If Dante's surprising and potentially hubristic claim preserves no trace of Augustine's influence beyond the larger contextual coherence, Dante makes of this idea the centre of his concern in *Monarchia* 3.iv.11, a few paragraphs after he has given the first and only open citation of *De doctrina christiana* in his works. The polemical thrust of the context in which he resorts to Augustine's authority should not obscure Dante's keen interest in the solution to the question offered in the treatise. Dante may be advancing a strictly political argument, but the point he makes has clear and momentous implications for his poetics. Inveighing against those readers who maliciously bend God's word for their political aims, he writes:

> Ego autem dico quod si talia fiunt de ignorantia, correctione diligenter adhibita ignoscendum est sicut ignoscendum esset illi qui leonem in nubibus formidaret; *si vero industria, non aliter cum sic errantibus est agendum, quam cum tyrampnis, qui publica iura non ad comunem utilitatem secuntur, sed ad propriam retorquere conantur.* (Monarchia 3.iv.10)

> Now I say that if such errors are done out of ignorance, the offender should be diligently corrected and then forgiven, just as one should forgive a person who is frightened by a lion in the clouds. *But if such errors are done deliberately, those committing them should be dealt with just as if they were tyrants who do not abide by the public laws for the common welfare, but instead try to twist them for their own advantage.*[54]

Appropriating Augustine's warning (and the Apostle's recommendation) for the exegetes who take their reading of the sacred text too far away from the 'right' one because of their ignorance, Dante concentrates here on readers who pervert their interpretation of the Scriptures so that they may advance a political agenda contradicted by that same text.[55] In *Monarchia*'s inflamed rhetoric, these readers are equated with tyrants who appropriate for their personal advantage the laws (*publica iura*) designed to serve the common good.[56] When they claim that one should read in Genesis' account of the creation of Sun and Moon a typological account of God's providential institution of Church and Empire they impose an illegitimate (because dialectically irrational) reading upon Moses' text. Church and Empire have been instituted by God only to provide mankind with guidance once original sin had rendered human will defective. Had God instituted two body politics to act as guides for mankind *before* Adam's fall, He would have acted irrationally: 'a stupid doctor ... who prepares a plaster for the future abscess of a man who had not yet been born' (3.iv.14–16). Whoever tries to read Moses' text as if it were saying so is bound to make a mistake on the level of pure dialectical thought: the author could not have meant that – *intentio Moysi esse non potuit illa quam fingunt*.[57]

The dialectical error of the partisans of the Church, however, brings about for Dante a graver sin. They are not just betraying the specific biblical author by violating his intention; they ultimately sin against the Holy Spirit, displacing the meaning willed by God from the text so that it may conform to their own interpretation. Dante had just stated:

> O summum facinus, etiamsi contingat in sompniis, *ecterni Spiritus intentione abuti*! Non enim peccatur in Moysen, non in David, non in Iob, non in Matheum, non in Paulum, sed in Spritum Sanctum qui loquitur in illis. *Nam quanquam scribe divini eloquii multi sint, unicus tamen dictator est Deus, qui beneplacitum suum nobis per multorum calamos explicare dignatus est*. (3.iv.11)[58]

> O worst of crimes, even if committed only in dreams *to abuse the intention of the eternal Spirit*! For the sin is not an offense against Moses, not against David, not against Job, not against Matthew, not against Paul, but against the Holy Spirit, who is speaking through them. *For although there are many scribes of the divine word, there is only one who dictates them, namely God, who has designed to make his will known to us through the pens of many writers.*

In the line of argumentation Dante develops in his political treatise, the hermeneutical error he detects in theocratic exegetes is a crime (*facinus*) against human laws and mores. However, it soon acquires a spiritual dimension in appearing as the antithesis of the highest good (*summum facinus* vs. *summum bonum*) and turning from crime into sin in the short span of a line. Reading self-servingly constitutes not only a violation of any intention the human biblical writers might have entrusted to their texts, but also a breaking off from Divine intentionality. Any subjective misreading is not a sin because it forces the text to signify something against the authority of the authors; it is a sin because it goes against the intention of the Holy Spirit. What is worse, bending the biblical text in order to advance one's own agenda amounts to an abuse of the interpretive freedom that the text affords to its readers.

The process of divine inspiration for the sacred texts described in the *Monarchia* passage is articulated in strict conformity with the Augustinian paradigm explored earlier: the human authors act as intermediaries between the ultimate author and His audience. The terms Dante uses to describe this process are, in turn, reminiscent of two central metapoetic pronouncements he had already made in the *Commedia*. Used to characterize the relation between God and biblical authors, the keywords *scribe* and *dictator* used in the *Monarchia* passage reflect the eerie lexical choice Dante made to describe his work as *scriba* in Paradiso 10.26–7 ('A sé torce tutta mia cura / quella materia *ond'io son fatto scriba*' [for my attention now resides / in that matter of which I have become the scribe]) and most of in all *Purgatorio* 24.52–4:

> 'Io mi son un che quando
> Amor mi spira, noto, e *a quel modo
> ch'e' ditta dentro vo significando.*'

'I am one who, when Love / inspires me, take note and, as he dictates / deep within me, so I set it forth.'[59]

As modern readers have noted, the lexical proximity of the passage in *Monarchia* to that of *Purgatorio* 24 is the sign that the *Monarchia* develops the distinction between immediate and ultimate author for biblical texts according to the same model of divinely inspired writing that the *Commedia* advances for itself.[60] What still needs to be stressed in these *loci paralleli* is that both the treatise and the poem address the problem in technically Augustinian terms. As the mediator of God's message, in the *Commedia* Dante invites a reading of his poetry that may move beyond the human agency of the text. Like the biblical authors, he presents himself as the 'scribe' – fully responsible for the rhetorical, human structure of the work. He is, however, receiving and transmitting a message, the ultimate author of which is God. Taking advantage of the hermeneutic and poetic window opened by Augustine, Dante has his poem claim the same *rhetorical* status that one should grant to the Scriptures.

Each element of the chain of texts presented in this section – Augustine's *De doctrina christiana*, Dante's *Commedia*, and his *Monarchia* – is marked by the same dichotomy between immediate and ultimate author. The former is responsible for the technical, human, poetic production of the text, while the latter dictates its spiritual, divine, and moral intention. Augustine had constructed this model for Holy Writ. Dante appropriates it for the hermeneutics he recommends for the poetry of Virgil, showing through Statius the difference between a good, 'constructivist,' and a bad, 'objectivist,' reading. Finally, as we can infer from the language of *Monarchia* and of the later *cantiche*, he transfers the Augustinian model of double biblical authorship into his poem. In so doing, he claims for his new work the status of a text that is both, like Virgil's, inescapably human and, like the text of the biblical authors, inescapably inspired by God. Were it not resting on such a foundation, the surprising claim made at *Paradiso* 25 that the *Commedia* is a collaborative work of heaven and earth would be little more than a precious rhetorical trope.

Dante's inspirational poetics, just as his active hermeneutics, amounts to a renunciation only of his *ultimate* authority over the poem. Far from implying that the poem's immediate author cannot guide and orient the process of signification set in motion by the words of the poem, this new nexus of poetics and hermeneutics only suggests that he is ready to give up his own (authorial claims to) authority and ground his text on a more solid foundation than the one he was able to provide for his earlier works. As Albert Ascoli has proposed, Dante's renunciation coincides with a final twist in his search for a foundational authorial paradigm that may authorize his poetic texts.[61] In other words, Dante's recourse to Augustine's hermeneutic and compositional model does not entail a free, 'collaborative,' and 'plurivocal' hermeneutics – a model of reading that, by emphasizing the role of individual readers in the construction of meaning, postulates the ultimate semiotic instability of the text. Just as Augustine strove to keep in check any aberrant interpretation of the sacred page, so too did the author of the *Commedia* for his own text. The *Commedia* is not designed to undergo any process of 'open-ended' interpretation. Just as in the Bible, so in the poem, 'openness' means more the acceptance of the mysterious artistic collaboration between God and Man, Holy Spirit and writer, than any insatiable search for meaning triggered by the failure of language. Not by chance, both Dante and Augustine agree on a fundamental principle, designed to limit interpretive freedom – that, as Dante put it in *Monarchia* 3.iv.6 – 'Concerning the mystical sense, one can be in error in two ways: either by seeking it where it is not, or by interpreting it otherwise than it ought to be interpreted'; or better, in Augustine's words quoted immediately after in the *Monarchia*: 'One must not assume that all the events narrated are symbolic [i.e., have further meaning].'[62] At the same time, however, the *Commedia* – just like the Bible – presents itself as an inspired text, thus lacking the automatic sacredness associated with texts *dictated* by God. It is a text in which human mediation is essential. By professing to play in the poem the role of inadequate mediator, Dante responds to the *need to claim* for his text an authority that is not based on the 'authorial' control of its meaning. His choice of incorporating the Augustinian model of interpretation in the *Commedia* is a rhetorical move. It represents a necessary and strategic detour that the author takes, in order to justify all that is human in his work, without relinquishing the option of founding the validity of his message on the higher authority of divine inspiration.

4 Augustine in Dante: Three Readings

> They said, 'You have a blue guitar,
> You do not play things as they are.'
> The man replied, 'Things as they are
> Are changed upon the blue guitar.'
> Wallace Stevens

This final section is devoted to a selection of three readings from the *Commedia*, one from each of its *cantiche*: Cato (from *Inferno*), Dido (from *Purgatorio*), and Aeneas (from *Paradiso*). These passages have two main features in common: they represent cases of heightened Augustinian intertextuality and they offer metapoetic resonances. In them, Dante's dialogue with Augustine on individual points of historiography, literary criticism, and theology opens up and involves his theory of poetic making. They are also cases in which the poetics of the poem are tested in action. Having been shaped by the interplay of several earlier texts and making room for them, these passages bring their sources into contact and exploit their interlacing, whether that intertextual encounter be dominated by collision or cooperation. I have chosen these examples because they revolve around three characters from the Roman world, a sensitive region in Dante–Augustinian relations. Marked as moments of heightened literary self-consciousness, they also embody a wide variety of possible models of textual interaction.

4.1 Cato and History

It is well known that Dante contests Augustine's polemical way of reading the history of the Roman Empire, as it is articulated mainly (but not solely) in the historical sections of *De civitate Dei*. The main thrust of Augustine's treatise was that Rome epitomized the essential features of the Earthly City, a community whose citizens had refused to acquire a genuine sense of transcendence and are focused only on this world. Like everything else under the sun, Augustine argued, Rome's power was transient, though its citizens deluded themselves in thinking otherwise; the morals they practised were only a travesty of ethics; and the religion they adopted an untenable heap of all-too-human superstitions. To Rome and its values Augustine contrasted the City of God – the Church militant, whose members 'live in this world but are not of this world' and practise Christian moral asceticism and reliance on a 'true religion.'[1] By presenting Rome's history as something more valuable than a mere foil for the 'true' eschatological history of the Church, Dante's approach to Rome's historical function is more nuanced. In opposition to Augustine, who saw Rome's historical role exhausted in the preparation for the coming of Christ, Dante values Rome as an essential instrument of God's writing of history, both in the ancient incarnation of Roman Empire and in its modern, Christianized continuation.[2]

Dante's disagreement with Augustine on matters of history was not merely ideological, but also, and essentially, hermeneutical. While they referred to and contemplated the same facts, Augustine and Dante did not agree on what kind of *reading* history called for and what *meaning* was to be ultimately extracted from it. As we shall see, Dante did not shun the contradictions Augustine had pinpointed in the history of the Empire; rather, he accepted them as part of God's way of writing history, a divine poetics. Second, together with the image of Rome that Augustine had indicted in his most detailed and bitter treatise against Roman cultural supremacy, Dante made room, in his political thinking, for the poetry in which Rome's providential mission was made manifest – both in the necessarily optimistic, but not naive, version that Virgil gave of Rome's mission (an 'imperium sine fine,' in *Aeneid* 1.279) as well as in the much darker account of its actual development that Dante could find in Lucan's *Bellum civile*.

In what follows, three texts will be used to summarize the sense that Dante has of the historical role of the Roman Empire: the section devoted to the legitimacy of Roman authority in *Convivio* 4.iv and v; the first part of Justinian's speech in the heaven of Mercury (*Paradiso* 6.1–96), which triggers Beatrice's gloss on the necessity of Incarnation (*Paradiso* 7.19–120); and, finally, the second book of the treatise on monarchy.³ In all three cases, Dante sets off from a consideration of Augustinian questions to proceed in a divergent direction by advocating a reading of sacred history in which Rome's ascent to power is an integral part of the divine plan for the redemption of humankind. In so doing, he advocates a method of 'reading' history that takes into account its ambiguities, a method that is embedded in the debate form that the argument takes. Unlike *Convivio* 4.iv.8, which creates a fictional interlocutor who may object to Roman legitimacy ('potrebbe alcuno gavillare'), the opening statement of *Monarchia* 2 responds to Augustine's wholesale condemnation of Rome by strategically internalizing the opposing point of view. The book's argument acknowledges from the start that the author had at a certain point entertained a crucial doubt, reminiscent of Augustine's position:

> Admirabar equidem aliquando romanum populum in orbe terrarum sine ulla resistentia fuisse prefectum, cum, tantum superficialiter intuens, illum nullo iure sed armorum tantummodo violentia obtinuisse arbitrabar.

> I, too, used to be amazed that the Roman people had prevailed over the whole world without encountering any resistance, for I thought that they had come to rule not by right but by sheer violence (since at that time I looked at the matter only in a superficial way).⁴

In book 5 of *De civitate Dei*, one of the most directly polemical sections targeting a positive exemplary approach to Roman history, Augustine devotes chapter 12 to a question that will become Dante's: what virtues did Roman citizens possess that made them worthy of God's support in their political expansion? Augustine's text reads:

> Proinde videamus, quos Romanorum mores et quam ob causam Deus verus ad augendum imperium adiuvare dignatus est, in cuius potestate sunt etiam regna terrena. (*De civitate Dei* 5.xii.1)

> Let us investigate, then, what are the customs of the Romans and for what reasons the true God deemed them worthy to expand their power, since earthly kingdoms, too, are in His control.

Thus set up, the argument can only be based on examples, and in fact, after having provided a contrastive double portrait of Caesar and Cato (to which we will return shortly), Augustine proceeds to review the claims to fame of several Roman heroes, unfavourably comparing their achievements with those that Christians may boast. The cast of characters Augustine introduces in chapter 18 comprises Brutus and Torquatus (who both killed their sons out of a sense of justice), Furius Camillus (defender of an ungrateful city), Mucius Scaevola, Curtius, and the Decii (who all sacrificed themselves defending Rome), Marcus Pulvillus (undeterred in the performance of his duty even to go as far as to disregard the news of his son's death), Marcus Regulus (who kept his word to Rome's enemies no matter what the consequences), Lucius Valerius, Quintius Cincinnatus, and Fabricius (all called to hold powerful offices, in which they were tempted by power and wealth and yet were able to remain faithful to their poverty). Significantly, the examples that make up the body of Augustine's historical survey of Rome's (relative) worthiness are for the most part coincident with the ones Dante has used in *Convivio* 4 and will again use to prove the opposite point.

Dante's way of answering his own Augustinian doubt is not merely defensive. Taking up the reasoning sketched out in *Convivio* 4, the whole of *Monarchia* 2 is devoted to an argument in favour of the legitimacy of the Roman ruling; but to the claim that the Roman people held universal 'imperium' legitimately, Dante adds an essential corollary that accepts Augustine's general framework while subverting his conclusions. Dante's pre-emptive strike at the core of the dilemma laid out in the first paragraph is that, upon closer inspection and by most convincing signs, he came to understand that Rome's success was the result of divine intervention: 'per efficacissima signa divinam providentiam hoc effecisse cognovi' (2.i.3).[5] For Dante, as for Augustine, the ultimate agent of Rome's irresistible rise to power is divine Providence; unlike Augustine, however, Dante sees God's intervention in history as sign of a harmonious collaboration between human and divine – at least in his militant prose works. His proof, so he states, is the wide array of most convincing signs that he can read in it.

In the rest of *Monarchia* 2, Dante's reasoning moves from the claims to nobility and virtue that Aeneas could stake for his progeny to rule over Asia, Africa, and Europe, to an account of the direct, miraculous interventions of God in Rome's difficult times (from the falling of the shield from the sky to the Capitoline geese), all of which are cited as an index of God's favour: from the virtuous behaviour of several leaders and exemplary characters of Rome's early and republican history (Cincinnatus, Fabricius, Camillus, Brutus, Mucius Scaevola, the Decii, and Cato), to the victories Rome scored in the long series of wars between Aeneas's arrival in Latium and Scipio's triumph over Hannibal. The cast of Roman self-sacrificing heroes is quite consistent with the one surveyed in *Convivio* 4 and *Paradiso* 6, and the same may be said for the catalogue of victories listed in the two texts, with the provision that Justinian's speech is perhaps more interested in straightforward victories than self-sacrifice and takes into account a wider span of time (to include the first four emperors of the new Christian dispensation, Titus, Constantine, Charlemagne, and of course himself).

The point in which Justinian's speech (in compact form) and Beatrice's (more extended) explanation in the following canto come into contact again with the argument developed both in *Convivio* 4.v.3–9 and in *Monarchia* 2 (and thus take leave of any remaining Augustinian safeguards) is in linking the history of centralized Roman rule with the project and process of human redemption. Connecting Christ's incarnation and passion with Roman jurisdiction, and hence legitimacy, is an essential step for *Monarchia*; nevertheless, this particular concern is shared by the two canti in *Paradiso* as well. In the defensive argument of the treatise, Christ's historical time on Earth, the span of time that Dante delimits using the label 'in utroque termino sue militie' (*Monarchia* 2.xi.7), is offered as a divine endorsement of Rome's power. At one end of the process, the birth of Jesus under the census launched by Augustus proves that the Saviour intended to be registered as a human being in that particular account of humankind; at the other end, Christ's self-sacrifice is said to function as retribution (*vendetta*) for Adam's sin only because the officer administering the punishment was rightfully holding authority over the whole human race. Justinian's insistence on the third 'bearer' of the imperial eagle in *Paradiso* 6.82–90 and Beatrice's insistence on the collective nature of Adam's sin (and hence of Christ's *persona* in His sacrifice) in *Paradiso* 7.85–92 speak to this same point.

The arguments most forcefully advanced in *Paradiso* and *Monarchia* are not completely new to Dante readers. He had already advocated a positive role for the Roman Empire in the fourth *trattato* of *Convivio*, putting forth several specific reasons. The first, which serves as a foundation for the reading of Roman history that Dante builds up in *Convivio*, is the idea of a collaboration between the Empire and the divine plan of salvation. In God's election of the Romans as the new 'chosen people,' and of their form of government as the ideal setting for the redemption of humankind, Dante sees the major argument in defence of the legitimacy of the classical Roman Empire, a legitimacy that extends to the Holy Roman Empire of his own time. The philosophically driven *Convivio*, it is worth noting, reaches the realm of history in a rather tangential way. In a digression motivated by a discussion of the notion of 'authority' (in its turn, prompted by the definition of 'nobility' contained in *Le dolci rime*), Dante devotes a portion of chapter 4 to a syllogistic argument echoing those developed in Aristotle's *Politics*, by which it is ascertained that the perfect form of political arrangement is the 'monarchy,' the rule of one over many. Before concluding his argument, Dante opens a 'sub-digression' in which he sets out a possible objection to his reasoning. If, he writes, it is possible to prove by logical argument that the Empire is necessary to humankind, it is more difficult to justify the historically contingent fact that God allotted to the Roman Empire (and to its heir, the Holy Roman Empire) the government of the world. There would seem to be no grounds for the Latin people to claim pre-eminence; their power could merely be the product of chance or, worse still, of mere violence.

To respond to this objection, and now moving into the historical part of his proof, Dante calls upon the intervention of God. It has been God himself who has chosen the Romans and their empire to rule the world. The evidence of God's election of the Roman Empire can be 'read' in history itself. Rounding off his eulogy of the heroes of the Roman Republic developed in chapter 4, Dante states:

> Certo e manifesto esser dee, rimembrando la vita di costoro e de li altri divini cittadini, non sanza alcuna luce de la divina bontade, aggiunta sopra la loro buona natura, essere tante mirabili operazioni state; e manifesto esser dee, questi eccellentissimi essere stati strumenti, con li quali procedette la divina provedenza ne lo romano imperio, *dove più volte parve esse braccia di Dio essere presenti*. (*Convivio* 4.v.17)

> It ought to be clear and beyond doubt, when one recalls the lives of these and other divine citizens, that so many wonderful actions did not occur without the natural goodness of these men being enhanced in some measure by the light from the divine goodness. It must be clear, too, that these thoroughly excellent men were instruments whereby divine providence favored the growth of the Roman Empire, *in which God's arms are often seen to have intervened*.[6]

However long and syntactically complex, the clear meaning of the passage is that the protagonists of Roman history who embodied the highest degree of virtue (their 'natural goodness') openly display God's intervention in time through their extraordinary actions. Their relationship to the Divine is one of instrumentality and participation in the providential plan. But there may be more: Dante's wording allows a stronger reading, one in which the progress of the Roman Empire emerges as 'sacred history.'

Anticipating one of his most daring descriptions in the *Commedia*, that of a 'sacred' artefact to which both heaven and earth have set their hands (*Paradiso* 25.2), Dante here treats the progress of the historical reality of the Roman Empire as preserving traces of the working together of human beings and divine providence. Just as the *Commedia* is presented as a text produced by a form of collaboration between human artistry and divine inspiration, so too imperial history is regarded as an artefact of collaboration.[7] The parallel is less far-fetched than it might seem, for Dante sets up his reasoning precisely in terms of reading history as a text. The opening passage of *Convivio* 4.v.1 had already presented the same picture. In the prefatory sentence that opens the chapter, Dante notes that the ways of God are hidden to men, when it is the case that even human actions often escape human understanding. The second part of the sentence introduces the theme of collaboration between human and divine powers on the level of textual interpretation: 'it is, rather, something truly wonderful when the realization of the eternal plan unfolds so clearly that our reason discerns that plan': *da maravigliare è forte, quando la essecuzione de lo etterno consiglio tanto manifesto procede con la nostra ragione*.

In the dialectics between temporal human thought (*la nostra ragione*), which has demonstrated the logical necessity of the Empire as the *unum* that can best guide multiplicity towards a unified goal, and eternal Divine providence (*etterno consiglio*), which has chosen the Roman people to exercise this function in time, what is noteworthy (*da maravigliare*) for Dante is the unique fact of their coming together in the history of the Roman Empire. The collaboration between human and Divine factors in the making of actual history is mirrored in the negotiation, on the level of hermeneutics, of the obscurity of God's plan and in the affirmation of the clarity of human logical argument. It is as if God's direct intervention in history had, in the case of the Roman Empire (but nothing prevents from extending the model to the rest of history), generated a kind of writing that can participate in both the divine and human realms.

Yet there is a problem. In the apparently peaceful picture Dante paints in his account of Rome's imperial power as God-willed, there still lingers a disturbing element. In the same breath that he declares the providential nature of the Roman Empire, Dante also insists on featuring Caesar as its founder. Bringing Caesar into the picture makes the reasons for God's choice harder to understand, for it appears that divine Providence has founded the Roman Empire on the personal thirst for power and the delusions of a fallible politician. Apparently contradicting the notion that Rome had advanced thanks to its 'god-like citizens,' Dante pinpoints as 'primo prencipe sommo' someone who did not have any personal merit to justify such a designation. By entrusting the creation of the Empire to Caesar, God has proved that He wants the Republic to succumb through intervention of a character unworthy of its virtues. Due to something that looks like a significant slip of the pen, *Convivio* 4 came close to stating the problem of the Roman Empire's traumatic birth without directly facing it:

> Se noi consideriamo poi quella per la maggiore adolescenza sua, poi che da la reale tutoria fu emancipata, da Bruto primo consolo *infino a Cesare primo prencipe sommo,* noi troveremo lei essaltata non con umani cittadini, ma con divini. (*Convivio* 4.v.12)[8]

> If we then consider her more advanced youth, after she was emancipated from the tutelage of the kings, from the time of Brutus, the first consul, *up until Caesar, the first supreme prince,* we will find that she was exalted not with human but with godlike citizens whose love of her was inspired not by a human but a divine love.

The text is open-ended: 'up until Caesar,' Rome had more-than-human citizens, but what about after his arrival? This early hint of the paradoxical nature of the new political formation is soon reabsorbed in the body of the argument. All the same, it is difficult not to perceive the uneasy sense that virtue, the rationally plausible motive behind the election of the Romans as those who had to assume the insignia of world power, dies with the Republic. Though born of virtue, the Empire seems to have very little virtue itself.

What Dante appears to bracket in his argument concerning the legitimacy of the Roman Empire are the same elements which Augustine used to buttress his indictment of Rome's apparently virtuous, but actually self-serving citizens. In the context of his review of Rome's claims to fame, Augustine pairs Caesar and Cato as central figures – different in their habits, but linked by their shared desire to excel:

> Laudat idem Sallustius temporibus suis magnos et praeclaros viros, Marcum Catonem et Gaium Caesarem, dicens quod diu illa res publica non habuit quemquam virtute magnum, sed sua memoria fuisse illos duos ingenti virtute, diversis moribus. In laudibus autem Caesaris posuit, quod sibi magnum imperium, exercitum, bellum novum exoptabat, ubi virtus enitescere posset ... Hoc illa profecto laudis aviditas et gloriae cupido faciebat. Amore itaque primitus libertatis, post etiam dominationis et cupiditate laudis et gloriae multa magna fecerunt. (*De civitate Dei* 5.xii.5)

> The same Sallust also praises Marcus Cato and Gaius Caesar as great and distinguished men of his own day. He says that for a long time the commonwealth had had no men of great virtue, but that, within his memory, there had arisen these two, outstanding in virtue even though different in character. He records in praise of Caesar that he desired a great command, an army and a new war in which his virtue might shine forth ... This, forsooth, was the result of that vaunted eagerness for praise and passion for glory! In this way, the Romans were led to do many great deeds, first by their love of liberty, and then by their desire for praise and glory.

As Augustine's passage suggests, Caesar's figure is laden with ambiguities. Although he was, in Sallust's perspective, 'a great and extraordinary man,' he decided to pursue war as a field in which his 'virtue' could shine. On account of this 'virtue,' which for Augustine amounted to little more than a thirsting after approval and a desire for glory, Caesar 'strove for great military power, a great army, and a grand, new kind of war.' Augustine's ironic praise of Caesar rests on topics that were commonplaces in Roman literature. The ambiguous portraits painted by Cicero (the philosopher, in his *De officiis*) and Lucan (the poet-historian, in his *Bellum civile*), for instance, match Augustine's highly critical treatment.[9] For Cicero, who writes a treatise in which ethics and politics are inextricably intertwined, Caesar is both an autocrat and a deluded individual. In *De officiis* 1.26, in discussing the dangers to which Justice is subject, Cicero mentions 'the temerity of Caesar, an individual who has overturned divine and human laws, merely on account of the conviction he had formed in and by himself to be worthy of acquiring the highest position in society.'[10] According to Cicero, Caesar's motive for action is the same that Augustine assigns him: 'gloriae cupiditas' – the desire to be recognized that affects any warmongering 'great soul.' Cicero's indictment is biting when it addresses Caesar's political profile directly, but it is similarly sharp when it targets him allusively. A few pages later in *De officiis*, Cicero returns to the issue of war, seen by some as the right terrain on which to show one's virtue. Anticipating again Augustine's argument and again redeploying the same charged language of desire, Cicero notes: 'Multi enim bella saepe quaesiverunt propter gloriae cupiditatem, atque id in magnis animis ingeniisque plerumque contingit' (For many often have sought war on account of their desire for glory, something that happens in most cases with great souls or minds, 1.74). Though indirect, the association here with Caesar's actions, his 'great soul,' and his just as great desire for glory, is no less clear than with Augustine.

Lucan offers basically the same characterization as Cicero of the man whom Dante lists as the first emperor when he treats the birth of the Principate as coinciding with the death of the Republic and of republican virtues. In Lucan's poem, the history of the birth of the Empire is turned into a series of paradoxes that coalesce around the figure of Caesar. The proem to his *Bellum civile* details several of them. In a historically recapitulatory and narratively anticipatory table of contents for his epic, Lucan surveys the evils of the civil wars: fraternal bloodshed, slaughter, hunger, and the collapse of civil society. He even lists the main field and naval battles in the civil wars: the clash at Pharsalus, Caesar's victories at Tapsus and Munda, the sieges of Perugia and Modena (set by Octavian and Anthony, respectively), the sea battle at Actium (in which Octavian defeated Anthony), and Caesar's defeat of Sextus Pompeius's army, in which freedmen were allowed to fight (vv. 38–43).[11] In the same breath as it decries the bloodshed that ended a political system, however, Lucan's text also suggests that the present age of imperial rule is so close to being a golden age that it retrospectively justifies all the evils necessary to produce it:

> Quod si non aliam venturo fata Neroni
> invenere viam ...
> iam nihil, o superi, querimur; scelera ista nefasque
> hac mercede placent.
>   (*Bellum civile* 1, 33–8)

> But if the Fates could find, to bring forth Nero, / no other way, ... / by god, we don't complain; those crimes, the guilt, / are pleasing at this price.

The difficulties involved in reading this passage reside primarily in determining whether a serious or ironic tone is implied in the final clause *scelera ista nefasque / hac mercede placent*. Both ancient scholiasts and modern readers have perceived the possibility that Lucan's conciliatory claim of Neronian allegiance should not be taken seriously. Semantics dictates that *scelera* and *nefas* are absolute negatives: they should not be accepted, no matter what the reward for it might be, especially because, by using these terms, Lucan is pointing to the bloodiest episodes of the internecine strife, the slaughterhouse of the civil wars. Yet the voice in the text insists that in the name of Nero even the breaking of human and divine laws at the core of the civil war was justified. If Lucan is presenting his reader with a panegyric, it is certainly one of his most acrobatic.

Finding praise for the current emperor in Lucan's prologue has appeared a paradox for both biographical and poetical reasons. On the one hand, this peculiar *elogium* came from a Roman aristocrat who was soon to be involved (allegedly) in the Pisonian plot to overthrow the tyrannical ruler he is now so ostentatiously praising. On the other hand, it came from a poet who drew (figuratively) a contrast between Cato's and Brutus's Republican virtues and Caesar's admirable, but lethal, will to power.[12] However one is to interpret Lucan's (chronologically) original intention and point of view when the proem was composed, the text of his epic reached Dante laden with the complication of this ambiguity. The *Commenta Bernensia*, one of the many commentaries on the *Pharsalia* that circulated widely in Dante's time, glosses Lucan's text with a double interpretation, and thus allows a potentially ironic reading of the prologue:

> 1.38 HAC MERCEDE PLACENT hac compensatione. Ideo quod gratularetur Italia Neronis imperium consecuta. Vel quod ante bella civilia dictatores erant, postea vero imperatores esse coeperunt et Caesares ab ipso Caesare nuncupati: quasi haec sint bellorum civilium benefici.

> These things we like because of this reward: because of this compensation. That is to say, either because Italy is rejoicing for having brought about Nero's ruling; or because before the civil wars there were dictators, while

thereafter one started to have emperors – called Caesars from Caesar himself – as if these were the advantages of civil wars.[13]

When compared to the more straightforward perspective exhibited by the *Adnotationes super Lucanum*, which repeat the tag *hoc lusit* (this is a joke) for every ambiguous statement in the text, the *Commenta Bernensia* introduce the possibility that Lucan's text could be taken earnestly. The scholiast admits that there is a chance that Lucan sincerely sees Italy as joyful at having succeeded in bringing about Nero's reign. Of course, another possibility is that the only positive effect of the civil wars has been the change of a label – from *dictator* to *imperator* (or *Caesar*, which amounts to the same) – in the discourse of intertwined *Realpolitik* and power in the last years of the Roman Republic. In this case, the final *quasi* would be ironic in nature.

However one decides to interpret the elements in the glossator's text, the import of the note goes beyond the fact that it mirrors, in its either/or form, the same indecision that affects the serious or ironic tone of Lucan's opening. In that text, peace has come from bloodshed; it was from the breaking of human and divine laws that the Empire came to life. The life of Nero, in his function as emperor, is presented in the *Bellum civile* as the paradoxical justification for Cato's death, and the Empire as the 'reason' (the rationale) for the death of the Republic. In Lucan's wording, Fate (which Dante might have translated with the Christian term 'Providence')[14] found no other way than this to make the Empire take its place in history; it found no other way to 'choose' the Roman people for His project of salvation than to destroy the very motives of its election.[15]

Whereas only the textual subconscious of Dante's prose allowed a hint of this ambiguity to surface, and the text of *Convivio* kept up a definite avoidance behaviour when faced with the paradox of the misguided founder of a God-willed empire, the *Commedia* would make of this ambiguity its fully conscious political core. Dante's treatment of Caesar in the *Commedia* recalls Lucan's in more than one aspect. It, too, is marked by a strong ambiguity. Dante places Caesar in the ambiguous space of the 'noble castle' in limbo,[16] having the Roman general surrounded by the epic heroes Hector and Aeneas, and thus presenting him as the culmination of a lineage that is wholly oriented towards the birth (and the *translatio*) of the Empire.[17] Still, Dante directs the reader away from the conciliatory solutions offered in *Convivio* 4. Even when it gives Caesar a relatively privileged place, the poem associates him with a high potential for violence, insisting on his fierce appearance. In the otherwise peaceful atmosphere of the Noble Castle in limbo, the 'griffin-like' gaze of the Roman and the arms that he bears associate him unmistakably with the violence that accompanied his ascent.

As was the case in *Convivio* 4, one may argue that in this poem too, the violence of Caesar's rise to power appears as a necessary evil compensated for by his being an instrument of divine Providence. On the other hand, even this argument is forced to acknowledge the distance between the new presentation of Caesar and the treatise's forgetfulness of the downside of history. The text of the *Commedia* leaves room for a question. If not 'Why did God destroy the Roman Republic?' one can ask at least: 'Why did He have to choose Caesar for this task?' It is true that the armed, griffin-like Caesar of *Inferno* 4 is the head of the same Empire which God has chosen and to which Dante's hopes and political allegiances are bound, and whose adversaries, the *Caesaricidae* Brutus and Cassius, are relegated – along with Judas – to the darkest, lowest point of Hell, precisely because they betrayed its founder (*Inferno* 34.64–7). Yet it is also true that Dante's poem does not refrain from pointing out the limitations of the Empire's first ruler.[18]

Dante's treatment of Caesar, *primo prencipe sommo*, is matched and balanced by that of Cato, the highest example of Roman virtue. Whereas, in the case of Caesar, Augustine had anticipated Dante's account in some respects, on the issue of Cato, Augustine and Dante part ways more radically. In the paragraph reviewed above, what determined the syntactic shift from third-person singular to third-person plural in the verbs expressing the most lamentable aspects of the pursuit of virtue was Augustine's subtle association of Cato with Caesar. In the framework of *De civitate Dei*, Roman 'virtue' is consistently characterized as at best misguided and at worst self-serving, and Cato is no exception. He, too, could be shown to have practised his stern morals mainly in an attempt to win praise. On the contrary, in Dante's political historiography, Cato, though a latecomer like Caesar, is consistently cast in a positive light, and Dante's investment in his figure is large from the start. Both in the enthusiastic praise that *Convivio* 4.v.16 and xxviii.15 lavish on the human virtues of this Roman statesman, and in the portrait painted of him in *Purgatorio* 1.34–9, Dante endows the character of Cato with arguably Christological overtones.[19] In spite of his being an anti-Caesar partisan, and of his having given up his own life to oppose the coming of the Empire, it is to his character as the pinnacle of Roman Republican virtue (in *Convivio* 4) and of human virtue in the universalizing perspective of the *Commedia* that Dante returns. Conspicuous for his absence from the first *cantica*, Cato stands in for all that was not only to be praised in Roman cultural lore but also to be saved.

Even within these premises, however, Cato from the start stands at the centre of the same historical paradox as did Caesar. According to *Convivio*, Cato's actions and claims to fame are located exactly at the same turning point in history as those of Caesar – the bloodstained transition from the Republic to the Empire. In Dante's reasoning, as we have seen, the virtues of the Republic, with Cato featured highest among its members and partisans, are what made God choose the Roman Empire for its mission in History; and yet Dante also acknowledges that the destruction of the Republic was necessary for the Empire to be born. The irony of the destiny which Cato shares with the Roman Republic is that their respective deaths are necessary to God's plan, in spite of their respective virtues, in order that the higher goal of salvation might be achieved – an outcome which can be attained only through the political advent of the Empire. The Roman Empire willed by God is the same political reality that could bring peace to earth only through the bloodbath in which Cato died, and could pave the way to salvation only through the destruction of the highest achievements of human ethical behaviour, whose symbol was the Utican.

Yet there is one more paradox concerning Cato that needs to be explored. When Dante focuses on Cato's character both in *Convivio* and in the *Commedia*, he could hardly be unaware that Cato ought not to be taken as a model. Augustine's treatment of him in *De civitate Dei* attests at least to this. Not only did Augustine associate Cato with Caesar in their *libido* for glory, he also deprived him of his most shining claim to glory – his heroic suicide. The parameters that Augustine adopts to discuss the figure of Cato are clear: his suicide needs to be addressed because Roman culture takes it as exemplary, and it can be indicted because it was not a heroic act, but rather a self-serving vindication of a misguided notion of *decorum*. One sentence suffices for Augustine to bring into focus the first point:

> Sed tamen etiam illi praeter Lucretiam, de qua supra satis quod videbatur diximus, non facile reperiunt de cuius auctoritate praescribant, nisi illum Catonem, qui se Uticae occidit; non quia solus id fecit, sed quia vir doctus et probus habebatur, ut merito putetur etiam recte fieri potuisse vel posse quod fecit. (*De civitate Dei* 1.xxiii)

> Apart from Lucretia, however, of whom we seem already to have said enough, those who counsel suicide do not easily find an example to put forward as an authority, unless it be that of Cato, who slew himself at Utica. He was not, of course, the only one who did so. He was, however, a man of such learning and probity that anyone might fairly think that his act could have been, and can be, rightly done.

What specifically comes under attack in the passage is the exemplary quality of Cato's behaviour, expressed in the repetition of the verb *posse* in the last sentence. Did Cato do something that could – or can – be done justly? The answer, of course, is no. The reasons that Augustine offers are characteristically all internal to the moral Roman system that he attacks. Cato's friends tried to dissuade him, arguing that killing himself in his situation would be a sign of weakness rather than strength. Cato did not recommend that his son also commit suicide, and actually encouraged him to seek Caesar's clemency, which proves that Cato was applying a double standard. The conclusion Augustine reaches on the issue emerges in the final question:

> Nullo modo igitur Cato turpe esse iudicavit sub victore Caesare vivere; alioquin ab hac turpitudine paterno ferro filium liberaret. Quid ergo, nisi quod filium quantum amavit, cui parci a Caesare et speravit et voluit, tantum gloriae ipsius Caesaris, ne ab illo etiam sibi parceretur, ut ipse Caesar dixisse fertur, invidit, ut aliquid nos mitius dicamus, erubuit? (ibid.)

> Cato, therefore, cannot, after all, have deemed it a disgrace to live under the victorious Caesar; otherwise, a father's sword would have redeemed his son from such a disgrace. What can we say, therefore, other than what Caesar himself is reported to have said: that although Cato greatly loved his son, whom he hoped and wished would be spared by Caesar, still more greatly did he hate – or let us put it more kindly and say blush – to give Caesar the glory of pardoning himself?

According to Augustine, Cato commits suicide not to give Caesar the final victory of being able to exercise clemency with him. Had Cato been pardoned by Caesar, the glory would have been wholly the victor's. Once again, Cato's virtue represents the epitome of Roman virtue only insofar as it embodies an egotistic motive.

Yet no trace of Augustine's indirect but firm indictment of Cato can be found in *Convivio*. In Dante's treatise, Cato is regarded only positively, as we have seen. Likewise, when we move into the *Commedia*, the paradox of Cato's treatment becomes a series of readerly surprises. The presence of Cato on the shores of purgatory as the first saved soul to make a direct appearance in Dante's poem is certainly high among these surprises. It is difficult to reconstruct an awareness of its originally shocking impact now that seven centuries of basically uninterrupted commentary on the poem have naturalized most of Dante's daringly idiosyncratic choices. Nevertheless, a measure of discomfort still remains. With few exceptions, for ancient and modern commentators alike, logic would require Cato to be located not *here* where we find him, but in Hell – or, more correctly, in the *Inferno*.

Benvenuto's gloss may be taken as an example of an early reaction. Faced with what he calls the 'rather huge mistake' ('error satis enormis') into which he thinks Dante has fallen when he chose Cato as guardian of purgatory, Benvenuto offers two alternative locations: either the suicides ('debebat melius reponi inter violentos contra se ipsos' [he should have placed him among the violent against themselves]) or the great souls of the first circle ('sufficiebat ponere ipsum inter viros illustres cum Socrate, Seneca, et aliis magnis viris' [it would have been enough to place him among the illustrious men, together with Socrates, Seneca, and other great men]) who had been forced to commit suicide. Modern readers mostly agree with Benvenuto, and find even more reasons for demoting Cato to hell. The question of Cato's political affiliation, which did not seem to bother early readers, becomes an irksome subject for post-Romantic critics. Singleton's gloss *ad loc.*, cited here only as one among many possible examples, suggests two alternative locations: 'We should expect to find Cato, as a suicide and a pagan and as the bitter opponent of Caesar, founder of the Roman Empire, in Hell with Pier della Vigna, or with Brutus and Cassius.'

Cato thus appears out of place and potentially out of harmony with the postulates of the poem. As a pagan, he should not have such a prominent role in a Christian poem. As a suicide, he should not be among the saved. And as a Republican partisan, he should not be on the good side of an imperial poet. Different remedies have been suggested. Critics have moved away from the urge to allegorize, which characterized Benvenuto's reading (and that of several of his contemporaries) and which imposed a sharp split between the historical and the allegorical character of Cato. Recent arguments have insisted, rather, on a combined effect that could have been exerted on Dante's classicizing poem by Virgil's *Aeneid* (in particular 8.670) and, again, Lucan's *Bellum civile* (the first two books, with the climactic point probably located at 2.312). No strategy, however, has been able to defuse the scandal of Cato's location in the poem.

Just like scholarly readers of the poem, so too ordinary cultivated members in Dante's first audience would have expected to find Cato somewhere, yet somewhere other than where they found him. Their first expectation, too, would have been *Inferno* 4. All the authors who helped grant Cato a place in history are present in limbo to testify in his favour. Cato was part of the common set of examples of precisely the classical virtues that are both encased in the first circle and confined by it. Readers could expect Cato to be there just as they could harbour no doubts that Dante's poem had made a strongly classicizing choice from the start. And yet, Cato is not to be found in limbo: he is not located among the pre- or non-Christian characters who left an honourable trace in the collective consciousness of the Latin West. The first readerly expectation having been frustrated, the second most plausible location for Cato's soul is *Inferno* 13. Dante could, that is, have joined Augustine in attacking, through Cato's suicide, the Roman ideal of Stoic virtue that he embodied. As we have seen, the main thrust of Augustine's censure was that Roman Stoic suicide was an essentially egoistic (or, at least, egocentric) act, in no way to be compared to the altruistic self-immolation of Christ and of his martyrs. Dante could hardly be unaware of this, and he might have been sensitive to its impact on his appreciation of Roman culture and ethics.[20] This second hypothesis induces a hermeneutic reorienting in the poem's readers. Dante's original audience is prompted to observe that he may well have chosen a classicizing framework for the poem, and yet, by endorsing Augustine's anti-Roman sentiment, he had to keep his classicism inside strictly Augustinian bounds. Apparently, however, even this second expectation is destined to be frustrated. Among the suicides, Dante only meets and interacts with Pier della Vigna and the equally eloquent though anonymous Florentine suicide, while Cato is not named in the canto. Despite his absence, however, the uncanny feeling that Dante's Cato may be connected with the circle of violence lingers with the readers of *Inferno* 13, especially because the poem, in an epic-historical allusion, evokes his name in the opening lines of *Inferno* 14. In describing the barren sands of the next *girone*, Dante alludes to an episode from Lucan's *Bellum civile*, where Cato leads his Republican army across the Libyan desert:

> Lo spazio era una rena arida e spessa,
> non d'altra foggia fatta che colei
> che fu da' piè di Caton già soppressa.
> (*Inferno* 14.13–15)

> ... an expanse of deep and arid sand, / much like the sand pressed long ago / beneath the feet of Cato.

At first sight, the allusion appears little more than a learned gloss on a detail in the infernal landscape. It serves, however, a deeper if subtler purpose. The evocation of Cato's name works as a retrospective signal. It alerts readers that Dante has not forgotten the Republican hero he had praised in *Convivio* 4. By evoking a particularly memorable line in Lucan, Dante reminds us that the canto we had just finished reading was in some way concerned with Cato. But in what way?

This third surprise again demands that we reorient our reading. The direction in which we should move, however, is not fully clear. There is a possibility that the late mention of Cato's name should be read as a confirmation that Dante has completely eliminated this character from the prosopographic horizon of the poem. On the other hand, the same lines could also be read as pointing back to the previous canto, putting it under the ambiguous sign of the Roman hero and indicting his suicide. It may also be the case that the allusion should be taken as a restrained reminder that the silence Dante maintains on Cato is no accident of his cultural memory. Readers are invited to look back and more closely at Dante's text to find traces of Cato among the suicides, as Augustine would have urged. Sounding Cato's name at the start of the new segment of the poem may, in sum, signal a silent inclusion among the suicides. It seems that readers are being asked to pick up and re-read *Inferno* 13, this time listening to subtle intertextual signals, and to match Piero, the modern example of a suicide, not only with Judas, his biblical antecedent, but also with a classical counterpart. And, indeed, in the canto of the suicides we find elements that evoke Augustine's treatment of Cato – in particular, the language in which Dante casts Pier della Vigna's self-defence.

In the course of his rhetorically masterful argument, while defending his innocence and refuting the rumours which were widespread in Dante's time about having betrayed the trust of his lord, Frederick II, Pier della Vigna echoes a recognizable Augustinian argument and even some of his terminology. A high point of his speech is the *narratio*, which contains the justification for ending his own life. The passage is famous for the way its elaborate phrasing folds back upon itself:

> 'L'animo mio, per disdegnoso gusto,
> credendo col morir fuggir disdegno,
> ingiusto fece me contra me giusto.'
> (*Inferno* 13.70–2)[21]

> 'My mind, in scornful temper, / hoping by dying to escape from scorn, / made me, though just, against myself unjust.'

Uttered through the de-humanizing means of the bleeding wound that Dante has opened in his arboreal body, Piero's words reproduce the internal debate that led him to give up his earthly life in order to preserve his honour. Having made *in foro interiori* the weaker case the stronger, Piero pays now the price for a self-induced erroneous judgment. He denounces himself in his words – and exposes them to the moral judgment of the reader, who should be able to read past the alluring surface they present. The language and syntax that Piero uses, however, do more than just expose the tortuous argument that brought him to suicide. His reasoning contains an allusion to one of the key arguments Augustine had put forward in *De civitate Dei* to indict the Roman Stoic tradition of the brave suicide as nothing less than self-murder. Augustine attacked the notion that there could be an honourable – or even, as we have seen, praiseworthy – suicide. No one, he argued, has the right to take his own life, not even when compelled by a desire to vindicate his own innocence or protest a wrong that has been done to him. Augustine weaves his argument using the same key terms and the same convoluted syntax that can be found in Piero's apologetic tirade:

> Profecto qui se ipsum occidit, homicida est, et tanto fit nocentior, cum se occiderit, quanto innocentior in ea causa fuit, qua se occidendum putavit: ... cur autem homo, qui mali nihil fecit, sibi malefaciat et se ipsum interficiendo hominem interficiat innocentem, ne alium patiatur nocentem, atque in se perpetret peccatum proprium, ne in eo perpetretur alienum?
> (*De civitate Dei* 1.xvii)

> No doubt, whoever kills himself is a homicide, and he becomes the more guilty of murder, the more he was innocent of the charge for which he had thought it right to kill himself ... Why should then a human being who has

done no evil, do evil upon himself? Why should he kill an innocent man by killing himself, so as to escape someone else's crime? Why should he commit against himself a sin that belongs to him, lest a sin that belongs to someone else be committed against him?

Curiously, Augustine's words have been left out of the traditional commentaries on *Inferno* 13 until very recently. To my knowledge, only Nicola Fosca, in his still unpublished commentary (available through the Dartmouth Dante Project), has used this passage in connection with Piero's speech. And yet the lexical and syntactical echoes are strong: the redoubled word play and logical turn on *nocentior* and *innocentior* anticipates Piero's own musing on being *ingiusto* against himself *giusto*; similarly, Augustine's insistence on the erring of the suicide's reasoning, who *se occidendum putavit*, resonates with Dante's *credendo*. The relevance of the intertext is also reinforced by contextual reasons. Augustine's tirade against Rome's cult of the Stoic martyrs precedes by only a few chapters his personal attack against Cato's choices in life and his seemingly exemplary suicide.

The intertext proposed here does more than enrich the reading of *Inferno* 13 by adding a new facet. It brings to the surface the missing element in the dialectics of surprises arranged by Dante around the figure of Cato. By engaging in a dialogue with Augustine's text, *Inferno* 13 casts the shadow of the ancient model over the main character in the canto of suicides. In so doing, Dante not only pre-emptively deconstructs one of Piero's self-defensive arguments, but also confirms that his poem had heeded Augustine's warnings against any political or ethical justification of suicide. For a responsive audience, one that is aware of the interplay between Dante's sources, Piero becomes a proxy for Cato, and the indictment of the former must implicate the latter. The allusion contained in Piero's words prepares the readers for the final surprise. The shock that educated first-time readers of the poem would have experienced in encountering Cato in *Purgatorio* 1 is stronger than we may have thought. When Cato approaches Dante and Virgil on the shores of Purgatory, his presence in the realm of the saved certainly astonishes readers because he is a character with a difficult history – one that would seem to foreclose the possibility of salvation. The 'veglio solo' of *Purgatorio* 1, however, surprises readers because the questions surrounding Cato's personality had apparently already been decided, in his disfavour, in the web of voices resonating through *Inferno* 13, if only deceivingly so.

By challenging Augustine on the issue of Cato, the *Commedia* seems to suggest that it was not necessary, not even for the polemical thrust of Augustine's argument, to repudiate *en bloc* Rome's republican past. History is an array of ambiguous signs and it requires hermeneutic agility to accommodate the ironies of God's writing. Just as with his ironic treatment of Caesar, so too with his re-evaluation of Cato, Dante suggests that Rome's history was able to provide examples which, once interpreted morally, could produce ethical behaviour. The following section will look again at the interpretation of signs. The focus will be love poetry, and the possibility that it can be just as ambiguous as history.

4.2 Dido and the Signs of Ancient Love

Having reached the threshold of the earthly paradise, being separated from it only by the narrow stream of Lethe, Dante hears from Matelda that the nature of the garden in which he finds himself has been 'dreamt in Parnassus by the ancient poets' who wrote about the golden age of mankind:

> 'Quelli ch'anticamente poetaro
> l'età de l'oro e suo stato felice,
> forse in Parnaso esto loco sognaro.'
> (*Purgatorio* 28.139–41)

> 'Those ancients who in poetry represented / the golden age, who sang its happy state, / perhaps, in their Parnassus, dreamt this place.'

Dante's reaction to Matelda's words is to turn to Virgil and Statius for confirmation. They meet his interlocutory gaze with a smile, acknowledging the role they played in foreshadowing the reality of the earthly paradise in their poetry. The episode of Matelda, opened by the contrastive reminiscence of the Ovidian account of Proserpina rape (49–51) and of Hero's and Leander's love, closes by suggesting the possible harmony between the classical perception of human perfection and its reality. The golden age and the earthly paradise are only two of the possible descriptions of the same reality.

The situation, however, begins to change in the following canto. When confronted with the first element of the mystical procession – the seven golden candlesticks that he mistakes at first for golden trees – Dante repeats his self-reassuring gesture. He turns back once again to Virgil. Yet, this time, he does so only to see his own amazement mirrored in the stupor of his guide. Belonging to a totally different cultural tradition and textual iconography, the significance of the candlesticks escapes the classical author. No classical, pre-Christian equivalents had been possible for them; the objects are completely new, unknown to both Virgil and the Christian neophyte.

> Io mi rivolsi d'ammirazion pieno
> al buon Virgilio, ed esso mi rispuose
> con vista carca di stupor non meno.
> (*Purgatorio* 29.55–7)

> Full of astonishment, I turned to my / good Virgil; but he only answered me / with eyes that were no less amazed than mine.

The game of puzzled glances that the poets exchange functions as a sign of the special nature of the events and of the theatre in which they take place. The dynamics of the mystical procession refer to a non-classical textuality, to a body of writing and of meaning from which Virgil is forever barred. Dante, too, is momentarily excluded from understanding the nature of the spectacle offered to his eyes, but his puzzlement will soon give way to a clearer perception. On the contrary, Virgil regresses from the role of involuntary and unconscious prophet to that of incompetent spectator of history.

Dante's act of turning to face Virgil is repeated for the third and final time in the instant in which Beatrice appears again to the Pilgrim, for the first time after his 'decennial thirst' had commenced with her death. The return of Beatrice is accompanied in the text by a heightened density of Virgilian allusions and two direct quotations – one in the original Latin and one in Dante's own vernacular. Beatrice's reappearance is marked first by an angelic choir singing two lines that join the invocation of Christ as '*Benedictus qui venis*' with the divided Virgilian line '*Manibus, oh, date lilia plenis*' (*Purgatorio* 30.19 and 21). The latter – originally designed to mourn, in *Aeneid* 6.883, the premature death of Marcellus – is now reinterpreted and reused by the angels as a joyful hymn to hallow life's conquering of death in the figure of Beatrice. At first sight, the text of the *Aeneid* seems to align itself, as was the case for the poetic anticipation of the golden age, with the truth of the biblical text. One could even go so far as to say that through the reverberation of the triumphant cry of the Gospel, the negativity of Virgil's line is redeemed. Once again, as in the case of Statius, it seems that one need only apply a better hermeneutic to rescue at least the open text, if not its non-Christian author. Similarly, the second element of Virgilian origin that appears in the episode – the Pilgrim's intended (but never uttered) quotation of Dido's words at the beginning of *Aeneid* 4 – might be cast in a positive, collaborative light:

> Tosto che ne la vista mi percosse
> l'alta virtù che già m'avea trafitto
> prima ch'io fuor di püerizia fosse,
>   volsimi a la sinistra col respitto
> col quale il fantolin corre a la mamma
> quando ha paura o quando elli è afflitto
>   per dicere a Virgilio: 'Men che dramma
> di sangue m'è rimaso che non tremi:
> conosco i segni de l'antica fiamma.'
> (40–8)

As soon as that deep force had struck my vision / (the power that, when I had not yet left / my boyhood, had already transfixed me), / I turned around to my left – just as / a little child, afraid or in distress, / will hurry to his mother – anxiously / to say to Virgil: 'I am left with less / than one drop of my blood that does not tremble: / I recognize the signs of the old flame.'

In parallel with the reinterpreted lines of *Aeneid* 6, so too Dido's famous admission of frailty could be present here as a transvaluated fragment of a salvaged text. Statius's successful example of salvific misreading is no less radical than the one the character of the Pilgrim attempts here. The three poets could still be united in their progress, each relying on the example set by the text of his immediate predecessor. It is not surprising, then, that the usual gesture is made to match the higher concentration of Virgilian echoes: Dante turns again towards Virgil. At this juncture, however, the character of the ancient Latin poet is no longer with him:

> Ma Virgilio n'avea lasciati scemi
> di sé, Virgilio dolcissimo patre,
> Virgilio a cui per mia salute die'mi;
>   né quantunque perdeo l'antica matre
> valse a le guance nette di rugiada
> che, lagrimando, non tornasser atre.
> (49–54)

But Virgil had deprived us of himself, / Virgil, the gentlest father, Virgil, he / to whom I gave myself for my salvation; / and even all our ancient mother lost / was not enough to keep my cheeks, though washed / with dew, from darkening again with tears.

His function as a guide fulfilled, Virgil returns to the eternal exile of limbo, leaving Dante to a better guide for the second stage of his journey. In the Pilgrim's reaction to his guide's sudden yet long predicted disappearance – a silent thrice-repeated invocation of his name – one finds the third Virgilian 'tessera' to the mosaic of classical quotations paraded in the episode. As is well known, the passage contains an allusion to the closing of the fourth book of the *Georgics*, in which, lending his voice to Orpheus's threefold lament for the final loss of Eurydice, Virgil laments the death of the poet, killed and dismembered by frenzied Maenads:

> tum quoque marmorea caput a cervice reuulsum
> gurgite cum medio portans Oeagrius Hebrus
> uolueret, *Eurydicen* uox ipsa et frigida lingua,
> a miseram *Eurydicen*! anima fugiente uocabat:
> *Eurydicen* toto referebant flumine ripae.
> (*Georgics* 4.520–7, my translation)

The whirling stream of the Hebrus carried the head torn from the pale neck while his voice and tongue – cold, for the breath was already leaving him – still called *Eurydice*, wretched *Eurydice*. The river banks were replying '*Eurydice*' all along.

The reuse of Virgil's text has been regarded as an instance of Dante's recuperation of the classical voice in his poem, a final homage to his departing guide. This homage once again contains a radical revision of the evoked antecedent. Whereas Virgil's Orpheus lamented the 'tragic' (not just in a technical sense) loss of Eurydice, Dante grafts the allusion onto a literally 'comic' development of the plot, which features the poet-protagonist's descent to the underworld and his return to the world above as a recovery – not a loss – of his beloved.[22]

There is yet one more feature of Dante's dialogue with his classical and post-classical 'sources' that is worth highlighting. The same shift in values that one witnesses in the oblique recovery of Virgil's own text affects other features of the episode. The assurance with which these cantos of the *Purgatorio* have proceeded in joining classical (tragic) texts as a foreshadowing of their Christian (comic) fulfilment is soon to be broken. When Beatrice addresses Dante, she will shatter the seemingly perfect initial harmony between the recuperation of Virgil's poetry and the new Christian dimension of the drama that unfolds in Eden. Her words speak to Dante's invocation of Virgil, to which she responds with a thrice-repeated injunction to stop weeping for Virgil's departure and instead begin to show repentance for his own sins:

> 'Dante, perché Virgilio se ne vada,
> *non pianger* anco, *non piangere* ancora;
> *ché pianger* ti conven per altra spada.'
> (55–7)

> 'Dante, though Virgil's leaving you, do not / yet weep, do not weep yet; you'll need your tears / for what another sword must yet inflict.'

The dense, classical intertextual grid of the episode has long been studied, and the dynamics of poetic palinode that these lines set in motion have received numerous interpretations, some of which have fruitfully stressed the ambiguous dialectics of recuperation and overcoming of ancient poetry, in which Dante would appear to be engaged here.[23] The dialogue between Virgil's ancient, classical, and Latin poetry and Dante's modern, Christian, and vernacular rendering of it has been cast as a dialectic involving but two sides and a binary series of oppositions. The strong presence of Virgilian quotations in the canto has been interpreted either as a final homage paid to his teacher, in which Dante shows the highest potentiality of pre-Christian culture epitomized in the *Aeneid*, or as a successful correction of the sombre perspective on life to which classical culture is condemned by its inescapable 'paganism.'[24]

Framing the question in terms of a strict duality between classical and Christian traditions, however, is not the only possible way of engaging these lines. The portions of text that exhibit Virgilian material are not the only ones worth noticing. When we reread Beatrice's words as something different from (and something more than) a point-by-point response to Dante's threefold silent invocation of his lost guide, the duality is complicated by a third element. Beatrice's threefold repetition of the verb 'piangere' apparently answers the threefold address to Virgil registered in the *Commedia*, but it actually cannot be read in these terms. No character in the poem speaks the words to which Beatrice allegedly replies; no character in the poem even thinks them out. In order for her statement to be an answer to Dante's Virgilian sentimentalism, Beatrice would not only had to have had access to the mind of the Pilgrim, but to the text of the *Commedia* as well.[25]

Pointing in the direction of Dante's awareness, a hypothesis has been advanced that matters had already become complicated in the Latin tradition concerning this passage. The episode of the *Georgics* had, in fact, been placed at a busy metapoetic intersection. Ovid had previously and allusively re-employed the same Virgilian passage at the end of his Orpheus episode in *Metamorphoses* 11. Beatrice's words can thus be taken as the first sign of a change of course in Dante's intertextual strategy. They are an anticipation of the radical move the *Paradiso* will register when Dante will shift from what one may call the Virgilian epic of development to the Ovidian epic of transformation.[26] At the beginning of the eleventh book of the *Metamorphoses*, Ovid had already echoed Virgil's Orpheus, concluding the scene of the poet's death with the allusive wording:

> Membra iacent diuersa locis; caput, Hebre, lyramque
> excipis, et (mirum!) medio dum labitur amne,
> *flebile* nescio quid queritur Lyra, *flebile* lingua
> murmurat exanimis, respondent *flebile* ripae.
> (*Metamorphoses* 11.50–3, my translation)

> You, Hebrus, received the head and the lyre, and – unbelievably – while it drifts mid-stream, the lyre *softly weeping* emits I don't know what kind of sound, *softly weeping* the dying tongue murmurs, a *soft weeping* is the answer from the river banks.

Suggestive as it may be on the level of Dante's diction (*piangere* could well be related to the *flebile* < *flere* = 'to weep'), the Ovidian parallel leaves the syntactically peculiar movement of the phrase – not to say its content – unaccounted for. To find a better parallel for Dante's phrasing one has to look in a different direction. The third polarity, and the third text, to interact with Dante and Virgil and to shape Beatrice's words is not Ovid, but rather a text with which the *Commedia* enters into a conversation no less ambiguous and complex than the one it engages with its classical sources.

In *Confessiones* 1.xiii, Augustine had attacked his own youthful infatuation with literature by focusing on Virgil's treatment of Dido in the *Aeneid*. The passage bears a striking resemblance with the wording and the syntactical movement of the words Dante attributes to Beatrice:

> Quid enim *miserius misero* non *miserante* seipsum et *flente* Didonis mortem, quae fiebat amando Aenean, non *flente* autem mortem suam, quae fiebat non amando te, deus lumen cordis mei, et panis oris intus animae meae et virtus maritans mentem meam et sinum cogitationis meae? ... et haec non *flebam*, et *flebam* Didonem 'exstinctam, ferroque extrema secutam,' sequens ipse extrema condita tua relicto te et terra iens in terram. et si prohiberer ea legere, dolerem, quia non legerem quod dolerem. (*Confessiones* 1.xiii.21)[27]
>
> What is more *pitiable* than a *wretch* without *pity* for himself who *weeps* over the death of Dido dying for love of Aeneas, but not *weeping* over himself dying for his lack of love for you, my God, light of my heart, bread of inner mouth of my soul, the power which begets life in my mind and in the innermost recesses of my thinking ... Over this I *wept* not a tear. I *wept* over Dido who 'died in pursuing her ultimate end with a sword' [*Aen.* 6.456]. I abandoned you to pursue the lowest things of your creation. I was dust going to dust. Had I been forbidden to read this story, I would have been sad that I could not read what made me sad.

The appearance of Augustine's text here is not unanticipated; two exceptional circumstances conjure it up. The first is the coincidence of Dante's Virgilian self-naming with Augustine's model. As Dante already made clear in *Convivio* 1.ii.1, speaking about oneself in a written text constituted a potentially serious breach of propriety, using Boethius and Augustine as two examples. Dante exempted both from the rhetorical norm for good reasons.[28] Whereas *Convivio* 1, in its defensive and post-exilic mode, was relying more on the Boethian model, the *Commedia* recalls more profoundly and directly the experience of Augustine.[29] Beyond the invoked 'necessity' imposed by the plot, the poem is authorized to name its protagonist-author by the Augustinian model of the conversion/confession-narrative it rehearses.[30]

The second corollary of recognizing that the first words Beatrice addresses to Dante are based on the passage from Augustine is that it joins the Virgilian echoes present in the canto (and culminating in Dido's words) with an explicitly Virgilian passage in the *Confessions*. To be sure, Augustine's context is deeply polemical, aimed as it is at an indictment of non-Christian literature. Still, even in the most polemical passage of his mature work, the very text that is condemned is uncannily allowed to speak again. Beatrice's rebuke to Dante employs the same words that the converted Augustine used to attack his unconverted self for his love of Virgil and the forgetfulness of his spiritual predicament ensuing from the enjoyment of poetry. And yet Dante is able, through an intra-textual allusion, to project these words on an Augustinian reading of the *Aeneid* that might undermine the main thrust of the argument developed in the *Confessions*.

The point Augustine was making in the *Confessions* was simple enough. He charged full speed against the *Aeneid* (immediately after this passage he will label his youthful love for poetry 'such a folly' – *talis dementia*) and attacked both its historical veracity and its moral value. The poem posed a moral threat to the Christian reader, he argued. When the enjoyment of literary fable takes over in someone's spiritual life, Augustine maintained, no room is left for that true self-knowledge which is necessary in order to come face to face with one's own misery. For the Augustine of the *Confessions*, attention to poetry is a diversion from the duty of spiritual introspection. It is a flight from the moral responsibility of self-analysis.[31] Beauty – mundane beauty – can be a defective and deceptive substitute for truth, and the appeal of poetry a hindrance to salvation. To the fascination of poetry, one may add, Augustine contrasted the usefulness of basic grammatical instruction. Whereas he discounts the *enjoyment* of poetry (under the rubric of *frui*), he values learning the elements of language as *tools* to be used (*uti*) for the decoding of God's written word: 'Such madness,' he notes, 'is considered a higher and more fruitful literary education than being taught to read and write ('Talis dementia honestiores et uberiores litterae putantur, quam illae quibus legere et scribere didici,' xiii.21).

A further element in the passage is worth noting. Just as it will be for Dante, Virgil's Dido is chosen as the first victim of Augustine's indictment of poetry. His attack on Virgil's fabrication of Dido's 'fable' follows the passage just quoted:

> Non clament adversus me venditores gramaticae vel emptores, quia, si proponam eis interrogans, utrum verum sit quod Aenean aliquando Carthaginem venisse poeta dicit, indoctiores nescire se respondebunt, doctiores autem negabunt verum esse ... Item si queram, quid horum maiore vitae huius incommodo quisque obliviscatur, legere et scribere an poetica illa figmenta, quis non videat, quid responsurus sit, qui non est penitus oblitus sui? (*Confessiones* 1.xiii.22)

Let there be no abuse of me from people who sell or buy a literary education. If I put the question to them whether the poet's story is true that Aeneas once came to Carthage, the uneducated will reply that they do not know, while the educated will say it is false ... Similarly, if I ask which would cause the greater inconvenience to someone's life, to forget how to read and write or to forget these fabulous poems, who does not see what answer he would give, unless he has totally lost his sense?

That Augustine's problems with Virgil coalesced around the Dido episode should not come as a surprise. After all, Dido was an easy target: Virgil had taken substantial liberties with her figure, departing from the most accredited historical accounts of her life in such crucial matters as chronology, moral standing, and choice of spouse. Her character and vicissitudes, too, were particularly suitable to be used as a platform to attack the *Aeneid*. Not only did Virgil's 'poetic' treatment of her character change the historical account of her life and end up slandering a chaste woman by accusing her of a sin (namely, breaching her vow to remain *univira*) that she did not commit at all historically, he also portrayed this morally faulty fiction as one of the most seductive, poetically successful, and long-lasting heroines of the Latin world.[32] In the *Aeneid*, she truly was presented as the prototype of the 'sympathetic sinner,' the foremost threat to the linear progress of the poem's God-willed epic development. Dido's story in the *Aeneid* could, thus, be for Augustine the epitome of the dangers that classical poetry entailed. Literally, Virgil's Dido was untrue; morally, the *Aeneid* had also associated with the fiction (*fabula*) of her life an oblique incitement to feel compassion for her self-induced misfortunes. From a Christian point of view, this feeling was always on the verge of becoming a sentimental complicity in the fascination of her 'sin.'

In this context, Dante's unuttered farewell to Virgil, 'conosco i segni de l'antica fiamma' (I know the signs of the ancient flame), needs to be re-evaluated. To be sure, it appears as the trigger of Beatrice's stern Augustinian rebuke. And yet, it is also the sign that if this rebuke is totally justified for the Pilgrim, who is about to perform his own rite of confession in front of her (and God), it is only partially justified when applied to Virgil's text. The coincidence of the rhyming words of Dante's farewell with those of the episode of Statius's conversion-through-poetry reminds attentive readers that Dante's adherence to Virgil's letter is not unfitting, and that it does not coincide with a form of textual idolatry. The inappropriate nature of the Virgilian quotation is actually invoked to guarantee its moral productivity. The love whose 'signs' Dante recognizes in himself is radically different from the love that Virgil wrote that Dido had felt. This difference does not, however, make the Virgilian line irrelevant. On the contrary, it paradoxically makes it all the more suited to Dante's situation, because it thematizes its divergence from the misguided authorial intention and its dangerous unhistorical fabrication. Dante renders Virgil's line with a significant variant: when he translates Dido's statement, *agnosco veteris vestigia flammae*, he chooses to translate the term 'vestigium' with a loaded word: *i segni*. In so doing, the text of the *Commedia* takes Dido's awareness that 'the traces' (that is, the remnants of her capacity for love) were still with her so long after her first husband's death and turns it into Dante's witnessing that a line of Virgil's text may be arbitrarily misread and reused; that poetry is the *locus* for a negotiation of signs.[33] By choosing a mistranslation, in other words, Dante bridges the distance between Augustine's *De doctrina christiana* and *Confessiones*. The text Augustine had devoted to the study of signs was, as we have been able to observe, a text not fully hostile to a recuperation of classical culture. Dante makes its lenient attitude clash with the no-less Augustinian assault on the fables of the ancient poets.

Beatrice's Augustinian rebuke surgically targets Dante's attachment to the figure of his first guide, and severs it. Her words reiterate the need of self-knowledge, self-deprecation, and conversion in the right moral direction. The Augustine whose stance Beatrice's words embody might have been right in claiming that love for literature was an impediment to be overcome in the path towards conversion and salvation in his own story. Yet, his indictment could not legitimately be generalized. Statius's case, doubling Dante's own experience, is there to suggest that Augustine himself had at a certain point held the opposite view. The Pilgrim's choice of the word 'sign' corroborates the intratextual allusion to the Statius episode and the Augustinian background on which Dante projected it. In his take on classical culture, Augustine had targeted Virgil's account of Dido, and Dante recuperates precisely that episode to cast his new encounter with Beatrice in Virgilian terms. Appropriating Dido's line to indicate the tokens of an ancient love – his own love for Beatrice – that is renewed by the return of the beloved, Dante projects again a Virgilian shadow on his work. If Augustine's theory of a charity-constructing hermeneutics loomed large beneath Statius's reading of Virgil, however, it still does in the passage at hand. At the exact moment in which Beatrice returns to displace Virgil, Dante recuperates precisely that locus in Virgil that Augustine had attacked in the *Confessions*, but the negative connotation that Virgil's poetry had assumed in that work is now balanced by the more favourable picture that *De doctrina christiana* offers of it.

Purgatorio 30 sets up a situation in which the Pilgrim is doubly mistaken. He is corrected once by Beatrice's direct Augustinian rebuke and then by the development of the classical – but by no means less Augustinian – argument begun in *Purgatorio* 22 with the entrance of Statius into the plot. The Pilgrim weeps for Virgil's disappearance in the highly literary threefold repetition of his name, and Beatrice – using the same argument that the mature Augustine of the *Confessions* had used – chides him. At the same time, the Pilgrim deploys on Virgil's text the same 'active,' ironic, and ultimately salvific reading that had proved to be successful in saving Statius before him. Beatrice does not object to Dante's appropriation of Virgil's line: nor could she, since a few lines before the angels had essentially performed the same appropriation on the Marcellus fragment from *Aeneid* 6. His autobiography centred on his love for Beatrice, Dante's use of Dido's line for his own love is not in itself a problem. Or, at least, it is not a problem for the one of the two 'Augustines' featured in the text – the author of *De doctrina christiana*. For the 'other' Augustine, the one whose condemnation of poetic *divertissement* in the *Confessiones* is echoed in Beatrice's words, the Pilgrim's memory of a poetic past coincides with his mistaking the 'comedy' of a Christian experience for a 'tragedy,' his projecting onto Virgil's departure the intertexual 'Orphic' burden of *Georgics* 4 and *Metamorphoses* 11.

No reconciliation seems to be possible between the two 'Augustines' whom Dante conjures up and contrasts in the episode, each blocked in his condemnation or recovery of classical poetry. Dante's almost perfect silence about him (or them) in the rest of the *Commedia* might be the sign that the problem of Augustine was not only political. Augustine might well have denigrated Rome as the antithesis of the City of God, thus taking an unacceptable stance for the poet of the (Holy) Roman Empire. He might well have made his position even worse by rejoicing at the collapse of that *civitas terrena* which Dante placed at the centre of his politics. Yet, what most deeply sets him apart from Dante is the unsolved strife at the core of his thought between his necessary dismissal of pre-Christian culture and his unceasing love for its poetic past. The conversion narratives of Dante and Augustine – similar in so many respects – diverge at the precise juncture in which Dante's name is uttered and necessarily registered, and the *Commedia* pauses, if for only a moment, to mark this spot with a densely allusive line.

4.3 Aeneas and the Bees

Paradiso 30 follows a series of liminal cantos and opens with the crossing of the threshold dividing the physical world and the metaphysical reality of the Empyrean.[34] This is perhaps the most important crossing in the protagonist's journey, and with it the poem registers a general reorientation that affects several elements in his experience. In this final section, I will focus only on a cluster of these, coalesced around the theme of the resurrection of the flesh. They form the theological background for the last case of Virgilian and Augustinian tangency that I will discuss in this book. My argument addresses questions of both theology and poetics, and attempts to bridge them, by suggesting that resurrection, the re-clothing of the souls with a new and perfected body, is not unrelated to the text's clothing itself with the rhetorical garb of Virgilian similes. In the context of the canto, the seamlessly perfected union of resurrected body and soul is both expressed by, and a sustaining element for, Dante's choice of deploying similetic language. By conforming to the reality of the Empyrean, the poetics of the poem dismisses as a foil any non-concretive understanding of form and matter, content and style, *verba* and *sententia*.

The canto addresses the theme of resurrection in at least three points.[35] First, Beatrice notes that, in an extraordinary fashion, as they cross into the Empyrean, Dante will be offered sight of the resurrected bodies of the saints:

> 'Noi siamo usciti fore
> del maggior corpo al ciel ch'è pura luce:
>   luce intellettüal, piena d'amore;
> amor di vero ben, pien di letizia;
> letizia che trascende ogne dolzore.
>   Qui vederai l'una e l'altra milizia
> di paradiso, e l'una in quelli aspetti
> che tu vedrai a l'ultima giustizia.'
>   (*Paradiso* 30.38–45)

'We have issued / from the largest body to the Heaven of pure light, /

light intellectual, full of love, / love of true good, full of joy, / joy that surpasses every sweetness. / Here you shall see both soldieries of Paradise, / one of them in just such form / as you shall see it at the final judgment.'

Although theologically difficult to argue for, the sense of Beatrice's words is clear: the souls that Dante will see appear to him in their final and fulfilled state. What Dante is allowed to see, in other words, is heaven after the elapsing of earthly time. The final judgment will only add the few souls who are still missing to fill up the ranks of paradise, but it will contribute nothing to the perfection of the souls who now (in earthly terms) inhabit it. They appear there with their bodies – their 'bianche stole' (as in line 129 of this canto) or their 'carne rivestita' (as from *Paradiso* 14.44).[36]

The second element that thematizes resurrection in the canto is Dante's own transformation as he enters the Empyrean. By passing into the 'pure light' of the last heaven, and thus leaving behind the 'body' of space and time, the poem suggests, Dante's presence in heaven proper entails a drastic change in his corporality. The metamorphosis is described, accordingly, in terms of light:

> Come sùbito lampo che discetti
> li spiriti visivi, sì che priva
> da l'atto l'occhio di più forti obietti,
>   così mi circunfulse luce viva,
> e lasciommi fasciato di tal velo
> del suo fulgor, che nulla m'appariva.
>   'Sempre l'amor che queta questo cielo
> accoglie in sé con sì fatta salute,
> per far disposto a sua fiamma il candelo.'
>   (46–54)

Like sudden lighting that confounds / the faculty of sight, depriving eyes / of taking in the clearest objects, / thus did a living light shine all around me, / leaving me so swathed in the veil of its effulgence / that I saw nothing else. / 'The love that calms this heaven / always offers welcome with such greetings, / to make the candle ready for its flame.'

An instantaneous flash of light envelops the protagonist and leaves him clothed ('swathed,' but perhaps also 'swaddled') in a veil of its 'effulgence.'[37] Something of the light that has touched Dante remains with him. Beatrice's words explaining what has just taken place follow so closely the transformation happening to Dante's body that they may seem to accompany it, and they too confirm that the appropriately ambivalent *salute* of heaven entails a transformation of matter (the wax made ready for the flame). The transformation that prepares Dante to experience the Empyrean involves his 'acquiring the characteristics of a resurrected body':

> Non fur più tosto dentro a me venute
> queste parole brievi, ch'io compresi
> me sormontar di sopr' a mia virtute.
> (55–7)

> No sooner had these few words reached my mind / than I became aware of having risen / above and well beyond my powers.

Marking the awareness that the protagonist has reached in almost perfect simultaneity with his own metamorphosis and Beatrice's explanation of it, the text indicates as 'an excess of one's own ordinary powers' the new state to which the protagonist is granted access.[38]

The third, and final, element that brings the issue of resurrection to the fore of the canto is the initial form in which the protagonist perceives the presence of the blessed souls, the angels, and their mutual continuous commerce. The first image of Paradise is one of natural beauty:

> E vidi lume in forma di rivera
> fulvido di fulgore, intra due rive
> dipinte di mirabil primavera.
>   Di tal fiumana uscian faville vive,
> e d'ogne parte si mettien ne' fiori,
> quasi rubin che oro circunscrive;
>   poi, come inebrïate da li odori,
> riprofondavan sé nel miro gurge,
> e s'una intrava, un'altra n'uscia fori.
> (61–9)

> And I saw light that flowed as flows a river, / pouring its golden splendor between two banks / painted with the wondrous colors of spring. / From that torrent issued living sparks / and, on either bank, they settled on the flowers, / like rubies ringed in gold. / Then, as though intoxicated by the odors, / they plunged once more into the marvelous flood, / and, as one submerged, another would come forth.

By way of a visual analogy, Dante perceives the form of heaven as two provisional earthly referents: the banks of a river and the stream flowing between them. As the protagonist and his guide were leaving the created world behind, the canto had opened with an image of change, the breaking of dawn on earth, that was taken as the *comparans* for the receding luminosity of the triumphant souls and the dawn of a new, all-powerful sun (10–15). As a balance to that image of change, and in accordance with the metaphysical quality of what follows, motion is now phrased in terms of a dynamic equilibrium. Sparks (the individual angels) fly out of the river of light, swarm towards the flowery meadows (the flowers being the resurrected souls), and then plunge back into the river itself – all at a constant rate of exchange. The images that the poem relates here are not in themselves a simile, but contain elements that the upcoming revisitation of the same passage will bring out. Phrased here as the record of an initially inadequate visual experience ('I saw'), they contain sub-similes, addressing individual aspects of the picture; and the text marks them with appropriately technical diction: 'quasi' and 'come' in lines 66 and 67 serve to signal the interpretive quality of these details, and the rest of the canto insists on their being sensory data (76–81).

What is now only partly similetic will become a full-fledged simile in the next canto, one that contains intertextual clues confirming the pertinence of the images to the theme of resurrection. At *Paradiso* 30.124, after having been perceived as morphing into intermediate images, heaven takes its final shape in Dante's eyes: it is a flower visited by bees. The first line of the next canto will take up again the image of the 'flower':

> In forma dunque di candida rosa
> mi si mostrava la milizia santa
> che nel suo sangue Cristo fece sposa;
>   ma l'altra, che volando vede e canta
> la gloria di colui che la 'nnamora
> e la bontà che la fece cotanta,
>   sì come schiera d'ape che s'infiora
> una fïata e una si ritorna
> là dove suo laboro s'insapora,
>   nel gran fior discendeva che s'addorna
> di tante foglie, e quindi risaliva
> là dove 'l süo amor sempre soggiorna.
>   (*Paradiso* 31.1–12)

In form, then, of a luminous white rose / I saw the saintly soldiery that Christ, / With His own blood, took as His bride. / But the others – who, even as they fly, behold / and sing the glory of the One who stirs their love, / and sing His goodness that raised them up so high, / as a swarm of bees that in one instant plunge / deep into blossoms and, the very next, go back / to where their toil is turned to sweetness – / these descended to the splendid flower, / adorned with many petals, and then flew up / to where their love forever dwells.

As has been recognized in Dante commentaries since the Renaissance, the simile casting the angels as bees, which occupies the second half of the passage, has its origin in book 6 of Virgil's *Aeneid*. The target of Dante's allusion is clear: the context of the simile he reuses for his depiction of heaven is Virgil's Elysian fields. It is there, in a secluded space, that Aeneas perceives the presence of the souls who are about to be reincarnated only as a sound (*murmur*) at first, and then as an unspecified image of humans shapes (*gentes populique*) in flight. The simile that follows takes the bees as signifier for the souls, in their swarming around the river of Lethe. Virgil's lines in question read:

Interea videt Aeneas in valle reducta
seclusum nemus et virgulta sonantia silvae,
Lethaeumque domos placidas qui praenatat amnem.
hunc circum innumerae gentes populique volabant:
ac veluti in pratis ubi apes aestate serena
floribus insidunt variis et candida circum
lilia funduntur, strepit omnis murmure campus.
                    (*Aen.* 7.703–9)

And now Aeneas sees in the valley's depths / a sheltered grove and rustling wooded brakes / and the Lethe flowing past the homes of peace. / Around it hovered numberless races, nations of souls / like bees in meadowlands on a cloudless summer day / that settle on flowers, riots of color, swarming round / the lilies' lustrous sheen, and the whole field comes alive / with a humming murmur.

In moving from the *Aeneid* to the *Commedia*, the simile does not remain intact: as he is wont, Dante modifies what he finds in his 'source,' in this case by distributing the elements of the original simile among the components of his *comparandum*. In Dante, the angels are assimilated to bees and the souls around which they swarm are pictured as flowers.[39]

Dante's varying of Virgil's text, however, goes beyond formal interventions. By framing this Virgilian passage within the context of resurrection, Dante brings to the fore both the theological background in which it had been traditionally framed and, with his insistence on its specific formulation as a simile, he intimates the role that Virgil's model could be asked to play in metapoetic discourse.

I will first briefly explore the background theology for the cited passage before dealing with the poetic aspects of the question. As has been noted by several readers of the canto, Virgil's text had reached Dante already framed in the charged context of arguments about resurrection. As a matter of fact, the *Aeneid* passage had been read as an instance of Virgil's shortcomings in theological matters. Theological objections to Virgil's 'philosophical' account of what Dante would call the 'status animarum post mortem' were, of course, well founded. The passage in question was clearly a case in which Virgil's poem bordered on (and even crossed into) Epicureanism. The letter of his text pointed undoubtedly to reincarnation.[40] The theme of reincarnation, taken literally, is of course incompatible with Christian doctrine, and it is significant that Fulgentius cites Virgil's passage precisely in this light. When the character of Virgil (*conductus narrator*, as he is about to define himself) recounts that in the Elysian fields Anchises, among other teachings, pointed out to Aeneas the souls who have come back from earthly life and are about to go back to life again (*reduces iterum animas iterum de vita*), Fulgentius's character passionately interjects:

> O uatum Latialis autenta, itane tuum clarissimum ingenium tam stultae defensionis fuscare debuisti caligine? Tune ille qui dudum in bucolicis mystice persecutus dixeras: 'Iam redit et uirgo, redeunt Saturnia regna; iam noua progenies caelo promittitur alto,' nunc uero dormitanti ingenio Academicum quippiam stertens ais: 'Sublimes animas iterumque ad tarda reuerti corpora.' Numquidnam oportuerat te inter tanta dulcia poma mora etiam ponere tuaeque luculentae sapientiae funalia caligare? (*De continentia Virgiliana* 161–2)

> O Roman spokesman for bards, should you really obscure your illustrious intellect in the fog of so foolish a line of defense? Are you not the one who once pleaded on mystic lines in the *Eclogues*: 'And now the virgin returns, Saturn's kingdoms return; / Now a new race is sent forth from high heaven'; and yet now is not your mind dozing off when you snore out something smacking of the Academy and say 'O Father, am I now to

believe that exalted souls go hence to heaven and once more return to their sluggish bodies'? Why, among such sweet apples, must you include sour blackberries and put out the torch of your luminous wisdom?

To the accusation of having mixed his intuitions of Christianity to come, which were contained in his fourth *Eclogue*, with a trite and untenable philosophical dogma of his day Virgil responds disarmingly, and perhaps ironically, by blaming it on his 'necessary' paganism: 'Si ... inter tantas Stoicas ueritates aliquid etiam Epicureum non desipissem, paganus non essem' (I would not be a pagan if I did not leaven so many Stoic truths with a pinch of Epicurean idiocy).

In Fulgentius's argument, the 'little bit of Epicureanism' which Virgil admits he has interspersed with so much (true) Stoic doctrine is the cycle of death and reincarnation that his poetry adumbrates. Late-antique and patristic accusations had been levelled at Virgil's account of the afterlife, and Dante's evocation of the *Aeneid* appears to underscore the necessary correction of Virgil that they required. However, if a literal reading of Virgil's text produces a theologically condemnable view of reincarnation as the inescapable destiny of any soul, an alternative symbolic approach is still possible. By citing Virgil's poetry in *Paradiso* 30 and 31, this is apparently the way Dante's text suggests we should read it. Dante's evocation contains a necessary distancing correction, but, once corrected, Virgil's text is recuperated in full. The dialectics of citation validates both points of view: by redeploying the *Aeneid* fragment in a discourse on resurrection, 'Dante enhances his critique of Virgil's misprision regarding the return to the body' (Rossi 1989, 312); however, in indicting him for not having grasped nor explored the full significance of what his verses were suggesting, Dante also points to those lines as potentially adequate to represent poetically the resurrected body and soul of the saints. In sum, even if Virgil could not be said to be in control of his poem's meaning, the *Aeneid* could still serve an illustrative purpose for a theologically crucial point of doctrine. Once framed in terms of resurrected bodies rather than reincarnated souls, Virgil's passage could support a Christian reading.

In this delicate operation, Dante could also count on Augustine's support. While arguing against Manichean objections to the doctrine of the resurrection of the flesh in *De civitate Dei*, Augustine had cited in a corroborative vein Virgil's passage and alluded to its larger context. The matter at hand – that is, his polemical take on the Manichean understanding of corporeal reality as an absolute negative – is perhaps responsible for the particularly lenient attitude Augustine maintains when citing Virgil's passage. The title sentence of his chapter makes clear that the focus is on the misguided notion that the flesh is responsible for all sins: 'Non igitur opus est in peccatis vitiisque nostris ad Creatoris iniuriam carnis accusare naturam, quae in genere atque ordine suo bona est' (It is not necessary, thus, to blame for our sins and vices the nature of the flesh – that would be an offense to our Creator – since the flesh is, in its *genus* and *ordo*, good. *De civitate Dei* 14.v.1). The argument comprises two complementary steps. First, Augustine avails himself of Platonic doctrine to oppose Manichean tenets. He notes: 'Non quidem Platonici sicut Manichaei desipiunt, ut tamquam mali naturam terrena corpora detestentur' (The Platonists are not, indeed, so foolish as the Manicheans; for they do not detest earthly bodies as the natural substance of evil). Second, he uses Virgil to correct the Platonic understanding of the four passions as deriving only from bodies – a restriction that would potentially associate Platonic doctrine with Manichean tenets. Virgil is a good authority on this point: even when they have reached the Elysian fields, he wrote, souls still have a desire to go back to their bodies. This apparently happens even after they have been completely purified, that is, freed from material existence and cleansed of any 'disease' that ensued from it. Based on Aeneas's marvelled reaction to Anchises' account of the corporeal destiny awaiting souls after their purgation, Augustine can conclude that bodies cannot affect souls. Or, at least, that the perturbations of the souls do not stem solely from their union with the bodies.

The passage deserves extended quotation, especially for the approbation with which Augustine cites Aeneas's words. Somewhat uncharacteristically, Augustine's argument takes a particularly gentle approach to Virgil's text:

> Quod si ita est, quid est quod Aeneas apud Vergilium, cum audisset a patre apud inferos animas rursus ad corpora redituras, hanc opinionem miratur exclamans: '*O pater, anne aliquas ad caelum hinc ire putandum est / Sublimes animas iterumque ad tarda reuerti / Corpora? Quae lucis miseris tam dira cupido?*'
>
> Numquidnam haec tam dira cupido ex terrenis artubus moribundisque membris adhuc inest animarum illi praedicatissimae puritati? Nonne ab huius modi corporeis, ut dicit, pestibus omnibus eas asserit esse purgatas, cum rursus incipiunt in corpora velle reverti?
>
> Vnde colligitur, etiamsi ita se haberet, quod est omnino vanissimum,

vicissim alternans incessabiliter euntium atque redeuntium animarum mundatio et inquinatio, non potuisse veraciter dici omnes culpabiles atque vitiosos motus animarum eis ex terrenis corporibus inolescere, si quidem secundum ipsos illa, ut locutor nobilis ait, dira cupido usque adeo non est ex corpore, ut ab omni corporea peste purgatam et extra omne corpus animam constitutam ipsa esse compellat in corpore. (*De civitate Dei* 14.v.3)

If this is true, however, how is it that, in Virgil, when Aeneas learns from his father in the underworld that souls will return again to bodies, he marvels at this belief, exclaiming: 'O father, can we believe that the souls rise up to heaven and then return once more to encumbering bodies? What dire lust for life thus holds them in such misery?' Does this 'dire lust,' deriving from earthly limbs and dying members, still dwell even in those souls whose purity is so much vaunted? Does not Virgil say that such souls have been cleansed of all 'bodily plagues,' as he calls them? Do they begin, then, even after this, to 'desire a return to bodies'? Hence, even if it were true (although the belief is an entirely vain one) that departing and returning souls pass through an incessant alternation of purification and defilement, we should still conclude that it cannot be truthfully said that all the culpable and vicious motions of such souls arise simply from their earthly bodies. For, according to the Platonists themselves, this 'dire lust,' as their distinguished spokesman calls it, is so far from deriving from the body that, of itself, it compels the soul to return to the body even after the soul has been cleansed of every bodily plague and established outside any kind of body.

Unsurprisingly, Augustine labels the 'literal' sense of Virgil's episode 'reincarnation,' an absurdity: in Christian terms, it is 'omnino vanissimum' to think that souls go back and forth between freedom from and subjection to corporeal defects. In using Virgil in a polemic against philosophical attacks on the dogma of resurrection, however, Augustine also opens up a 'refocused' reading of the passage. Instrumental as it may be, his resorting to Virgil's 'philosophical' authority paves the way for its recuperation in a discourse on resurrection. Proving, via Virgil, that Christian doctrine is free from bias against the flesh, Augustine anticipates Dante's redeployment of a Virgilian passage in the context of a canto concerned with resurrection.[41]

The intertextual connection that Augustine's argument establishes with Virgil's Elysian context supports a theological use of Virgil's *Ae-*

neid. But Dante does not insist, as Fulgentius and Augustine had, on a strictly argumentative use of Virgil's text; rather, he specifically recuperates a similetic passage. What does his choice entail? Of course, there is no doubt that Dante easily and competently rejects the doctrinal subject of Virgil's 'visionary comparison' (he is not suggesting a reintroduction of 'reincarnation' as a viable philosophical option), as it is similarly clear that the theology on which the canto is based does not run counter to Augustine's approach to the dogma of resurrection (there is no trace whatsoever of any Manichean suspicion of the flesh in Dante's thinking – rather, the opposite is perhaps true).[42] The strictly theological questions that had marked Virgil's reception and redeployment appear to have receded into the background, but this is so only because Dante approaches them via the allusion to Virgil's simile. Dante's choice of 'doing theology in similes' is of some consequence. Similes, Dante's example shows, can be made to bear the weight of theological truth. As the interplay of the redoubled image in *Paradiso* 30 and 31 suggests, they are not merely a provisional, sensory-dependent instrument to approach 'things as they are'; they can convey that truth in full.

A final example may help to clarify the point, suggesting that similes can work as effectively as dialectical demonstrations do in conveying the metaphysical substrate of the universe. The texts are drawn again from a series of passages from the neighbouring cantos. A retrogressive chain of references marks the stretch of cantos between 31 and 28 in *Paradiso*, triggered by recurrent image of God as a *punctus*. When they reach the opening of *Paradiso* 30, readers encounter the image of the receding darkness to convey the waning from Dante's sight of the 'triumph' of the souls around God:

> Non altrimenti il trïunfo che lude
> sempre dintorno al punto che mi vinse,
> parendo inchiuso da quel ch'elli 'nchiude,
>   a poco a poco al mio veder si stinse:
> per che tornar con li occhi a Bëatrice
> nulla vedere e amor mi costrinse.
> <div align="center">(<i>Paradiso</i> 30.10–15)</div>

Nor otherwise the victory that revels / in eternal joy around the point that overcame me / and seems enclosed by that which it encloses / little by little faded from my sight, / so that, compelled by seeing nothing and by love, / I turned my eyes to gaze on Beatrice.

The definition of the Godhead as the 'point' around which the souls move in harmony, apparently surrounding what in truth He contains, looks back at the previous use of the term *punto* in *Paradiso* 29.9, as 'il punto che mi avea vinto' (the point that overcame me). In addition, it also rehearses the long account of the angelic hierarchies by which, in *Purgatorio* 28 (a canto in which, incidentally, the term *punto* is used six times), Beatrice responds to the protagonist's doubt about the apparent discrepancy between the cosmological view of the universe and its metaphysical arrangement: the 'essemplo' and 'essemplare' of lines 55–6.[43] Dante's doubt was simple. Apparently the universe has at its centre the Earth, which is surrounded by seven planetary heavens, which in turn are surrounded by the heaven of the fixed stars and the *Primum mobile*; beyond them – that is, from an earthly point of view, 'around them' – there is the Empyrean, the 'seat' of God and heaven proper. What the protagonist now sees, however, is the reverse image: God is at the centre, and around Him whirl nine concentric circles of angelic orders. The discrepancy between the physical appearance of the universe and its metaphysical truth – things as they appear, and things as they are – is what puzzles Dante, and Beatrice will devote a good deal of the canto to address this issue.

A curious detail about the passage is that what Beatrice accounts for in her long and rigorous explanation had already been anticipated in the second *cantica*, in a daring metaphor used by Virgil. In inviting Dante to look upwards, condemning earthly goods and their enticements, Virgil had lamented that humans seem to be blind to God's summonings – His *richiamo*:

> 'Chiamavi 'l cielo e 'ntorno vi si gira,
> mostrandovi le sue bellezze etterne,
> e l'occhio vostro pur a terra mira;
>   onde vi batte chi tutto discerne.'
>   (*Purgatorio* 14.148–51)

'The heavens call to you and wheel about you, / revealing their eternal splendors, / but your eyes are fixed upon the earth. / For that, He, seeing all, does smite you.

Five cantos later, returning to the same point, Virgil apparently invited Dante once more to look away from earthly goods and aspire to heaven. This time, however, he framed his invitation in a figure of speech:

> 'Li occhi rivolgi al logoro che gira
> lo rege etterno con le rote magne.'
> (*Purgatorio* 19.62–3)

'Raise your eyes to the lure / the Eternal King spins with His majestic spheres.'

The metaphor Virgil uses is now drawn from the art of falconry and is based on a paradoxical ambiguity along the vertical axis. While Virgil is inviting Dante to look up at the heavens, the metaphor he constructs suggests the opposite direction. The 'lure' is supposed to call the falcons 'down' towards the *falconiere*, not 'up' towards the sky. The paradox is apparently even greater when we resolve the metaphor: God, the falconer, whirls around himself the lure, the 'great wheels' of heaven; Man, the falcon, is drawn to Him by the heavenly beauties (the 'eternal beauties' of *Purgatorio* 14). The logical paradox at the heart of Virgil's metaphor, we should note, does not affect the message. Dante immediately complies with the ethical imperative contained in Virgil's words to him: 'Quale il falcon ... tal mi fec' io' (19.64 and 67). The paradoxical situation is the same as *Paradiso* 28: the tenor of the metaphor places God at the centre of the universe, the heavens revolve around Him, and they draw in Man from the outskirts. In *Paradiso*, Dante will be faced with the revelation and direct experience of the metaphysical truth, and he will still not see how *essemplo* and *essemplare* can go together. Yet, he already had received, in an ambiguous metaphor, the essence of what Beatrice's account will explain to him. While, before the experience, the intellectual content of the metaphor was inert, after the experience, the metaphor becomes the perfect embodiment of that content. Held in the balance between an experience that can be communicated fully only to those whom grace will grant its redoubling and the need to relate it, the *Commedia* proceeds by way of 'examples.' Far from discarding them as inessential additions to the poet's thoughts, the poem now vindicates *similitudines et repraesentationes* as one of the vehicles for its truth.

Notes

Introduction

1 In *Paradiso* 10.109, with its problematic reference to the 'avvocato de' tempi cristiani,' the mention is made no less in passing – if indeed it is Augustine who is meant.
2 Traditional treatments of Dante's thematic debt to Augustine may be found in Calcaterra 1942, 247–80, Chioccioni 1952, and Fallani 1976, 185–203; more recently, see Mazzoni 1960 and on his line Sarteschi 2002, 171–94. On conversion narrative, in addition to the essays on 'The prologue scene,' 'The firm foot,' and 'The significance of *terza rima*' (all in Freccero 1986), see Masciandaro 1972, Wingell 1981, Cassell 1989 (and, *contra*, Cioffi 1989), Took 1990, D'Andrea 1993, 53–69, and Caputo 2003, 49–67. On the moral architecture of Dante's afterlife (specifically Purgatory), see Barolini 1992, 99–110, which mobilizes Augustine's conception of transient temporal goods and desire. On History and its necessary hermeneutics, see Mazzotta 1979, 147–91, and Davis 1957 and 1984, 198–289; but see also Thomson 1978. On the interplay of Virgilian and Augustinian elements in the poem, see Hawkins 1999, 197–228, but also Ahern 1982. On the Augustinian frame for the dialectics of letter and spirit, as it applies to the peculiar fictionality of Dante's poem, Freccero's essays on 'Infernal irony,' 'Medusa,' and 'Bestial sign and bread of angels' (all collected in Freccero 1986) remain seminal. Mazzotta 1979, 233–74 tackles similar questions under the heading of Allegory, bringing new Augustinian intertexts to bear on the discussion; Barolini 1992, 166–74 goes back to the same central issue of the poem's rhetorical status as it confronts (in an Augustinian vein, but with non-Augustinian results) Dante's representation in the temporal medium of language of the a-temporal reality of Paradise.

3 For this background the best, most systematic, sources are Minnis 1988 and Minnis and Johnson 2005.
4 See Hollander 1976, Mazzotta 1979, 238–43, Dronke 1986, 28–9, and Harwood-Gordon 1991, esp. 3 and 158.
5 On the instrumental quality of Dante's argumentative stance in the treatises and his real allegiances, see Barański 2000, 57–65.
6 On the issue, see Hollander 1976; Barolini 1992, 122–42 and 194–217; and Barański 1987 and 1996, 153–82.
7 Once again, the necessary reference is to the seminal work in this field initiated by Barolini (esp. 1992) and Ascoli (esp. 2008).
8 On the twist and turns in Dante's intellectual history, with particular reference to the intertwined questions of philosophy and literature, see the critical survey in Ascoli 1995. Key texts in the articulation of the debate on style are Auerbach 1965, 25–66; Hollander 1983, 81–115 ('Travisamenti danteschi dell'*Eneide*') and 117–54 ('Tragedia nella *Commedia*'); Battaglia Ricci 1983; Barański 1994 and 1996, 41–77 ('I trionfi del volgare: Dante e il plurilinguismo') and 79–128 ('La linguistica scritturale di Dante'). See also Barolini 1984, 275ff. and 1989. For an argument seeing a strong continuity rather than a break in Dante's poetics, as they are presented in *De vulgari eloquentia* and appear to guide the writing of the poem, see Moevs 2005, 178–80.
9 The most recent overview of the problem is in Barański 1996, 69–77 and 129–51.
10 The dictum 'The fiction of the *Commedia* is that it is not a fiction' derives from Singleton 1977. The most detailed treatment of the concept of '*fictio*' in Dante to date is Paparelli 1960; for some reservations about Paparelli, see Mengaldo 1968, 47 and his note (1979) at *De vulgari eloquentia* 2.iv.2, and cf. *infra*.
11 Several attempts have been made by various early commentators (among whom Boccaccio plays a prominent role) to bring Dante back to his classical authors. But see Battaglia Ricci 1983, passim; and most recently Hawkins 1999.
12 When I bring together *Convivio* and *De vulgari*, I *almost* conflate them. On account of theoretical and chronological considerations that I have examined elsewhere (Marchesi 2001b), I believe that, while *Convivio* 1–3 and *De vulgari eloquentia* may actually be taken as a compositional and ideological unity, *Convivio* 4 is a different creature, one which in many respects looks ahead to the *Commedia*. The claim to historicity for epic narratives that Dante stakes in *Convivio* 4, and the reduced poetic-allegorical density that characterizes the text and its interpretation endow the fourth book with

a transitional status (on the transitional role of *Le dolci rime*, see Barolini 1984, 81–2). The same phenomena do not seem to recur, however, in the previous three sections. The ambiguous status of *Convivio* 4 (at once culminating part of the work as we have it today, and strangely at odds with the principles guiding the first three treatises) is actually responsible for many of the current arguments that see continuity between the treatise and the *Commedia* (see, e.g., the introductory essay in Boyde 1981, Scott 1995, Dronke 1997, and Barański 2004). Downplaying the possible chronological and ideological hiatus that exists between the first block of *Convivio* and its final section has led readers, on occasion, to project on the former some of the latter's specific acquisition. On the issue, see Nardi 1942 and Corti 1983 (insisting on matters of philosophy as marking the transition from the treatise to the poem) and Dronke 1997, 52–4 (arguing against the existence of any real break, again on philosophical grounds). In addition to philosophical issues, my work invites one to measure Dante's shifting allegiances in his intellectual history on the basis of more strictly poetic (or poetologic) considerations.

13 The poem reclaims the Florentine dialect, thus providing Machiavelli with the strongest argument to set Dante against himself in his *Discorso* 18 (=775b, 20–35).

14 This happened to the dismay of Renaissance theorists of vernacular poetics such as Pietro Bembo, who objected to the loss of linguistic 'decorum' in some areas of the *Commedia*. See Bembo's *Prose*, 128ff.

15 See Zumthor 1981, 15.

16 The lexical and logical proximity of the three passages can still be measured in their English translations. *Convivio* 1.xii.1: 'If flames of fire were seen issuing from the windows of a house, and someone asked if there were a fire within, and another answered in the affirmative, I would not be able to judge easily which of the two was more deserving of ridicule'; *De doctrina Christiana* 2.i.2: 'Natural signs are those that signal something else by themselves, without entailing any will or desire to signify, as in the case of smoke indicating the presence of fire'; *Commedia*: 'And if from seeing smoke we argue there is fire / then your forgetfulness does clearly prove / your faulty will had been directed elsewhere.'

17 On *De doctrina christiana* as an antecedent for Dante's sense of God's way of communicating with Man, see Barański 1995b (esp. 157), now (in Italian) in Barański 2000, 41–76.

18 For the label *alia rhetorica*, see Curtius 1953. For Dante's sense of rhetoric in the encyclopedia of the sciences during his post-exile years, see Mazzotta 1993.

19 See, for instance, Hollander 1983 and Picone 1993a and 1993b, both passim.
20 See Bloom 1975.
21 For Dante's widespread redeployment of biblical writing, see A. Lanci and V. Truijen, *Scrittura*, in *ED*, 5:93b–99a (with essential bibliography); Hollander 1973; the proceedings of the conference *Dante e la Bibbia* (Barblan 1988); Battaglia Ricci 1983; Higgins 1992; Rigo 1994, 60–108; Kleinhenz 1997; Pertile 1998; Hawkins 1999, 1–95; and, most recently, Nasti 2007.
22 Seemingly anachronistic, they call to mind modern (or postmodern) critical perspectives. For a constructivist theory of hermeneutic, see Barthes 1974 and Iser 1978. See, however, the critical survey in Ascoli 2008, 34–7 – from which see especially Hult 1986, 263–300; Dagenais 1996, 8–29; and Stock 1996, 174–206, and 2001, 8–23. I borrow the terms 'readerly' and 'writerly' (which translate the French *lisible* and *scriptible*) from Barthes 1974; but see also Ianucci's Introduction in Dante: Contemporary Perspectives, xiii–xiv.
23 See Hawkins 1999, esp. 19–35, 72–95, and 197–212. See also Cook 1999 and, most recently, Holmes 2008, 38–52 and passim.
24 On the centrality of the hermeneutic process in Dante's thought, see also Franke 1997. The metaphysical basis of Dante's poetics is laid out in Moevs 2005, esp. chapter 5 and Conclusion.

Chapter 1: Linguistics

1 Wittgenstein's present approach is, thus, not free from a hint of self-revision: in the *Philosophical Investigations* he is reworking and, in many ways, revolutionizing his earlier take on language as articulated in the *Tractatus*. On the issue, see Baghramian 1988 and, in cursory but effective form, Kirwan 2001, 186–90. For the relevance to Dante's own revisions, see Fortuna and Gragnolati 2010.
2 See, for instance, the summarizing gloss Servius appends to Virgil's line 'hinc metuunt, cupiuntque, dolentque, gaudentque' (thence they fear, desire, suffer, and rejoice), which ascribes the fourfold analysis of passions to 'omnes philosophi' (*ad Aen.* 6.733).
3 On the role of Augustine in Wittgenstein's thinking, see Spiegelberg 1979, Bearsley 1983, Gallagher 1982, and Lo Piparo's preface to Vecchio 1994. From the complementary perspective, see also Watson 1982.
4 For the problematic dating of the works, see Petrocchi 1997, 102, Mengaldo 1968, 3, Corti 1983, 142–5, and Vasoli's note to *Convivio* 1.v.10.
5 On the problem of the discrepancy between the statements in *Convivio* 1.v.7 and *De vulgari eloquentia* 1.i.3, see the summary of the proposals in Men-

galdo 1968, 50. The line of argument I defend here goes back to the observation by Parodi 1915, 267–8, and was fostered by Contini 1976, 37–41. The same solution is offered more recently by Barański 1996, 46–57 and Tavoni 2010. On the whole question, see the commentary *ad loc.* by Marigo 1968, 9, Grayson 1965, 54–76, and Pagani 1982, 102–12. *Sed contra*, see Vinay 1959, esp. 240–5 and again Pagani 1982, 192–243. Other *loci* in the two works can be used to reconstruct Dante's (complex but harmonious) notion of the relationship between Latin and the vernacular. See their discussion in Mengaldo's entries for *ED*: *Gramatica* (3:259–64); and *La lingua latina* (3:592–6). See also Brugnoli's entry *latino* 3:591–2. A catalogue of the parallels also can also be found in Weiss 1942 (with limitations due to issues of chronology).

6 Mengaldo's text reads here *diversibus temporibus*, perhaps to be emended to *diversis* as in Marigo's edition.

7 For the number of grammatical (artificial) languages that one may assume Dante thought existed, see Mengaldo's note to *De vulgari eloquentia* 1.i.3: *Quam* [*scil., locutionem*] *Romani gramaticam vocaverunt. Hanc quidem secundariam Greci habent et alii, sed non omnes* ('The Romans called [this other kind of language] *gramatica*. The Greeks and some – but not all – other peoples also have this secondary kind of language'). Mengaldo does include biblical Hebrew, basing his argument on the authority of Isidore, *Etymologiae* 10.3. *Sed contra*, see Marigo 1968, *ad loc*.

8 Dante does not explicitly say anything about the relationship with Latin that the Slavic and Germanic languages might have (the *iò* peoples), which make up for the first branch of the first post-Babelic *idioma tripharium* (see *De vulgari eloquentia* 1.viii.2–4). They might be included in the 'others' – those *non omnes* that have failed to create their own inter-linguistic idiom and were thus forced to adopt a 'foreign' grammatical language. For the few antecedents of Dante's emphasis on the affirmative particle as language-defining, see Mengaldo's entries 'Oc,' Oil,' and 'Tripharius' in *ED*. Apparently none is just as radical.

9 The same notion of the vernacular's primacy can be found, couched in a political rather than psychological argument (and, accordingly, with a political terminology), at 1.xii.5: *E così lo volgare è più prossimo quanto è più unito, che uno e solo è prima ne la mente che alcun altro* ('And so a man's vernacular is nearest to the extent that it is most closely related to him, for it is in his mind first and alone before any other').

10 On the dichotomy between the maternal and paternal images Dante associates with the two distinct spheres of natural and artificial language, see Cestaro 2003, 49–76.

11 For a basic summary of Dante's linguistics, see also Mazzocco 1993, 108–58 and Fumagalli 2001, 1–18.

12 Dante's argument continues by pointing out that his prose commentary will help further the cause of the vernacular in the struggle for (theoretical) pre-eminence with Latin, by showing its potential as a language for philosophical investigation: 'Ché per questo comento la gran bontade del volgare di sì [si vedrà]; però che si vedrà la sua vertù, sì com'è per esso altissimi e novissimi concetti convenevolmente, sufficientemente e aconciamente, quasi come per esso latino, manifestare; [la quale non si potea bene manifestare] nelle cose rimate per le accidentali adornezze che quivi sono connesse, cioè la rima e lo tempo e lo numero regolato' (For by means of this commentary the great goodness of the vernacular of sì will be seen, because its virtue will be made evident, namely how it expresses the loftiest and the most unusual conceptions almost as aptly, fully, and gracefully as Latin, something that could not be expressed perfectly in verse, because of the accidental adornments that are tied to it, that is, rhyme and meter; *Convivio* 1.x.12).

13 Lansing's translation systematically renders Dante's *manifestare* with the English *to express:* for reasons that I hope will momentarily become apparent I have modified his translation throughout, opting for a more neutral rendering 'to convey.' See below, note 31.

14 The antecedents of Dante's definition and its corollaries are outlined in Mengaldo 1978, 162–99.

15 The passage in the original reads: 'Chè per questo comento la gran bontà del volgare di sì [si vedrà]; però che si vedrà la sua vertù, sì come per esso *altissimi e novissimi concetti* convenevolmente, sufficientemente e acconciamente, quasi come per esso latino *manifestare* ...'

16 The passage in full reads: 'Et cum loquela non aliter sit necessarium instrumentum nostre conceptionis quam equus militis, et optimis militibus optimus conveniant equi ... optimis conceptionibus optima loquela convenit.'

17 The reading depends on the nuance we give to the clause 'nichil aliud,' which may be taken to mean either 'nothing but' or, in a slightly lighter vein, 'in the end.'

18 Those who have seen Dante situate his embryonic philosophy of language very close to the philosophical mainstream of his age were probably right. Dante's insistence on the conceptual nature of language assimilates his perspective to the views of the *Modistae* – be it Boethius of Dacia or his Italian counterpart Gentile da Cingoli. The Latin treatise, in particular, defines language by way of contrasting *vulgare* and *gramatica* (the living language of vernacular poetry and the Latin of philosophical culture), in an argument which does borrow terms and structures of thought from

the Modistae. Taking up the arguments of Marigo 1968 (passim, but most importantly at pp. lxi–lxv), see Corti 1981, 33–76 and 1983, 38–44, Alessio 1984, and Shapiro 1990 (in particular the appendices), and, most recently, see Lombardi 2007 and Benedictis 2009. For the interplay between the two treatises on this point, see also Weiss 1942 and Mengaldo 1968, 50–8.

19 For a treatment of Dante's adherence to this model, see Colish 1983 and Eco 1994 (esp. 40–6). For a general bibliography on modistic philosophy, see Bursill-Hall 1971. See also deMan 1986, 73–105.
20 On Latin as ideal language see also Eco 1992 and, in passing, Agamben 1999, 53–6.
21 The *locus classicus* for this argument is Benjamin's 'The Task of the Translator' (in Benjamin 1996).
22 On the issue, see Ascoli 2008, preliminarily at 5–7 and 37–40, but also 150–61 and passim.
23 On the private-language argument, see chapter 3.3 in Steiner 1975 and, in a more technical vein, Fann 1969. Cf. also below, after note 22.)
24 For the Aristotelian source of the idea (*Pol.* 1.2, 1252a and ff.), see Vasoli's gloss *ad loc.*
25 A somewhat similar progression is analysed in *Convivio* 4.xii.16–17, in an argument about desire: 'Per che veder si può che l'uno desiderabile sta dinanzi a l'altro a li occhi de la nostra anima *per modo quasi piramidale*, che 'l minimo li cuopre prima tutti, ed è quasi punta de l'ultimo desiderabile, che è Dio, quasi base di tutti' (emphasis mine).
26 For this terminology, see Baghramian 1988, 29–33 (on Frege, Russell, and Wittgenstein of the *Tractatus*).
27 For Dante's treatment of the illustrious vernacular as a 'utopian reality,' see Marchesi 2001a.
28 Augustine's Latin reads: 'Quae utrum, sicut vultus aut dolentis clamor, sine voluntate significandi sequantur motum animi, an vere ad significandum dentur, alia quaestio est et ad rem quae agitur non pertinet' (*De doctrina christiana*, lines 14–17).
29 Markus 1957 (esp. 71–6), Colish 1983, and Manetti 1987 remain essential contributions to the study of Augustine's theory of signs. For a useful systematic approach to Augustine's treatment of language, see Ando 1994 and Vecchio 1994 (esp. 95–112).
30 See Mazzoni 1967, who cites Thomas Aquinas citing Augustine on this point (79).
31 For a brief but suggestive analysis of Dante's recurrent emphasis on the expressive power of language in poetry (the semantics of *isfogare*), see the observations in Rigo 1994, 11–44. The radical dichotomy between the

expression and the communication of an idea in at least one authoritative ancient tradition should discourage conflating the two notions in one English verb: 'to express.'

32 For a treatment of Dante's progressive reframing of the poem, see Barolini 1984 (chapter 1.4) and, from a different perspective, Steinberg 2006, 61–94.
33 Musa's translation is here slightly modified (lines 1 and 3).
34 It is the promise following the *mirabile visione* of Beatrice in bliss: 'non dire più di questa benedetta infino a tanto che io potesse più degnamente trattare di lei' ('to say no more about this blessèd one until I would be capable of writing about her in a nobler way,' *Vita nuova* 42.1). On the technical quality of the adverb 'degnamente,' see below the discussion of Isidore's definition.
35 A fuller treatment both of the way *Vita nuova* signifies and of the peculiar status of the poetics outlined in chapter 25 can be found in chapter 2. For a discussion of the consequences that the principles thus set forth will have on the hermeneutics and poetics of the *Commedia*, see chapter 3.
36 In addition to the instances surveyed below (*Inf.* 32.4; *Par.* 2.37, 15.41, 18.86, 19.12, 23.68, 75,122, and 127), all referring to a technical, poetic sense, the verb 'concepire' and the noun and adjective derived from its past participle 'concetto' have a wide use in the poem, ranging from the physical act of conceiving a child (*Inf.* 12.13, of the Minotaur; *Purg.* 28.113, said metaphorically of the generative power of the earth) to that of forming an image (*Par.* 3.60, the memory of Piccarda's features), an idea (*Inf.* 26.73, of Virgil's foreknowledge of Dante's desire to speak to Ulysses; *Par.* 29.81, on angelic memory of individual events; 29.130, on their inconceivable multitude; and 29.139, on their love for the Creator), or finally articulating a discourse (*Par.* 19.12, on the choral quality of individual self/selves in heaven; 24.60 and 132, in Dante's response to the examination on Faith, for which, see below; and 22.33, in Benedict's prologue to his *vita*). The catalogue of the passages can be found, with some commentary, in Salsano, *Concetto*, *ED* 2: 133–4; see also Ledda 2002, 243–98 and 316–19. A special case is *Paradiso* 15.37–48, for which see below. Though the term *concetto* is absent from the passage, *Purgatorio* 19.42, 'forti cose a pensar metter in versi,' deserves passing mention, since it contains the three key notions of Dante's proto-neo-Positivist philosophy of language lined up in one verse: things, thought, words. Like the invocation in *Inferno* 32, this one also will bracket the middle element in favour of a direct poetic connection: events (*cose*) and poetic words (*versi*) can be made to match, in spite of any resistance to understanding (*pensar*) that they may exercise.

37 For this argument, see Hollander 1980, 115–29.
38 On the role of *convenientia* in this passage and at *Inferno* 31.67–9 (Nimrod's speech), see Mazzotta 2005, 171–7.
39 My translation. For the *crux* in the passage, all editors seem to agree on the meaning but not on the text to print: see O'Donnell's note *ad loc.* The role of the will as spur to the production of language is recuperated from previous passages: see, for instance, 1.6.8 and 10 and 1.8.13.
40 Related passages in Augustine are not difficult to find: see *De Trinitate* 9.vii.12 (Atque inde conceptam rerum veracem notitiam, tamquam verbum apud nos habemus, et dicendo intus gignimus; nec a nobis nascendo discedit), or *Sermo* 288.3 (*De voce et verbo*). The Christological dimension of Augustine's semiotics is explored in detail by Markus 1957 and Ando 1994, in reference to arguments advanced mainly in *De magistro*.
41 The verb *spirare* has both meta-poetic and linguistic connotations that are sometimes difficult to separate. In a group of passages, the meta-poetic meaning appears to prevail: as, for instance, in *Purgatorio* 24.53, *Paradiso* 1.19, or, metaphorically, in *Paradiso* 2.8. In other cases, the verb translates the basic act of 'speaking' into the exceptional conditions for communication that Dante enforces in heaven: see, at least, *Paradiso* 4.18, 19.25, 24.32, 54, and 82, and 26.3 and 103.
42 On this specific kind of poetic solution to ineffability, see Chiarenza 1972, Botterill 1988, Brownlee 1991, and Barolini 1992 (54–8), critical of Carugati 1991. See also Hawkins 1999, 213–23.
43 On the issue of the Pauline quality of Dante's experience (and its Augustinian connections), see Barolini 1992, 147–50. For a recent contribution and a summary of the critical debate, see Gragnolati 2005, 162–74.
44 Perhaps the clearest case of the dictation–notation relationship that Dante presented as essential to his poetic mission is in *Purgatorio* 24; in conforming to that system, the invocation preceding the dance of the souls appears to embody the new poetics controlling Dante's poem. See Freccero 1986, 213–14. Mazzotta 1979, 202–11 discusses the *Purgatorio* passage in terms of what I have labelled 'incarnational poetics.' For a fuller treatment of Dante's poetics as alluded to in *Purgatorio* 24, see chapter 3 below.
45 For the value that the term 'conceiving' assumes here as related to a 'receiving' (rather than 'producing'), see *Paradiso* 29.136–41, which rephrases the reception of 'the first Light' (God) in the angelic intelligences as a conception.
46 On the choral quality of the Eagle's speech and an Augustinian antecedent for it, see Lombardi (forthcoming), citing early commentators pointing to

Augustine's *uti/frui* distinction for the soul's *dolce frui* (19.2). On the anti-Augustinian quality of the political philosophy expounded in the passage, see Hollander's commentary *ad loc.*

47 Of course, since it does not relate to the poet, but only to the character, this is not to be counted among the 'official' invocations in the poem. However, the author is having the character ask someone ('La Grazia') for something connected to the way ('bene') in which he is going to talk ('esprimere') about something ('li miei concetti'). The philosophizing character, in sum, is made to preface his doctoral defence with something that, had the situation been that of a poem, would be an invocation.

48 The coming together of conceptual and ethical concerns in the passage is a case of what *Epistle* 13.40 characterizes as the practical purpose of the *Commedia*, labelling it a work 'non ad speculandum, sed ad opus inventum' (conceived, not for speculation, but with a practical object). (Notably, this is a language that reverberates in the text of *Monarchia* 1.ii.6: 'materia presens non ad speculationem per prius, sed ad operationem ordinatur' [the present subject is not directed primarily towards theoretical understanding but towards action].) Perceiving an ethical dimension in Dante's profession of faith also helps us to feel Augustine's presence in the background of the episode. As commentators have not failed to notice, the final proof in the validation process that Dante is asked to provide for his reliance on Scripture as both divinely inspired and trustworthy is lifted almost verbatim from Augustine's treatment of the same issue in *De civitate Dei* 22.5: 'Hoc nobis unum grande miraculum sufficit, quod eam [namely, Christ's resurrection] terrarum orbis sine ullis miraculis credidit' ('The one great miracle – that the whole world has come to believe without any miracles at all – is in any case enough for us.'). An underlying homology informs both Augustine's argument and Dante's handling of linguistics in the canto: the final form of validation for Scripture has less to do with its content (that is, with the concepts it signifies) than with the historical manifestation of its readers' ethical choice.

49 Only Buti has favoured victory over the Devil; the second reading (victory over human intellects) has had numerous champions: Benvenuto, Serravalle, Landino, Lombardi, Costa, Tommaseo, Bianchi, Campi, and del Lungo. Scartazzini's reading was anticipated by Daniello, Vellutello, Venturi, and Portirelli, and followed, unacknowledged, by Poletto, Tozer, Mestica, Barbi, Steiner, Grabher, Trucchi, Momigliano, Porena, Sapegno, Mattalia, Giacalone, and Singleton.

50 Carroll has been followed, in turn, by Torraca, Pietrobono, Chimenz, Bosco-Reggio, and somewhat ambiguously by Barbi and Pasquini-Quaglio.

Chapter 2: Poetics

1 On the issue of the growing weight of and attention to the *lictera* in medieval literary culture after the twelfth century, see Minnis 1988, 73–159. On Dante's participation in this widespread cultural movement, see Barański 2004, 54–9 and Ascoli 2008, 39–41.
2 For the prehistory of *Convivio*'s canzoni as non-allegorical, see Barolini 1984, 25–9 and below, note 18.
3 For the common source of the two passages, see Crespo 1972, 97–9 and the discussion of the tradition behind the issue in Mengaldo's note *ad loc*. Additional, post-classical material on the problem can be found in Paparelli 1960, 42 (Matthew of Vendôme, *Ars versificatoria* 3.2=Faral, p. 167) and 43 (Geoffrey of Vinsauf, *Documentum* 2.3.2=Faral, p. 284).
4 See, especially, his *ED* entries *Convenienza* (1:187a–b) and *Ornatus* (4:200a–203a).
5 Direct references to *Vita nuova* in *Convivio* can be found at 1.16, 2.ii.1–5, and 2.xii.4. In all of them, Dante strives to build, by obscuring the main divergences, a strong sense of continuity between the two works. In the first passage we read the declaration of mutual reinforcement quoted above. In the second we witness the acrobatic re-interpretation of Dante's second love as love for Lady Philosophy (see De Robertis's note at *Vita Nuova* 35.1, and Ascoli 2008, 72–5). In the third we are faced with the puzzling declaration that 'quasi come sognando' (almost as if in dreams) Dante had seen in the *libello* many of the philosophical truths that he now will expound in the *Convivio*. On the issue, see D'Andrea 1993.
6 On Dante's often quite polemical treatment in the minor works and his eventual overcoming of Brunetto's model in the *Commedia*, see Mazzotta 1979, 138–41, Armour 1983, and Davis 1984, 137–97. More recently, see the development of this argument in Freccero 1991, Mazzotta 1993, 29–33, and Bisson 1992. For Solomon as an alternative model for Dante's writing of *Convivio*, see Barański 2004, 27–34, citing Dronke 1997, and anticipating the publication of the doctoral thesis by P. Nasti, now in Nasti 2007, 43–85.
7 For a similar account of the potential imbalance between philosophical prose and poetry, see Ascoli 2008, 109–18 and 203–18.
8 To find the same principles at work, see also *Convivio* 1.x.12 and 1.xii.13.
9 Barański 2004 arrives at exactly the opposite result while assessing exactly the same texts: in his reading, the literal force of *partite e diverse* is subsumed under the wider theoretical frame of Dante's conciliatory 'distinguishing between *ornamento* and *sentenza* without separating them' (47–8).

10 The argument may, again, cut both ways: 'the *need* for prose (i.e. exegesis)' that Dante predicates on his 'serious' poetry may be conceived as 'the mark of its importance' (as noted by Barański, in private correspondence).
11 The same metaphors are activated in Dante's submission of a poem to Lippo Pasci de' Bardi: 'Lo qual ti guido *esta pulcella nuda*, / che ven di dietro a me sì vergognosa / ch'a torno gir non osa, / *perch'ella non ha vesta in che si chiuda*: / e priego il gentil cor che 'n te riposa / *che la rivesta* e tegnala per druda, / sì che sia conosciuta / e possa andar là 'vunque è disiosa' (*Rime* 48.13–20). On the literariness of the lyric, see Sebastio 1993; on the 'metatextual lexicon' activated in the poem, see now Barolini 2009, 92.
12 On the debate about the value of *fictio*, see Paparelli 1960. Mengaldo discusses the notion in his *Introduzione*, 47 and his note at *De vulgari eloquentia* 2.iv.2. See also Dronke 1986 (chapter 1) and Mazzotta 1993, 21. For the opposite reading of Dante's definition, stressing its potential continuity with the poetics of the *Commedia*, see Moevs 2005, 8–9 and 179ff. remarking that the definition is basically content-free.
13 Barański 2004, 36–8.
14 One can, of course, argue the point both ways: the sweetness of poetry, one may say, is in turn endangered by the eminently intellectual pleasure that prose can elicit (both *bellezza* and *bontade* engender *diletto*, with *bontade* being even more efficient in doing so: see, again, *Convivio* 2.xi.4–5).
15 For this argument, see Barolini 1984, 81–2.
16 For the claim to historicity that the *Commedia* will make both for itself and the *Vita nuova*, see Hollander 1976, Barolini 1992, and Cristaldi 1994 (esp. 101–15 and 165–80). The *libello* does not make such a claim in its metapoetic section. It implies, however, precisely that claim in deciding to treat Beatrice as a *figura Christi* in his/her coming into history. For Beatrice's Christological analogy, see most incisively Mazzoni 1997.
17 On the different role prose plays in the two works and on the historical status of the narrative in the *libello*, see De Robertis's commentary at *Vita nuova* 14.13 that contrasts 'sposizione digressiva' and 'narrativa.' See also Grayson 1972, 68–71, Harrison 1988 (chapter 4), and Barolini 2006; see too the interesting observations of Carrai 2006, 83–9. On the issue of the *divisioni*, see Stillinger 1992, 44–109. Symptomatic, even if perhaps motivated by external concerns, is the decision of the first editor of the *libello*, Boccaccio, to exile the *divisioni* into the margins of the text as purely ancillary material: see his autograph edition in the ms. Chigiano L.V. 176, that contains the famous editorial disclaimer 'maraviglierannosi molti.' On Boccaccio's editorial strategy, see most recently Houston 2010.
18 In *Convivio*, the allegorical interpretation of his text that Dante advocates

is used as an antidote to history. (Following Ascoli 2008, the term is here used to denote the author's personal and intellectual individual circumstances, and Dante's avoidance behaviour on this point is seen in relation to what Ascoli calls Dante's pursuing of 'coherence, or at least the appearance thereof' [p. 52].) Dante's choice of framing the erotic *canzoni* of *Convivio* 2 and 3 as allegorical is designed to undercut, by de-historicizing them, any potentially biographical readings of the *donna gentile* episode in the final sections of *Vita nuova*, as well as its segue in the other 'canzoni ... d'amor ... materiate' which may become part of *Convivio* (1.i.14). By suggesting an authorially endorsed model of interpretation that dissolves the narrative implications of the *canzoni*, the treatise strives to counteract 'errant' readings of the poetic texts to which it is applied, readings that would make it incompatible with Dante's previous work. It is noteworthy, however, that, in order to defuse the narrative contradictions marking the two *prosimetra*, Dante opted in favour of a theoretical continuity of these two texts. When, in *Convivio*, Dante established the legitimacy of allegorical interpretation on an allegedly convergent process of authorial composition, he certainly renounced the option that *Vita nuova* had afforded for inspirational and expressive poetics; in the end, however, his turn to allegory conformed to, and reinforced, the mode of signification advanced in the metapoetic section of the *libello*.

19 See Barolini 1984, 80–4.
20 For an account of Dante's poetics, see Barański 2005a. On Hollander's position in the debate about the authenticity and the significance of the epistle, see Hollander 1993; *contra*, see, most recently, Barański 2005b. The case for authenticity having been made much stronger by Azzetta 2003, there is hope that the debate on *Ep.* 13 will move into addressing interpretive questions on their own merits. As outlined above, I agree with Barański's diagnosis of the letter as non-representative of Dante's revolutionary practice in the poem; in light of the precedent of *Vita nuova*, however, I think that his observations do not automatically impose a verdict of spuriousness for the text. As self-commentator of both his first and last works, Dante anticipates the coy behaviour of T.S. Eliot's endnotes to the 1922 edition of *The Waste Land*, which famously claim that 'Miss [Jessie L.] Weston's book [*From Ritual to Romance*] will elucidate the difficulties of the poem much better than my notes can do.' (On the issue, see J. Grayson 1992, 48–50.)
21 See also: 'Alie vero sacre scripture non tantum sententiarum sed verborum etiam cunctis dignitatibus exornantur, quia sicut dicit Ieronimus, a fonte sacre pagine omnis scripturarum dignitas emanavit' ('Holy Writ is adorned by all possible forms of elegance – not only of meaning but also

of style. This is because, as Jerome says, all elegance in writing comes from the source of the holy page.' All translations from Bene's text are mine). For an introduction to the issues of dating and intellectual background of the *Candelabrum*, see, in addition to Alessio's edition, Vecchi 1958.

22 On the Stoic nature of the argument, see Cicero's negative portrayal of the *dicere philosophorum more* in *De oratore* 1.liii.227–30, and passim. For the Stoic rhetorical tradition, see in general Moretti 1995.

23 Augustine phrases the division in a recapitulating sentence at 4.i.1: *De inveniendo multa iam diximus ... adiuvante Domino de proferendo pauca dicemus* ('We have already said much concerning discovery [or *inventio*?] ... With the help of God we shall say a few things concerning teaching [or *elocutio*?]'). According to a different interpretation of the summation cited above as more sensitive to the structural model of the rhetorical treatises, book 4 might be seen as devoted to the *elocutio* after the *inventio* has been treated in 1–3. Suggestive as it may be, this division is reductive, given, in particular, the care with which Augustine repeatedly points out that his book *is not* (designed to take the place of) a traditional manual of rhetorical instruction. On the matter, see the series of articles by Press (1980, 1981, 1984).

24 For the theme of the correspondence between the speaker and the rhetoric he has to practise, see also Dante's statement at *Convivio* 1.i.16–17 on the way one should properly understand the relationship between *Vita nuova* and *Convivio*: '... *veggendo sì come ragionevolmente quella fervida e passionata, questa temperata e virile esser conviene. Chè altro si conviene e dire e operare ad una etade che ad altra*' ('... seeing that it understandably suits that one to be fervid and passionate, and this one tempered and mature. For it is proper to speak and act differently at different ages, because certain manners are fitting and praiseworthy at one age which at another are unbecoming and blameworthy'). The sentence is usually glossed with a reference to 1 Cor. 13:11 (Busnelli-Vandelli), which is not entirely pertinent. Dante's phrasing is more probably indebted to Cicero's notion of rhetorical *prepon* at *Orator* 21.71, most likely mediated by (or, at least, in tune with) Horace's *Ars Poetica* 99–118. On Dante's relation to Cicero as rhetorician, see below (note 30); for common themes in Cicero and Horace, see Grant-Fiske 1924.

25 Augustine's argument outlines the paradox of what Auerbach (1965, 33–8) will label the Christian '*sermo humilis*.'

26 Italics signal my divergence from Robertson's translation.

27 A detailed commentary may be found in O'Donnell's edition (2: 170–3). For other examples of the similar notion in Augustine, see also Auerbach

1965, 47–50; to Auerbach's examples one may add also *De catechizandis rudibus* 13.

28 For the notion of *idonei auctores*, see Kaster 1978, 181–209. For the problems caused by the inclusion of Frontinus and the puzzling exclusion of Cicero, see Mengaldo's gloss *ad loc.* and Barański 2001b, 19–23.

29 Psalms directly translated (or alluded to in their vernacular garb) appear in *Convivio* at 2.i.6 (Ps. 113:1–2 vs. *Purgatorio* 2.46–48 and *Ep.* 13.21); 2.iii.11 (Ps. 8:2); 2.v.12 (Ps. 18:1); 3.iv.8 (Ps. 99:3, ex Vinc. Beauvais, *Spec. hist.* 25.12); 4.viii.4 (Ps. 8.4); 4.xv.1 (Ps. 62:11); 4.xix.7 (Ps. 8:5–7 and 8:2); 4.xxiii.8 (Ps. 103.9, contaminated with Job 14:5); 4.xxviii.2 (Ps. 65:8 and 12). For a commentary on Dante's diversified use of the texts, see the debate between Negri 1925 and Rostagno 1925. See also Groppi 1962, 34–47 and A. Penna, *Salmi* in *ED* 4:1078–9. On the issue of vernacular renderings of psalms, see L.G. Kelly 1997.

30 On the contrary, the Latin of Cicero and Boethius is deemed 'sweet': 'Boezio e Tullio (li quali con la dolcezza di loro sermone inviarono me, come detto è di sopra, ne lo amore, cioè ne lo studio, di questa donna gentilissima Filosofia)' (*Convivio* 2.xv.1: 'Boethius and Tully, who with the sweetness of their discourse guided me, as has been said above, along the path of love – that is, into the pursuit of this most gentle lady Philosophy'). Dante's note 'as has been said above' refers only to the circumstance that Boethius and Cicero acted as propaedeutic texts. The stylistic note does not refer to the earlier section – and Cicero's Latin is constantly (and cavalierly) translated.

31 On the necessary resistance to translation of Nimrod's speech, see Dronke 1986 (chapter 1.4 and *Excursus* 2), Hollander 1992, and Dragonetti 2006, 257–75. *Contra*, see Mazzotta 2005, 177, citing Nohrnberg 1996 (whose argument on Nimrod is developed on pp. 168–71).

32 Similar considerations might be in order for the second citation of a psalm, in *Purgatorio* 5.24: Dante stresses here the musical style (alternate: *verso a verso*) of the song, but not the quality of the words. *Purgatorio* 19.73, with the quotation of Psalm 118:25 (*Adhaesit pavimento anima mea*), offers a peculiar case of performative speech: the song is at the same time the expression of the souls' *confessio oris* (it describes their sin while on earth), a sign of their *contritio cordis* (they now meditate on what they sing and weep), and a description of their *satisfactio operis* (they actually lie prone on the ground). When their condition is described as 'amara' (117), their singing may be involved as well. If so, the adjective would contrast the sweetness of the Siren who has just occupied the centre of Dante's last purgatorial dream (*Purgatorio* 19.19). On the practice of psalm citation by incipit, see

Kleinhenz 2007, esp. 183–8. On the issue, see Hollander 1975 and Freccero 1986, 186–94.

33 On the oxymoronic quality of the penitents' singing, see Trone 1995. If it were not for the numerous interpretive problems connected to the episode of Matelda – many of which derive precisely from Dante's reticence on the song she sings for him – one could propose to see in her songs a new hint to the sweetness of the Psalms. Even if we do not know the lyrics of her song in *Purgatorio* 28.80 (later she alludes to Ps. 91:5–6, *Delectasti*), we know that in *Purgatorio* 29.3 she sings a line from Ps. 31 ('Beati quorum tecta sunt peccata') 'as an enamoured lady.'

34 Dante has already spelled out the complementary opposition of Highest Justice and Highest Mercy in God in the symmetrical episode of Manfredi (*Purgatorio* 3.124–9).

35 For the use of the fiftieth Psalm, see Freccero 1961 and Hollander 1983.

36 Italics signal my departure from Robertson's translation.

37 The same assessment, with additional reference to parallel texts in Augustine, may be found in Vecchio 1994, 74–9.

38 One can see, for instance, the heightened sense of the textual nature of Holy Writ Augustine demonstrates at *De doctrina christiana* 2.xii.17–18, when he compares different translations of the same passages, sketching out a three-step typology of complementing translations (both right), reciprocally illuminating translations (one of which is more accurate than the other), and contradictory renderings (one of which is to be refused and the text is simply in need of philological emendation).

Chapter 3: Hermeneutics

1 On the role that Augustine's 'rule of charity' may have played in shaping Dante's recommended hermeneutics, see Ascoli 2008, 34–43, discussing several recent contributions on the subject.

2 The admission is put forth at *Vita nuova* 25.5: 'E segno che sia picciolo tempo, è che se volemo cercare in lingua d'*oco* e in quella di *sì*, noi non troviamo cose dette anzi lo presente tempo per cento e cinquanta anni' ('And proof that it is but a short time is the fact that if we look into the Provençal and the Italian literatures, we will not find poems written more than one hundred and fifty years before the present time').

3 De Robertis's complex note *ad loc.* deserves to be quoted in full: '*Per prosa*: cioè in linguaggio non figurato, com'è normalmente quello della prosa. Ma qui Dante si riferisce alla particolare funzione che la prosa ha nella *Vita nuova*, di "aprire" appunto "la ragione" delle rime. Per cui il capitolo vale non

solo come interpretazione del parlar poetico per metafore, ma come "poetica" dello stesso libro.' (*In prose:* that is, in straightforward language, as it is wont to be that of prose. But here Dante refers to the peculiar role that prose assumes in *Vita nuova;* namely, that of 'opening' the 'meaning' of the poems. The chapter, thus, serves both as an assessment of the metaphoric quality of poetic language and as an exposition of the 'poetics' of the book itself.) The opposite approach may be found in Picone 2005, 184–7.

4 See also the closest parallel to the expression in 25.10 *lo verace intendimento* ('true meaning'), for which see below. A radically divergent reading is in Stone 1994.

5 On the vexed question of the relationship of continuity with or break between Dante's first works, see Vasoli's detailed *Introduzione* to his edition of the *Convivio* (liii–lxiv). As will be clear in the following pages, my work develops under the influence of De Robertis's argument on the radically different poetic status and rhetorical aim of the two works, as developed in De Robertis 1951 and 1970.

6 In the extensive bibliography on the canto the following readings prove useful: Pézard 1952; Brugnoli 1969; Whitfield 1981; Stephany 1983; Scrivano 1992; Franke 1994; Martinez 1995; Grlick 1995; Iannucci 1997 (in polemic with Scott 1996). For a quite recent essay on the role of Statius in the poem, with a detailed and up-to-date bibliography, see Glenn 1999.

7 A history of the tradition opposed to Dante's choice can be found in Rossi 1993. For the general problem of the poem's unnatural naturalization in the critics' response, and its consequent loss of unexpectedness, see Scarano 2001 and, in English, Botterill 1994, 1–9 ('Re-reading Dante: An Unscientific Preface').

8 Most notably by Lewis 1956 and Padoan, both 1959 and 1970. *Sed contra,* see the arguments of Pézard 1952, passim, and Renucci 1954, 334, taken up in Paratore's entry, *Stazio, ED* 5:419–25, and Paratore 1968, 71–8. Along the same line, but with different arguments, see Brugnoli 1969 and Hollander 1980, 123–4. See finally Shoaf 1978, 195–9.

9 Cf. Hollander's proposal of seeing *Thebaid* 2.358–62 as the place in which one can find, following Dante's suggestion, an echo of Virgil's fourth *Eclogue* and thus a trace of what Dante wants his readers to see as Statius's 'secret' Christianity (1980, 206–8).

10 Statius is mentioned in several pre-comedic *loci*: as authority on the matter of Thebes, in *Convivio* 3.vii.10, 3.xi.16, and 4.xxv.6, 8, and 10; and as one of the 'regular poets' in *De vulgari eloquentia* 2.vi.7. A summary of Dante's evolving notion of the canon of *auctores* from *Vita nuova* 25, to *Convivio* 4.xxv–xxviii, to *De vulgari eloquentia* 2.vi.7, to the diptych *Inferno* 4–*Purgatorio* 22, is in Picone 1993a.

11 The idea is advanced by Renucci 1954, 122–3, and tolerated, almost as an afterthought, by Brugnoli 1969, 125.
12 Even a brief survey of the textual presence in Dante's works of Statius's *corpus*, like the one sketched out by Paratore, *ED* 5:419–25, shows how constantly and closely Dante had read both the *Thebaid* and the unfinished *Achilleid*. On the question of Statius's influence on Dante's lower hell, see Cowan 1982. The basic function of the *Thebaid* as keynote text for several later episodes in lower hell had already been suggested by Ettore Paratore, in his reading of *Inferno* 14 (1968, esp. 227–39 and 247–8). See also Hagedorn 1997.
13 For a fuller discussion, see below, chapter 4. A partial reappearance of the rhyme series, deprived this time of the thematic word *dramma* (lit., 'one eighth of an ounce'), is in both *Paradiso* 23.119–23 and 31.125–9. Dante is not alien from these rhyme games: on the retrospective relevance of the complementary series (*Achille*/*faville*/*mille*/(*sortille*) for the diviners of *Inferno* 20, see Hollander, 1980, 194–8.
14 For Dante's insistence on the technical words 'savio' and 'poeta,' previously almost exclusively Virgil's patrimony, but now shared by Statius, see Barolini 1984, 256–69.
15 On the ambiguous image of love's fire, see the reading of *Purgatorio* 30.48 in Hawkins 1999, 125–42. On the imaginative link between 'sins of ingegno' and a fiery punishment in the system of Dante's hell, see Corti 1981, 79–85, and 1983, 142–5. On the same theme, but from a different perspective, see also Mazzotta 1979, 147–91.
16 On the notion of 'family romance,' see Bloom 1975, 122–3 (citing a letter from John Freccero on *Purgatorio* 30). On the lexical juxtaposition of *mamma* and *matre*, see Hollander 1980, 124–5. On the surprising gendering of the metaphor, see Jacoff 1988, and Cestaro 2003, 138–45.
17 In a different, physicalist perspective, the episodes of the 'failed' and successful embraces between poets have been treated by Heilbronn 1977, 1978, and Iliescu 1971. See also Wei Wei 2003 and, in a wider perspective, Gragnolati 2007. For a possible political dimension of the episodes, see Kleinhenz 1988.
18 For this notion, see Minnis and Scott 1991, especially the chapter 'The Human *Auctor* as Efficient Cause' (75–94). For the relationship between *investiganda* and Aristotelian causes in the *accessus ad auctores* (on which the Epistle to Cangrande at 6.18 models itself), see also Nardi 1961. For an alternative and less fortunate scheme of *investiganda* in a commentary to a poem (explicitly discarded, for instance, by Bernardus Silvestris), see Servius, *Ad Aen.*1.*proem*.

19 The structure of Virgil's answer echoes (in a further distancing gesture) the exchange between the angel and John fallen on his knees in Revelation 19:10: *et cecidi ante pedes eius ut adorarem eum et dicit mihi vide ne feceris, conservus tuus sum et fratrum tuorum* ('And I fell down before him so that I may worship him, but he said "Do not do that: I am a fellow servant with you and your brethren'''; already alluded to in *Purgatorio* 19.133–8). Virgil's words point to the absence of the clear moral connotation present in the Angel's statement: 'conservus ... sum.' Dante, in other words, appears to cast the character of Virgil as certainly doing the right thing in refusing the deferential embrace, but solely on account of a partial and inadequate perception of propriety (*decorum*).

20 The Pilgrim will be just as careful. When the same situation is proposed again, a few cantos later, in the episode of Guinizzelli, Dante appears to have learned from the example set by Statius here. Unsurprisingly through a Statian reminiscence (Hypsipyle at *Thebaid* 5.720ff.), Dante makes clear he knows how to deal with the issue of embracing one's own precursors. The homage he pays to his 'maestro' of the *Vita nuova* years goes a long way in the canto, but it does not lead to any confusion with his texts (see *Purgatorio* 26.94–6). For the suggestion of a Statian echo in *Purgatorio* 26 see Cestaro 2003, 141–2. On a possible role played across *Inferno* and *Purgatorio* by the figure of Hypsipyle, see Wetherbee 1988, esp. 87. Cf. also Glenn 1999, 105–7.

21 For a rapid examination of the stratified citation, see Moore 1896, 293–4, who proposes the two sources as alternatives. Incidentally, this is the place in which Moore admits that a thorough study of Augustine's influence on Dante would be necessary. On a possible typology of the sources for Statius's simile, see Delcorno 1989, 216–18. See also Mazzotta, 1979, 221–2. For Dante's involvement with Cicero's philosophical treatise in the years immediately preceding the *Commedia*, see Marchesi 2001b.

22 For the context of Augustine's statement and its relevance in the cultural debate of his time on the *liberales disciplinae*, see O'Donnell's commentary on the *Confessions* (2:269–78).

23 See the counter-definition of material goods that Dante gives at *Purgatorio* 14.97 as those 'from which sharing is forbidden' ('in cui v'è di consorzio il divieto'). On the issue, in an Augustinian light, see Hawkins 1999, 200–9.

24 Returning for a moment to the perspective of the minor works, Dante's recuperation of Augustine's construction and indictment of the Jews' alleged literalism may be shown to be partly political, partly linguistic. From the point of view of politics as developed in *Convivio*, Jews appear to have resisted (unsuccessfully) the linguistic and political transfer of power and

knowledge to Rome, and their former election (established on linguistic grounds in *De vulgari eloquentia* 1.vii.8) has turned into cultural isolation. From the point of view of language, Dante's indictment of the Jews targets their linguistic entrenchment in the 'untranslated' Hebrew of their Bible.
25 In Mandelbaum's rendering, Virgil's text reads: 'To what, accursed lust for gold, do you / not drive the hearts of men?'
26 Mandelbaum's translation of Dante's passage can also serve as a translation for Virgil's text, so literal is Dante's rendering in this case as well: 'The ages are renewed; / justice and man's first time on earth return; / from Heaven a new progeny descends.'
27 The authorial voice in *Vita nuova* 25 had used the same prefatory language as Statius when it introduced the potential objections to the use of a controlled figurality in the *libello*: 'Potrebbe qui dubitare persona degna da dichiararle onne dubitazione' (It may be that at this point some person, worthy of having every doubt cleared up, could be puzzled, para. 1).
28 Dante's decision to have Virgil make this mistake has a clear element of irony, since avarice and prodigality had been two related sins punished in the first of the few 'double-circles' of hell for which Virgil had acted as a perfectly competent guide (cf. *Inferno* 7.40–8). For the Aristotelian moral structure of *Purgatory* evoked in the term 'dismisura,' see Cogan 1999, 87–119.
29 The text I quote here diverges from the one printed by Petrocchi and translated by the Hollanders, whose rendering I have thus modified. In line 40 Petrocchi adopts 'Per che non reggi' ('by what means you guide') over 'perché non reggi' ('why cannot you ... restrain'). His choice is based on the attempt, in the end misguided, to make Dante's 'translation' of Virgil's text as respectful of the original context as possible. My argument runs exactly in the opposite direction: the point of Statius's reference to Virgil's text is his deliberate and literal misquoting, aimed at proving that a text's meaning is independent from its context and from whatever its author might have 'intended' for it. For the reading supported here, see Ronconi 1958, 85–6, Consoli 1967, 15, and Hollander 1983, 88–90; on the status of literalism in medieval habits of translation, see D. Kelly 1997 (with bibliographic indications).
30 On the possible Ovidian source for the elaborate apology registered in Canto 13, see D'Ovidio 1907, 143–333, esp. 157–60.
31 This interpretive line has support from early commentators: see Barolini 1984, 260, citing Francesco da Buti. The most detailed review of the positions taken by Dante scholars on the problem can be found in Chiamenti's long bibliographical note (1995, 131–7), to be supplemented (mainly for American contributions) by Hollander's note at *Purgatorio* 22.40–1. Chia-

menti's views on the other misreading in the canto and its relationship with *Purgatorio* 30 are to be found earlier on pages 79–81.
32 A detailed survey of the allegorical readings of Virgil's text is to be found in both Comparetti 1966, 96–118, and the entry by Consoli, *Virgilio*, in *ED* 5:1031.
33 On Dante's changing poetics, see Barański 1994 and 1995a, 33–45.
34 On the question of Dante's self-revisionary attitudes, see Ascoli 1995. See also the debate between R. Hollander and L. Pertile in the *EBDSA* (7–8 October 1996) on the *Commedia*'s attitude towards *Convivio*.
35 On the use of the term 'charismatic' to indicate readers who advocate holy ignorance and an immediate reading of Scripture, see Simonetti's note *ad Prol.* 20.
36 The potentially crucial two-pronged critique of Augustine's enterprise stemmed from the unbalanced relation between the object of study and the means he proposed to use. His proposal of deploying technical, utterly human, knowledge in the understanding of a sacred, divinely inspired text reflected vaster cultural ambiguities. His call to deploy 'classical' philosophical and rhetorical principles in the service of Christian truth risked clashing with the essential need to keep this truth alternative to the classical world view. When fully human tools are used to approach the Word of God, they are doomed to prove, at best, insufficient to illuminate its spiritual core. At worst, a 'classical,' philosophical, and rhetorical reading of the Scriptures such as the one Augustine apparently proposed risked reducing them to a second-rate collection of stylistically flawed and rhetorically inadequate writings. A purely human hermeneutics is, after all, always misguided and at times even potentially misleading, insofar as it is forced to eliminate the specific difference of biblical writing.
37 For the nexus of rhetoric and hermeneutics in Augustine's discourse, see in general Murphy 1974, 47–64, and more recently, with a stricter focus, Eden 1990.
38 On the notion of *dispensatio* (or *dispositio*, both translations of the Greek *oeconomia*) *temporalis*, see *De doctrina christiana* 1.xxxv.39.
39 In the case of St Paul's and the consul Cornelius's conversions, for instance, Augustine maintains that the necessary human mediation for salvific acts speaks optimistically in favour of, not against, the dignity inherent in the condition of man: *Prooemium* vi, line 90. See also *De doctrina christiana* 2.ii.3, where a similar statement is repeated. For the appeal that this notion could have exerted on the poet of Paradise, whose very structure *is* a form of divine condescension, see *Paradiso* 4.43–4 with Hollander 1969, 192–201, Freccero 1986, 221–6, and Barolini 1992, 143–65.

40 For the use of the term in Augustine to indicate the Bible, see Simonetti's note at *De doctrina christiana* 1.xxxv.39, referring the reader to several passages, in particular *De civitate Dei* 17.3 (*veteris instrumenti*) and 20.4 (*prius de libris instrumenti novi, postea de veteris*). Augustine's choice of an ambivalent word, one that might mean both 'pact' and 'tool,' is significant of the double perspective he takes on Scripture.

41 For the opposition between 'things to be used' and 'things to be enjoyed,' see at least the *abrégée* of Augustine's thought at *De doctrina christiana* 1.iv.4. The notion is, however, as fundamental as it is widespread in all of Augustine's works. See, for example, *De civitate Dei* 8.8 and 19.2. For Augustine's antecedents in operating the distinction (Cicero's split between *utile* and *honestum*, Seneca, Varro), see Simonetti's *Introduzione* xvii–xx.

42 The notion is reinforced by a second passage at 2.ix.14: 'In his omnibus libris timentes Deum et pietate mansueti quaerunt voluntatem Dei' ('In all of these books those fearing God and made meek in piety seek the will of God') and the recapitulating sentence that opens book 3.

43 The notion of the *regula caritatis* was already active in Augustine's thought before the writing of the *De doctrina christiana*. Cf., for instance, the slightly different wording for the same concept in *De Genesi ad litteram* 1.21: 'Aliud est enim quid potissimum scriptor senserit non dignoscere, aliud autem a regula pietatis errare' ('It is not the same thing not to understand what above all the writer intended, and go astray from the rule of piety'; my translation). See also *De civitate Dei* 11.33: 'etsi voluntatem auctoris libri hujus [Genesis] indagare nequivimus, a regula tamen fidei, quae per alias ejusdem auctoritatis sacras litteras satis fidelibus nota est, non aberravimus' ('Even if I was not able to expound the will of the author of the present book, I did not depart from that rule of faith that is made known to those who have faith by other passages of the Scriptures of the same weight'; my translation).

44 As one of the *genera quae controversiam in omni scripto facere possint* (as in Cicero's *Topica*, 96), the *discrepantia scripti et voluntatis* (or *diffinitio legalis*) is discussed in Cicero, *De inventione* 1.56; 2.123, 128, 137, 139, and 143; *Partitiones oratoriae* 136 and 180; in the pseudo-Ciceronian *Rhetorica ad Herennium* 1.19; 2.13–14; and in Quintilian, *Insititutio oratoria* 7.vii.1 and x.1. In Augustine, the label for the problem oscillates between 'voluntas' and 'intentio' (see, for example *Contra Adimantum*, PL 42, 149: '[manifeste appareat] et istorum fraus, qui particulas quasdam de Scripturis eligunt, quibus decipiant imperitos, non connectentes quae supra et infra scripta sunt, ex quibus voluntas et intentio scriptoris possit intelligi' ('[It will be evident] also the fraud that characterizes these individuals, who pick and

choose some little bits of the Scriptures, with which they deceive the inexperienced, avoiding to draw any connection with what is written before and after, by means of which one can understand what is the *will* and the *intention* of the writer'; my translation). The distinction is quoted *ad litteram* in Hugh of St Victor, *Eruditio didascalica*, PL 176, 808. The principle according to which the dianoetic (intentional) meaning of a text is to be retrieved through the inspection and collation of parallel passages in the Bible has a rhetorical, particularly legalistic lineage. See Eden, 1990, 47–53 and 1987, 69–82. In the latter she traces the lineage of the notion from Aristotle, to Cicero, to Quintilian.

45 The standard tag to characterize the Pauline 'literal' or Augustinian 'carnal' reading of the Scripture sounded *littera, cui soli Judaeus innititur*. See also *De doctrina christiana* 3.xxxiv.49: 'Hic ergo Israhel spiritalis ab illo Israhele carnali, qui est unius gentis, novitate gratiae, non nobilitate patriae, et mente, non gente distinguitur' ('Therefore this spiritual Israel is to be distinguished from that carnal Israel which is one people by newness of grace, not by nobility of descent, by their minds and not by their race'). The foundational text of the Apostle is at 2 Cor. 3:5–6: 'Sed sufficientia nostra ex Deo est: qui et idoneos nos fecit ministros novi testamenti: non littera, sed Spiritu: littera enim occidit, Spiritus autem vivificat' (But our sufficiency comes from God, who made us competent to be ministers of a new covenant, not of the letter but of the Spirit; for the letter kills, but the Spirit gives life). On this distinction was based the cultural operation of turning the Hebrew Scriptures into the 'Old' Testament by establishing their subordinate functionality to the 'New' Testament (see, for instance, *De civitate Dei* 17.3).

46 Attesting the authority of the poets on divine matters, Dante calls Lucan's *Bellum civile* 'Scriptura paganorum' (a propos of *BC* 9.580, one of Cato's most Christian-sounding *epiphonema*). See also Marchesi, 'Lucan at Last' (forthcoming).

47 For further Augustinian (and meta-poetic) elements disseminated in the immediately preceding cantos, see the discussion of the verb 'manifestare' in chapter 1.5, note 45.

48 English-speaking translators seem to agree in their renderings. Mandelbaum's translation reads: 'The good with which this court is satisfied / is Alpha and Omega of all writings / that Love – loud or low – reads out to me.' Similarly, Singleton's version reads: 'The good that satisfies this Court is Alpha and Omega of all the scripture which Love reads to me, either low or loud.' For motives that will be clear shortly, I think that these renderings, with their shared stress on the volume of Love's voice, might

be misleading on a crucial point. Particular attention should be devoted to the loaded term *scrittura*, which has already been used for Virgil's *Aeneid* at *Purgatorio* 6.34, still in the context of a discussion of alternative hermeneutics. On the ambiguous status of the word 'scriptura/scrittura,' and on the role of mediation that Dante constantly assigns to it in the *Commedia*, cf. esp. (all in the third *cantica*) *Paradiso* 4.43 (on how paradise appears to Dante as the result of an accommodating metaphor); 13.128 (on the perversion of the Scripture's interpretation by heretics); 19.83 (on the role Scripture plays in supplementing the mysterious nature of God's judgments); the present passage at 26.17 (on the 'rule of charity' as the guiding principle of the interpretation of God's tripartite writing: creation, Old Testament, New Testament); 29.90 (on the perversion or abandonment of the Scriptures by present-day preachers); 32.68 (on the presence of a biblical indication – plain and clear, in Augustinian terms – of the God-willed gradation in the distribution of grace among the souls). In a slightly different sense, see also *Paradiso* 12.25 (on the *regula* of a religious order).

49 Scripture is the subject of the verb for the following commentators (in roughly chronological order): Benvenuto, Anonimo Fiorentino, Serravalle, Daniello, Porena, and Sapegno (with limitations). On the contrary, Love is the subject for Lombardi, Portirelli, Costa (with limitations), Campi, Poletto, Giuliani, Tozer, Carroll, Torraca, Mestica, Casini-Barbi, Steiner, Del Lungo, Vandelli, Grabher, Chimenz, Giacalone, Singleton, Bosco-Reggio (with limitations), and Pasquini-Quaglio.

50 On Augustine's principle, see Tracy 1990; as it becomes fruitful for Dante, see Mazzotta 1979, 294–7. On the semantic ambiguity of some expressions in Dante, see Wlassics 1975 ('Ambivalenze dantesche,' 7–34).

51 Cf. Valente's entries *Forte* (adj., adverb, and noun) in *ED* 2:980–2 and Salsano's entries *Lieve* and *Lievemente* in *ED* 3:648–9. For a proposal to see in the 'dark wood' of *Inferno* 1 (a 'selva selvaggia e aspra e *forte*' [that wood, savage, dense and harsh]) a metaphoric equivalent of the 'obscurity' of the Scriptures, see Warner 1995, interpreting the Pilgrim's predicament at the beginning of the *Commedia* as the dramatization of the poet's struggling with biblical hermeneutics.

52 On the issue, and the Augustinian connection, see the trenchant assessment in Barolini 1992, 11–13.

53 Dante may have thought that the seven candelabra were only a thin allegorical veil, but their interpretation has caused difficulties and disagreements among modern readers. For a more extended presentation of the question (with relevant bibliography), see Marchesi 2002.

54 On the puzzling simile of 'the lion in the clouds,' see Scott 1983.

55 On the Christian notion of 'diligent correction,' see Matt. 18:15–17. The target of Dante's attack is one who for 'an excessive zeal for the Church' takes his interpretation of the Bible one step too far. In practice, as Nardi's gloss reminds us here, this class includes the pope and the theocratic faction of the Guelph party (see *Monarchia* 3.iii). It may include Dante himself. He has, however, the same self-assurance in his 'political' *Epistles*. On the issue, see Hollander 1999 and Ascoli 2008, 229–73 (on *Monarchia*).

56 The context is shaped by the same principle of universality that the *Commedia* lays out in *Paradiso* 6.100–8 for the Empire, incidentally indicated by a 'sign': 'L'uno al publico segno i gigli gialli / oppone, e l'altro appropria quello a parte, / sì ch'è forte a veder chi più si falli' ('For some oppose the universal emblem / with yellow lilies; others claim that emblem / for party: it is hard to see who is worse'). For Dante's insistence on the need to preserve 'semiotic freedom' to God's signs in history, see chapter 4.1.

57 The present example of Dante's hermeneutic practice may be used to clarify his theory of interpretation, in particular when it comes to the necessary balance of interpretive freedom and correct response to the intention of the text. The fact that Dante declares his opponents' reading 'wrong' does not mean that he is limiting the potential multiplicity of meanings the biblical text can produce, nor does his belief in the ultimately divine authority of the text keep him from saying that their interpretation is illogical.

58 The (once again) puzzling reference to the sin of misinterpretation as grave even when committed only in dreams can be glossed, I believe, with a passage in Dante's *Epistle* 5, 20, where the tag *velut sompniantes* refers to the self-deception of those who pretend not to heed God's (and the emperor's) authority, lulling themselves with the words 'Dominus non habemus' (from 3 Reg. 22:17 and Ps. 13:1, 52:1). On the confluence of biblical and political language in Dante's political epistles, see Pertile 1998, 14–21.

59 The proximity of the *Commedia*'s lexicon to the one used in the *Monarchia* is even greater in Bonagiunta's reply to Dante's statement: 'Io veggio ben come le vostre *penne* / di retro al *dittator* sen vanno strette, / che de le nostre certo non avvenne' ('I clearly understand that your pens follow / faithfully whatever Love may dictate, / which, to be sure, was not the case with ours,' 58–60).

60 On a groundbreaking reading of these lines as setting up a model for the God-inspired poem, see Mazzotta 1972 (developed in 1979, 193–226). See also Hollander 1980, 82–6, and Gorni 1981, 13–21. To be noted are also Scott 1965, Martinez 1983, esp. 54–6, and Pertile 1993a, and, in the frame of *leu* and *clus* poetics, Barański 1998. On this particular 'knot' of poetics and the presence of a metaphor from falconry side by side, if not before the one

from 'calligraphy' contained in Dante's *penne*, see also Pertile 1993b, taking up an argument by Musa 1966. Pertile's reading brings into the discussion as a strategic element of their exchange the *equivocatio* on *penne* (feathers/quills) to separate the inadequate reading given by Bonagiunta (and by Dante himself in *De vulgari eloquentia* 2.iv.11: 'et si anseres natura vel desidia sunt, nolint astripetam aquilam imitari' [and, if nature or their own incompetence has made them geese, let them not try to emulate the star-seeking eagle]) of the falconry metaphor. On the vernacular intertextual dynamics of the passage, see, more recently, the contributions by Lazzerini 1996 and Brugnolo 2000.
61 See Ascoli 1993, 64–5.
62 Dante's Latin reads: 'Circa sensum misticum dupliciter errare contigit: aut querendo ipsum ubi non est, aut accipiendo aliter quam accipi debeat.' Augustine's original reads: 'Non sane omnia quae gesta narrantur etiam significare aliquid putanda sunt' (*De civitate Dei* 16.2).

Chapter 4: Augustine in Dante

1 See O'Donnell 1983. On Augustine's political thought in general, see Bigongiari 1964 and Weithman 2001, 240–5.
2 On the difficult compromise that Dante is able to form between the idea that the Roman Empire is at the same time essential to God's plan for humanity and a violent force in history, see Armour 1989, 170–5. Relevant to the present discussion, in particular insofar as they highlight Augustine's double standard for Roman history (negative in its main thrust, somewhat positive on particular points of argumentation) and its main supporter Virgil, are Davis 1957, 40–56, Nardi 1967, 215–28, Freccero 1986, 152–4, and Mazzotta 1979, 59 as well as 170–87. See also Ferrante 1984, esp. chapter 2. On Dante's strained dialogue with Augustine on this point, see Ascoli 2008, 253–63.
3 A further text worth consideration is *Ep.* 5, which reiterates the key arguments in defence of contemporary imperial legitimacy that are developed in the treatises and the poem, from Henry's titles as 'divus et Augustus et Cesar' (5), to the God-willed nature of imperial power (8–10), all significantly argued in a similarly historical and syllogistic vein as they appear in *Monarchia* 2. For an expanded version of the argument developed here, see Marchesi 2010.
4 It is perhaps better not to try and endow Dante's words with a biographical import (as suggested, for instance, by Muresu 1979, 27–30), a move which would leave us hard-pressed to locate a text in Dante's corpus expressing anti-Roman (or merely sceptical) sentiments.

5 *Signum* is a keyword both for the argument of *Monarchia* 2 and for *Paradiso* 6 (where it recurs five times: vv. 27, 32, 82, 100, 103). Concern with signs, their 'meaning,' and their 'reading' was central for the Roman sections of *Convivio* 4, for which see below.
6 Italics mark my departure from Ryan's translation, which here misses the crucial image, reducing 'God's arms' to His 'powerful intervention.'
7 The same concept is addressed in *Monarchia* as well, almost in the same language, and in very close connection to the issue of 'reading' history: 'Veritas autem questionis [namely, that Roman predominance came about *de iure*] patere potest non solum lumine rationis humane, sed etiam radio divine auctoritatis: que duo cum simul ad unum concurrunt, celum et terram simul assentire necesse est' (2.i.7). On the pairing of heaven and earth, which is a recurrent feature across Dante's repeated assessment of God's historical semiotics, see also *Paradiso* 7.48: 'Per lei [i.e., the cross] tremò la terra e 'l ciel s'aperse.' Scott 1996 makes the connection with the other *terminus* of Christ's *militia* on earth, the angelic hymn linking the glory of God in heaven (*in altissimis*, or *excelsis* in the Greater Doxology) and peace on earth (*in terra*) from Luke 2:8.
8 See also the similar phrasing and argument at 4.v.10: 'infino a la sua perfettissima etade' ('until its most perfect age').
9 On Dante and Lucan, see Paratore 1968, 55–121, Raimondi 1977, 65–94, and, with limitations, Marsili 1986. See also the more recent treatments by Brownlee 1993, De Angelis 1993 (with notes on Cato's salvation), Scott 1996, 69–84, Schnapp 1997, and Schildgen 2001.
10 Cicero's text reads: 'Temeritas C. Caesaris, qui omnia iura divina et humana pervertit propter eum, quem sibi ipse opinionis errore finxerat, principatum.' On the political dimension associated with the *De officiis*, see Brunt 1986. For the problem of Cicero's political stance in his last philosophical work, see Gabba 1979. See also Dyck 1996, *ad loc*.
11 Unsurprisingly, *Paradiso* 6 reviews much of the same events in a similarly ambivalent light: Caesar's (and Augustus's) civil wars are part of the triumphal 'flight of the eagle.' See esp. vv. 61–78.
12 An outline of the modern critical debate on the issue can be found in Dewar 1994. See Conte 1966, Hinds 1988, esp. 26–9, and Fantham 1992, 13. See, finally, the problematizing position of Barchiesi 2001: '[When reading Lucan 1.40–2,] it is hard to avoid the impression that Caesar, that is Nero, is one of the disasters listed by the poet, a deadly catastrophe like Munda, Perugia and Modena. But the effect works only if we look from the start with the eyes of an anti-Neronian partisan. Lucan's own position, and the internal history of the *Pharsalia*, continue to be uncertain data on which to ground our interpretation' (75–6).

13 On the problematic dating of the commentary, see Ussani 1903. See also Zetzel 1981, 75–80 and 195–6 and Werner 1994.
14 The relevant passage detailing the semantic shift can be found in *Monarchia* 2.x.9: commenting upon the Ennian lines containing Pyrrhus's answer to the Roman embassy which are preserved in Cicero's *De officiis* 1.xii.38, Dante writes: *Hic Pirrus 'Heram' vocabat fortunam, quam causam melius et rectius nos 'divinam providentiam' appellamus* ('Here Pyrrhus called fortune "Hera"; we call that same cause by the more appropriate and accurate name "divine providence"'). The whole idea stems probably from Boethius, *De consolatione philosophiae* (in particular, book 4, Prose vi); this is a context Dante might have kept in mind also earlier than in the *Monarchia*, namely, when defining the illustrious vernacular as *cardinale*: see *De vulgari eloquentia* 1.xviii.1 and *De consolatione philosophiae* 4.vi.15. Mengaldo's note *ad loc.* is perhaps too hasty in treating the two texts as unrelated.
15 For the position Lucan takes vis-à-vis Virgil's Augustan allegiance in poetics, see Ahl 1993 and Hardie 1993. On Nero as epitome of vice, see also Augustine's *De civitate Dei* 5.19.
16 On the topographical and moral ambiguity of the noble castle in *Inferno* 4, see at least Forti 1977, 9–48 and the note to *Inferno* 4.69 in Mazzoni 1965.
17 Dante is most likely following Virgil's example on this point. In *Aeneid* 5.826–35, Anchises did decry the same iconographically marked antagonism between Caesar and Pompey and their potential for violence.
18 The mythologeme of Caesar appears to be productive in other areas of the poem less directly involved with this character. Stull and Hollander (1991, 12–19) are probably right in proposing a Lucanian source, Caesar's 'fraudulent' speech in *Bellum civile* 1.299–302, for Ulysses' speech in *Inferno* 26.
19 For the presence of a suicide, a pagan, and an adversary of Caesar among the saved souls in purgatory, see Hollander 1969, 124–6, and Hollander and Rossi 1986, 66. My argument develops along the same lines. On Cato in the context of a redemptive kind of suicide, see Mazzotta 1979, 58–64 and Ferrante 1984, 205–10.
20 On Dante's reaction to Augustine's indictment of Cato in *De civitate Dei* 1.xx and the Lucanian source of his Christological treatment, see Hollander 1969, 124–9, and Mazzotta 1979, 47–65. For Virgilian elements in Augustine's polemical treatment of Roman culture, see McCormack 1998, 175–224.
21 For an evaluation of Piero's elaborate rhetoric, as potentially infecting other areas of the canto, see Spitzer 1959, Paratore 1968, 178–220, and Jacomuzzi 1972, 43–77.
22 For a brief history of the gloss connecting Dante's invocation to the paral-

lel text in *Georgics* 4, starting with Bernardino Daniello's teacher Trifon Gabriele, see Hollander 1993a, 317. On the connection, which extends also to Beatrice's threefold rebuke, see Jacoff 1991. For Edward Moore's interpretation, see Moore 1896, 21. Notably, *Georgics* 4.563 is the only place in Virgil's corpus in which the Latin poet mentions his name. Dante, invoking the 'necessity' of relating literally Beatrice's words, is about to do the same. Dante's internal signature of his work might, thus, be linked to Virgil's own *sphragis*.

23 On the palinodic meaning of the syntagm 'other sword' in the passage, see Storey 1989, esp. 93.

24 For this line of interpretation, see Singleton 1958, 74ff., Mazzotta 1979, 185–8, Ryan 1982, Stefanini 1991, esp. 96–7 and 100, and Gorni 1997. For the pairing of the two Virgilian quotations and the recontextualization imposed on the first one, see Freccero 1986, 206–8. For a reading that emphasizes a different intertextual grid, see also Shapiro 1982.

25 'Volsimi ... per dicer a Virgilio: "[...]" Ma Virgilio ... Virgilio ... Virgilio.' While Beatrice may plausibly have read in Dante's mind the first Virgilian allusion to the 'tokens of the ancient love,' the threefold address belongs only to the text of the poem. These are words that only the readership of the *Commedia* can access. Diegetically, they are uttered outside the plot.

26 For the changing role that Ovid played in Dante's culture, see Picone's series of essays (1992a, 1993b, 1994). See also Brugnoli 1995. For two essential collections of essays on Dante's Ovidian allegiance, see Sowell 1991 and Jacoff and Schnapp 1991. On further pointedly Ovidian allusions in the canto, see Levenstein 1996.

27 On this passage as a source of Dante's non-Augustinian portrait of Dido in *Inferno* 5, see Mazzotta 1979, 160–70, and Scott 1979.

28 Dante breaks here the norm according to which it is not becoming to speak of oneself, the same norm from which he had exempted Augustine in the *Convivio* – hence, his insistence on the *necessity* of his recording. See also note 22 above.

29 See Freccero's argument in 'Dante's Prologue Scene' (Freccero 1986).

30 See also the explicit link with the sacrament of confession made at *Purgatorio* 31.1 and 4–6.

31 To the Augustinian (but not only) moral imperative of 'knowing oneself,' Dante will allude shortly, in yet another commixture of confessional, Ovidian and Virgilian motives: 'Li occhi mi cadder giù nel chiaro fonte; / ma veggendomi in esso, i trassi a l'erba, / tanta vergogna mi gravò la fronte' ('My lowered eyes caught sight of the clear stream, / but when I saw myself reflected there, such shame weighed on my brow, my eyes drew

back / and toward the grass'). In a last attempt to escape from Beatrice's *pietade acerba* ('stern pity'), the Pilgrim is forced to lower his eyes. He is met, however, with the narcissistic – Ovidian – image of his own self. His flight from himself, a 'mistake' from the point of view of the confessional liturgy to be performed in the canto, represents, however, also a 'correct' gesture because it subtracts the Pilgrim from the fascination with one's own self. Self-knowledge comes to Dante from the outside, from the defining gaze of Beatrice (in a gesture that intends, perhaps, to reassess Augustine's position on the point). On the reuse, in the simile immediately following, of Virgilian material, see Mazzotta 1979, 187–8. On the theme of Narcissus, see Dragonetti 1965, Brownlee 1978, and Picone 1977.

32 Augustine's is neither the first nor the only polemic voice raised against Virgil's treatment of Dido. For bibliographic information on Dido's Virgilian, non-Virgilian, and anti-Virgilian *Nachleben* in Late Antiquity and the Middle Ages, see Pease 1935, 3–79, Courcelle 1984, Miller Ortiz 1986, and Ruff 1994. For the reception of the 'historical' Dido among Dante's early commentators, see Marchesi 2004, 70–85.

33 Dante knows perfectly well how to translate the word *vestigia* literally – and he does so in *Paradiso* 31.81, another locus of dialogue with Augustine (cf. below). On the valence of 'antica,' see most recently Holmes 2008, 116–18.

34 On liminality and transition, see Moevs 2005. In the rich bibliography on this canto and the next, see Longen 1975, Scott 1977, Shaw 1981, Rossi 1981, 1985, and 1989, Hollander 1988, Dronke 1989, Kleinhenz 1995, and Iannucci 1995.

35 A fourth point has been proposed by Rossi, 1981 and 1985, who has suggested that Beatrice too is involved in the post-resurrection mode in which the canto frames Dante's vision. He links the term 'bando,' appearing here on line 34, with its previous deployment in *Purgatorio* 30.13 ('novissimo bando'), an unambiguous end-of-days context.

36 On the metaphoric field of bodies as garments at resurrection, see also *Purgatorio* 30.15: 'La revestita voce alleluiando.'

37 Shaw 1981, 201, and Hollander 1993a, 14–15, insist on the Pauline resonance of these lines – especially for the link they establish with blindness. On the 'fasciare' as a technical term for infancy, see *Purgatorio* 7.100 ('in fasce' to mean 'during infancy'), to be compared with 16.37 ('fascia' as mortal body); for the pertinence of the image, cf. vv. 82–3 'Non è fantin che sì sùbito rua / col volto verso il latte' (No infant, / [...] will thrust his face / up to his milk with greater urgency).

38 On the technical features of this body, see Bynum 1995, and Gragnolati 2005, 139–78 (citation from 174).
39 Lansing 1977, 38–9.
40 For the 'philosophical' reading of *Aeneid* 6, see what Servius has to say about this precise passage, *ad Aen.* 721: 'AD CAELUM HINC IRE PUTANDUM EST miscet philosophiae figmenta poetica et ostendit tam quod est vulgare, quam quod continent veritas et ratio naturalis.' (*From here one should think they go to heaven:* the author mixes poetic fictions with philosophy and includes both what is popular and what falls within the confines of truth and natural reason). For the Dantean tag, see *Ep.* 13.8.
41 The Manichean (and perhaps also Platonic) bias against corporeality is absent from Christian doctrine because the notion of resurrection entails that human bodies will be utterly changed at the end of time: the flesh will not be flesh anymore. Augustine develops this argument elsewhere (*Contra Adimantum* 12.5), basing it on the authority of 1 Cor. 15:51–8, incidentally the same text in which we find the expression 'in novissima tuba canet' (the last trumpet will sound, 52).
42 Dante had even offered a somewhat idiosyncratic argument proving the necessity of the resurrection of the flesh in the coda of *Paradiso* 7.145–8. For Dante's only limited dependence on theological antecedents in his reasoning, see Chiavacci Leonardi's commentary *ad loc.*
43 On the Augustinian resonance, via *Inferno* 5, contained in the tag 'il punto che mi vinse,' see most recently Moevs 2005, 156–8. For the failure of hermeneutics that is evoked and redressed in this context, see Mazzotta 1979, 163–70, and Freccero 1986, 152–66.

Works Cited

Abbreviations

ED = *Enciclopedia Dantesca* (Roma: Istituto dell'Enciclopedia Italiana, 1970–8), 6 vols.
All commentaries to Dante's poem are consulted through and cited from the Dartmouth Dante Project (see http://dante.dartmouth.edu/).

Primary Works

DANTE

La Commedia secondo l'antica vulgata. Ed. Giorgio Petrocchi. Florence: Le Lettere, 1994.
– *The Inferno, Purgatorio, Paradiso.* Trans. Robert and Jean Hollander. New York: Doubleday, 2001–7.
Convivio. Ed. C. Vasoli and D. De Robertis, in *Opere Minori* 1, ii. Milan-Naples: Ricciardi, 1988.
– *Il Convivio (The Banquet). Translation with introduction and notes, and Italian verse text*. Trans. Richard Lansing. New York: Garland, 1990.
Epistola a Cangrande. Ed. E. Cecchini. Florence: Giunti, 1995. [Translations in the present work are the author's.]
Monarchia. Ed. B. Nardi. Milan-Naples: Ricciardi, 1979.
– Dante, *Monarchia*. Ed. and trans. P. Shaw. Cambridge, UK: Cambridge University Press, 1995.
– Dante's *Monarchia*. Ed. and trans. R. Kay. Toronto: Pontifical Institute of Mediaeval Studies, 1998.
Rime. Ed. G. Contini. 2nd ed. Turin: Einaudi 1946.

Vita nuova. Ed. D. De Robertis. Milan-Naples: Ricciardi, 1980.
– *Vita nuova*. Trans. Mark Musa. Oxford: Oxford University Press, 1992.
De vulgari eloquentia. Ed. P.V. Mengaldo, in *Opere Minori* 2. Milan, Naples: Ricciardi, 1979.
– *De vulgari eloquentia*. Ed. and trans. S. Botterill. Cambridge: Cambridge University Press, 1996.

AUGUSTINE

The City of God against the Pagans. Trans. R.W. Dyson. Cambridge: Cambridge University Press, 1998.
Confessions. Trans. H. Chadwick. Oxford: Oxford University Press, 1991.
Confessions. Text and commentary by James J. O'Donnell. 3 vols. New York: Oxford University Press, 1992.
L'istruzione cristiana. Ed. M. Simonetti. Milan: Mondadori 1994.
– *On Christian Doctrine*. Trans. D.W. Robertson, Jr. London, New York: Macmillan Publishing Co., Collier Macmillan Publishers, 1958.

FURTHER PRIMARY SOURCES

Bembo, Pietro. *Prose della volgare lingua*. Ed. C. Dionisotti. Turin: UTET, 1960.
Bene Florentini Candelabrum. Ed. G.C. Alessio. Padua: Antenore, 1983.
Boccaccio, Giovanni. *Esposizioni sopra la Comedia*. Ed. G. Padoan. Milan: Mondadori, 1965.
Cicero, M. Tullius. *De officiis*. Ed. M. Winterbottom. Oxford: Clarendon Press, 1994.
Fulgentius, Fabius Planciades. *Expositio Virgilianae continentiae secundum philosophos moralis*. In R. Helm, ed., *Fabii Planciadis Fulgentii V. C. Opera*, 81–107. Leipzig: Teubner, 1898.
– 'The Exposition of the Content of Virgil.' In *Fulgentius the Mythographer*, trans. L.G. Whitbread, 119–53. Columbus: Ohio State University Press, 1971.
Isidori Hispalensis Episcopi. *Etymologiarum sive originum libri XX*. Ed. W.M. Lindsay. Oxford: Clarendon Press, 1911.
Lucanus, M. Annaeus. *De bello civili libri X*. Ed. D.R. Shackleton Bailey. Leipzig: Teubner, 1997.
– Lucan, *The Civil War*. Trans. M. Fox. London: Penguin, 2009.
– *M. Annaei Lucani Commenta Bernensia*. Ed. H. Usener. Leipzig: Teubner, 1896.
Machiavelli, Niccolò. *Discorso ovver Dialogo circa la lingua fiorentina*. Ed. B.T. Sozzi. Turin: Einaudi, 1976.
Honoratus, Maurus Servius. *Servii Grammatici qui feruntur in Vergilii carmina*

commentarii. Ed. Georgius Thilo and Hermannus Hagen. Leipzig: Teubner, 1881.

Critical Studies

Agamben, G. 1999. *The End of the Poem: Studies in Poetics.* Trans. D. Heller-Roazen. Stanford, CA: Stanford University Press.
Ahern, J. 1982. 'Binding the Book: Hermeneutics and Manuscript Productions in *Paradiso* XXXIII.' *PMLA* 97.5: 800–9.
Ahl, F. 1993. 'Form Empowered: Lucan's *Pharsalia.*' In *Roman epic,* ed. A.J. Boyle, 125–42. London and New York: Routledge.
Alessio, G.C. 1984. 'La grammatica speculativa e Dante.' *Letture Classensi* 13: 69–88.
Ando, C. 1994. 'Augustine on Language.' *Revue des Études Augustiniennes* 40: 45–78.
Armour, P. 1983 'Dante's Brunetto: The Paternal Paterine?' *Italian Studies* 38: 1–38.
– 1989. *Dante's Griffin and the History of the World: A Study of the Earthly Paradise.* Oxford: Oxford University Press.
Ascoli, A.R. 1989. 'The Vowels of Authority (Dante's *Convivio* IV.vi, 3–4).' In *Discourses of Authority in Medieval and Renaissance Literature,* ed. K. Brownlee and W. Stephens, 23–46. Hanover and London: University Press of New England.
– 1990. '"Neminem ante nos": Historicity and Authority in the *De vulgari eloquentia.*' *Annali d'Italianistica* 8: 186–231.
– 1993. 'The Unfinished Author: Dante's Rhetoric of Authority in *Convivio* and *De vulgari eloquentia.*' In *The Cambridge Companion to Dante,* ed. R. Jacoff, 45–66. Cambridge: Cambridge University Press.
– 1995. 'Palinode and History in the *Oeuvre* of Dante.' In *Dante Now,* ed. T.J. Cachey, 155–87. Notre Dame, IN: University of Notre Dame Press.
– 2008. *Dante and the Making of a Modern Author.* Cambridge: Cambridge University Press.
Auerbach, E. 1965. 'Sermo humilis.' In *Literary Language and Its Public in Late Latin Antiquity and in the Middle Ages,* 2nd ed., trans. R. Manheim, 27–66. Princeton: Princeton University Press.
Azzetta, L. 2003. 'Le chiose alla *Commedia* di Andrea Lancia, l'*Epistola a Cangrande* e altre questioni dantesche.' *L'Alighieri. Rassegna dantesca* 44: 5–76.
Baghramian, M., ed. 1988. *Modern Philosophy of Language.* London: J.M. Dent.
Barański, Z.G. 1987. 'La lezione esegetica di *Inferno* I: Allegoria, storia e lette-

ratura nella *Commedia.*' In *Dante e le forme dell'allegoresi,* ed. M. Picone, 79–97. Ravenna: Longo.
- 1994. 'Dante commentatore e Commentato: Riflessioni sullo studio dell'*iter* ideologico di Dante.' *Letture Classensi* 23: 135–58.
- 1995a. '"Tres enim sunt manerie dicendi ...": Some Observations on Medieval Literature, "Genre," and Dante.' In '"Libri poetarum in quattuor species dividuntur": Essays on Dante and "Genre,"' ed. Z.G. Barański. *The Italianist* Supplement 2.15: 9–60.
- 1995b. 'Dante's Signs: An Introduction to Medieval Semiotics and Dante.' In *Dante and the Middle Ages: Literary and Historical Essays,* ed. J.C. Barnes and C. Ó Cuilleanáin, 139–80. Dublin: Irish Academic Press.
- 1996. *'Sole nuovo, luce nuova': Saggi sul rinnovamento culturale in Dante.* Turin: Scriptorium.
- 1998. *''Nfiata labbia* and *Dolce stil novo*: A Note on Dante, Ethics, and the Technical Vocabulary of Literature.' In *Sotto il segno di Dante: Scritti in onore di Francesco Mazzoni,* ed. L. Coglievina and D. De Robertis, 17–35. Florence: Le Lettere.
- 2000. *Dante e i segni.* Naples: Liguori.
- 2001a. 'L'esegesi medievale della *Commedia* e il problema delle fonti.' In *'Chiosar con altro testo': Leggere Dante nel Trecento,* 13–39. Fiesole: Cadmo.
- 2001b. 'Three Notes on Dante and Horace.' *Reading Medieval Studies* 27: 5–37.
- 2004. 'Il *Convivio* e la poesia: Problemi di definizione.' In *Contesti della 'Commedia,'* ed. F. Tateo and D.M. Pegorari, 9–64. Bari: Palomar.
- 2005a. 'Dante Alighieri: Experimentation and (Self-)Exegesis.' In Minnis and Johnson 2005, 561–82.
- 2005b. 'The *Epistle to Cangrande.*' In Minnis and Johnson 2005, 583–9.
Barblan. G., ed. 1988. *Dante e la Bibbia: Atti del Convegno Internazionale promosso da 'Biblia.'* Florence: Olschki.
Barchiesi, A. 2001. *Speaking Volumes: Narrative and Intertext in Ovid and Other Latin Poets.* London: Duckworth.
Barolini, T. 1984. *Dante's Poets: Textuality and Truth in the 'Comedy.'* Princeton: Princeton University Press.
- 1989. 'True and False See-ers in *Inferno* XX.' *Lectura Dantis* 4: 42–54.
- 1992. *The Undivine Comedy: Detheologizing Dante.* Princeton: Princeton University Press.
- 2006. '*Cominciandomi dal principio infino a la fine*: Forging Anti-Narrative in Dante's *Vita Nuova.*' In *Dante and the Origins of Italian Literary Culture,* 175–92. New York: Fordham University Press.

– 2009. *Commentary to* Dante Alighieri, *Rime giovanili e della Vita nuova.* Milan: Rizzoli.
Barthes, R. 1974. *S/Z.* Trans. R. Miller. Oxford: Basil Blackwell.
Battaglia-Ricci, L. 1983. *Dante e la tradizione poetica medievale: Una proposta per la 'Commedia.'* Pisa: Giardini.
Bearsley, P. 1983. 'Augustine and Wittgenstein on Language.' *Philosophy* 58: 229–36.
Benedictis, R. De 2009. *'De vulgari eloquentia:* Dante's Semiotic Workshop.' *Italica* 86.2: 189–211.
Benjamin, W. 1996. *Selected Writings.* Ed. M. Bullock and M.W. Jennings. Cambridge, MA: Belknap Press.
Bigongiari, D. 1964. 'The Political Ideas of St. Augustine.' In *Essays on Dante and Medieval Culture,* 93–103. Florence: Olschki.
Bisson, L.M. 1992. 'Brunetto Latini as a Failed Mentor.' *Medievalia et Humanistica* 18: 1–15.
Bloom, H. 1975. *The Anxiety of Influence: A Theory of Poetry.* New York: Oxford University Press.
Bocassini, D. 2007. 'Falconry as a Transmutative Art: Dante, Frederick II, and Islam.' *Dante Studies* 125: 157–82.
Botterill, S. 1988. *'Quae non Licet Homini Loqui:* The Ineffability of Mystical Experience in *Paradiso* I and the *Epistle to Can Grande.' Modern Language Review* 38.2: 332–41.
– 1994. *Dante and the Mystical Tradition: Bernard of Clairvaux in the 'Commedia.'* Cambridge: Cambridge University Press.
Boyde, P. 1981. *Dante Philomythes and Philosopher: Man in the Cosmos.* Cambridge, UK: Cambridge University Press.
Brownlee, K. 1978. 'Dante and Narcissus (*Purg.* XXX.76–99).' *Dante Studies* 96: 201–6.
– 1991. 'Pauline Vision and Ovidian Speech in *Paradiso.'* In *The Poetry of Allusion: Virgil and Ovid in Dante's 'Commedia,'* ed. R. Jacoff and J.T. Schnapp, 202–13. Stanford, CA: Stanford University Press.
– 1993. 'Dante and the Classical Poets.' In *The Cambridge Companion to Dante,* ed. R. Jacoff, 100–19. Cambridge, UK: Cambridge University Press.
Brugnoli, G. 1969. 'Stazio in Dante.' *Cultura neolatina* 29: 117–25.
– 1995. 'Forme ovidiane in Dante.' In *Aetates Ovidianae: Lettori di Ovidio dall'Antichità al Rinascimento,* ed. I. Gallo and L. Nicastri, 239–56. Naples: ESI.
Brugnolo, F. 2000. 'Due schede per l'ornitologia poetica duecentesca (Iacopo Mostacci, Cino da Pistoia).' In *Carmina semper et citharae cordi: Études de philologie et de métriques offertes à Aldo Menichetti,* 191–9. Geneva: Slatkine.

Brunt, P.A. 1986. 'Cicero's *Officium* in the Civil War.' *Journal of Roman Studies* 76: 12–32.
Bursill-Hall, G.L. 1971. *Speculative Grammars of the Middle Ages: The Doctrine of 'Partes orationis' of the Modistae.* The Hague: Mouton.
Bynum, C.W. 1995. *The Resurrection of the Body in Western Christianity 200–1336.* New York: Columbia University Press.
Calcaterra, C. 1942. *Nella selva del Petrarca.* Bologna: Cappelli.
Caputo, R. 2003. *Il pane orzato: Saggi di lettura intorno all'opera di Dante Alighieri.* Rome: Editrice Universitaria di Roma–La Goliardica.
Carrai, S. 2006. *Dante Elegiaco: Una chiave di lettura per la 'Vita nova.'* Florence: Olschki.
Carugati, G. 1991. *Dalla menzogna al silenzio: La scrittura mistica della 'Commedia' di Dante.* Bologna: Il Mulino.
– 2002. 'Mistica, Ermeneutica, Dante.' *Modern Language Notes* (Italian issue) 117(1): 1–16.
Cassell, A.K. 1989. *Lectura Dantis Americana: 'Inferno I.'* Philadelphia: University of Pennsylvania Press.
Cestaro, G. 2003. *Dante and the Grammar of the Nursing Body.* Notre Dame, IN: University of Notre Dame Press.
Chiamenti, M. 1995. *Dante Alighieri traduttore.* Florence: Le Lettere.
Chiarenza, M.M. 1972. 'The Imageless Vision and Dante's *Paradiso.*' *Dante Studies* 90: 77–91.
Chioccioni, P. 1952. *L'agostinismo nella 'Commedia.'* Florence: Olschki.
Cioffi, C. 1989. 'St. Augustine Revisited.' *Lectura Dantis* 5: 68–80.
Cogan, M. 1999. *The Design in the Wax: The Structure of the 'Divine Comedy' and Its Meaning.* Notre Dame, IN: University of Notre Dame Press.
Colish, M. 1983. *The Mirror of Language: A Study in the Medieval Theory of Knowledge.* 2nd ed. New Haven: Yale University Press.
Comparetti, D. 1966. *Vergil in the Middle Ages* (1872). Trans. E.F.M. Benecke. Hamden: Archon Books.
Consoli, D. 1967. *Il significato del Virgilio dantesco.* Florence: Le Monnier.
Conte, G.B. 1966. 'Il proemio della *Farsalia.*' *Maia* 18: 42–53.
Contini, G. 1976. 'Dante come personaggio-poeta' (1957). In *Un'idea di Dante*, 33–62. Turin: Einaudi.
Cook, E. 1999. 'Scripture as Enigma: Biblical Allusion in Dante's Earthly Paradise.' *Dante Studies* 107: 1–20.
Corti, M. 1981. *Dante a un nuovo crocevia.* Florence: Sansoni.
– 1983. *La felicità mentale: Nuove prospettive per Cavalcanti e Dante.* Turin: Einaudi.
Courcelle, P. 1984. *Lecteurs païens et lecteurs chrétiens de l'Enéide.* Paris: Institut de France.

Cowan, B. 1982. 'Dante's "Novella Tebe."' *The Comparatist* 6: 16–23.
Cristaldi, S. 1994. *La 'Vita Nuova' e la restituzione del narrare.* Messina: Rubbettino.
Crespo, R. 1972. 'Brunetto Latini e la *Poetria Nova* di Geoffroi de Vinsauf.' *Lettere Italiane* 24: 97–9.
Curtius, E.R. 1953. *European Literature and the Latin Middle Ages.* Trans. W.R. Trask. Princeton: Princeton University Press.
Dagenais, J. 1994. *The Ethics of Reading in Manuscript Culture: Glossing the 'Libro de buen amor.'* Princeton: Princeton University Press.
D'Andrea, A. 1993. *Strutture inquiete: Premesse teoriche e verifiche storico-letterarie.* Florence: Olschki.
Davis, C.T. 1957. *Dante and the Idea of Rome.* Oxford: Clarendon Press.
– 1984. *Dante's Italy and Other Essays.* Philadelphia: University of Pennsylvania Press.
De Angelis, V. 1993. '... e l'ultimo Lucano.' In *Dante e la 'bella scola' della Poesia: Autorità e sfida poetica*, ed. A. Iannucci, 154–203. Ravenna: Longo.
Delcorno, C. 1989. *Exemplum e Letteratura: Tra Medioevo e Rinascimento.* Bologna: il Mulino.
deMan, P. 1986. 'Conclusions: Walter Benjamin's "The Task of the Translator."' In *The Resistance to Theory*, 73–105. Minneapolis: University of Minnesota Press.
De Robertis, D. 1951. 'Il libro della *Vita Nuova* e il libro del *Convivio*.' *Studi Urbinati* 25: 9–27.
– 1970. *Il libro della Vita Nuova.* 2nd ed. Florence: Sansoni.
Dewar, M. 1994. 'Laying it on with a trowel: The Proem to Lucan and Related Texts.' *Classical Quarterly* 44: 199–211.
D'Ovidio, F. 1907. *Nuovi Studi danteschi: Ugolino, Pier della Vigna, i simoniaci e discussioni varie.* Milan: Hoepli.
Dragonetti, R. 1965 'Dante et Narcisse.' *Revue des études italiennes* 11: 85–146.
– 2006. 'Dante face à Nemrod: Babel mémoire et miroir de l'Eden?' In *Dante: La langue et le poème.* Paris: Belin.
Dronke, P. 1986. *Dante and Medieval Latin Traditions.* Cambridge: Cambridge University Press.
– 1989. 'Symbolism and Structure in *Paradiso* 30.' *Romance Philology* 43: 29–48.
– 1997. *Dante's Second Love: The Originality and the Contexts of the Convivio.* Leeds: Society for Italian Studies.
Dyck, A.R. 1996. *A Commentary on Cicero, 'De Officiis.'* Ann Arbor: University of Michigan Press.
Eco, U. 1992. 'The Quest for a Perfect Language.' *Versus: Quaderni di Studi Semiotici* nos. 61–3.

- 1994. *The Search for a Perfect Language*. Oxford: Blackwell.
Eden, K. 1987. 'Hermeneutics and the Ancient Rhetorical Tradition.' *Rhetorica* 5: 59–86.
- 1990. 'The Rhetorical Tradition and Augustinian Hermeneutics in *De doctrina christiana*.' *Rhetorica* 8: 45–63.
Fallani, G. 1976. *L'Esperienza teologica di Dante*. Lecce: Milella.
Fann, K.T. 1969. *Wittgenstein's Conception of Philosophy*. Oxford: Blackwell.
Fantham, E., ed. 1992. 'Introduction' to Lucan, *De bello civili. Book II*. Cambridge, MA: Harvard University Press.
Ferrante, J. 1984. *The Political Vision of the 'Divine Comedy.'* Princeton: Princeton University Press.
Forti, F. 1977. *Magnanimitade: Studi su un tema dantesco*. Bologna: Pàtron.
Fortuna, S., and M. Gragnolati. 2010. 'Dante after Wittgenstein.' In *Dante's Plurilingualism: Authority, Knowledge, Subjectivity*, ed. S. Fortuna, M. Gragnolati, and J. Trabant.
Franke, W. 1994. 'Resurrected Tradition and Revealed Truth: Dante's Statius.' *Quaderni d'Italianistica* 15: 7–34.
- 1997. 'Reader's Application and the Moment of Truth in Dante's *Divine Comedy*.' In *Dante: Contemporary Perspectives*, ed. A.A. Iannucci, 261–80. Toronto: University of Toronto Press.
Freccero, J. 1961. 'Adam's Stand, *Purg*. XXX, 82–84.' *Romance Notes* 2: 115–18.
- 1986. *The Poetics of Conversion*. Edited and with an introduction by Rachel Jacoff. Cambridge, MA: Harvard University Press.
- 1991. 'The Eternal Image of the Father.' In *The Poetry of Allusion: Virgil and Ovid in Dante's 'Commedia,'* ed. R. Jacoff and J.T. Schnapp, 62–76. Stanford, CA: Stanford University Press.
Fumagalli, M.C. 2001. '"L'Alto Volo" and the Return to the Real.' In *The Flight of the Vernacular*, 1–18. Amsterdam: Rodopi.
Gabba, E. 1979. 'Per un'interpretazione politica del *De officiis* di Cicerone.' *Atti della Accademia Nazionale dei Lincei, Rendiconti, Classe di Scienze morali, storiche e filologiche* 34: 117–41.
Gallagher, K.T. 1982. 'Wittgenstein, Augustine, and Language,' *The New Scholasticism* 56: 426–70.
Glenn, D.C. 1999. 'Women in Limbo: Arbitrary Listings or Textual Referents? Mapping the Connection in *Inferno* 4 and *Purgatorio* 22.' *Dante Studies* 117: 85–116.
Gorni, G. 1981. *Il nodo della lingua* in *Il nodo della lingua e il verbo d'amore: Studi su Dante e altri duecentisti*. Florence: Olschki.
- 1997. 'Beatrice agli Inferi.' In *Omaggio a Beatrice (1290–1990)*, ed. R. Abardo, 143–58. Florence: Le Lettere.

Gragnolati, M. 2005. *Experiencing the Afterlife: Soul and Body in Dante and Medieval Culture.* Notre Dame, IN: University of Notre Dame Press.
– 2007. 'Nostalgia in Heaven: Embraces, Affection and Identity in the *Commedia.*' In *Dante and the Human Body: Eight Essays,* ed. J.C. Barnes and J. Petrie, 117–37. Dublin: Four Courts Press.
Grant-Fiske, Mary A., and George Converse Fiske. 1924. 'Cicero's *Orator* and Horace's *Ars Poetica.*' *Harvard Studies in Classical Philology* 35: 1–74.
Grayson, C. 1965. '*Nobilior est vulgaris*: Latin and Vernacular in Dante's Thought.' In *Centenary Essays on Dante, by the members of the Oxford Dante Society,* 54–76. Oxford: Oxford University Press.
– 1972. *Cinque saggi su Dante.* Bologna: Patron.
Grayson, J. 1992. 'In Quest of Jessie Weston.' *Arthurian Literature* 11: 1–80.
Grlic, O. 1995. 'Dante's Statius and Augustine: Intertextuality in Conversionary Narrative.' *Medievalia et Humanistica* 21: 73–84.
Groppi, F. 1962. *Dante traduttore.* 2nd ed. Rome: Herder.
Hagedorn, S.C. 1997. 'A Statian Model for Dante's Ulysses.' *Dante Studies* 115: 19–43.
Hardie, P. 1993. *The Epic Successors of Virgil: A Study in the Dynamics of a Tradition.* Cambridge, UK: Cambridge University Press.
Harrison, R.P. 1988. *The Body of Beatrice.* Baltimore: Johns Hopkins University Press.
Harwood-Gordon, S. 1991. *A Study of the Theology and Imagery of Dante's 'Divina Commedia': Sensory Perception, Reason and Free Will.* Lewiston, NY: Edwin Mellen Press.
Hawkins, P.S. 1999. *Dante's Testaments: Essays in Scriptural Imagination.* Stanford, CA: Stanford University Press.
Heilbronn, D. 1977. 'The Prophetic Role of Statius in Dante's Purgatory.' *Dante Studies* 115: 53–67.
– 1978. '"Io pur sorrisi": Dante's Lesson on the Passions (*Purg.* XXI, 94–136).' *Dante Studies* 116: 67–74.
Higgins, D. 1992, *Dante and the Bible: An introduction.* Bristol, UK: University of Bristol Press.
Hinds, S. 1988. 'Generalizing about Ovid.' In *The Imperial Muse: Ramus Essays on Roman Literature of the Empire, to Juvenal through Ovid,* ed. A.J. Boyle. Berwick, UK: Victoria.
Hollander, R. 1969. *Allegory in Dante's 'Commedia.'* Princeton: Princeton University Press.
– 1973. 'Dante's Use of the Fiftieth Psalm (A Note on *Purg.* XXX, 84).' *Dante Studies* 91: 145–50.

- 1975. 'Purgatorio II: Cato's Rebuke and Dante's scoglio.' Italica 52: 348–63.
- 1976. 'Dante Theologus-Poeta.' Dante Studies 94: 93–136.
- 1980. Studies in Dante. Ravenna: Longo.
- 1983. Il Virgilio dantesco. Florence: Olschki.
- 1988. 'Paradiso XXX.' Studi Danteschi 60: 1–33.
- 1992. Dante and Paul's 'Five Words with Understanding.' Occasional Papers, no. 1, Medieval and Renaissance Texts and Studies. Binghamton, NY: Center for Medieval and Early Renaissance Texts and Studies.
- 1993a. Dante's Epistle to Cangrande. Ann Arbor: University of Michigan Press.
- 1993b. 'Le opere di Virgilio nella Commedia.' In Dante e la 'bella scola' della poesia: Autorità e sfida poetica, ed. A.A. Iannucci, 247–343. Ravenna: Longo.
- 1999. 'Dante as Uzzah? (Purg. X 57 and Epistle XI 9–12).' In Sotto il segno di Dante: Scritti in onore di Francesco Mazzoni, ed. L. Coglievina and D. De Robertis, 143–51. Florence: Le Lettere.

Hollander, R., and A.L. Rossi. 1986. 'Dante's Republican Treasury.' Dante Studies 104: 59–82.

Holmes, O. 2008. Dante's Two Beloveds: Ethics as Erotic Choice. New Haven: Yale University Press.

Houston, J. 2010. Building a Monument to Dante: Boccaccio as Dantista. Toronto: University of Toronto Press.

Hult, D. 1986. Self-fulfilling Prophecies: Readership and Authority in the First 'Roman de la Rose.' Cambridge: Cambridge University Press.

Iannucci, A.A. 1995. 'Paradiso XXXI.' In 'Divine Comedy,' Introductory Readings III: 'Paradiso,' ed. T. Wlassics, 470–85. Lectura Dantis Virginiana 16–17. Charlottesville: University of Virginia.
- 1997. 'The Mountainquake of Purgatorio and Virgil's Story.' Lectura Dantis 20–21: 48–58.

Iliescu N. 1971. 'Gli episodi degli abbracci nelle strutture del Purgatorio.' Yearbook of Italian Studies 1: 53–63.

Iser, W. 1978. The Act of Reading: A Theory of Aesthetic Response. Baltimore: Johns Hopkins University Press.

Jacoff, R. 1988. 'Transgression and Transcendence: Figures of Female Desire in Dante's Commedia.' Romanic Review 79: 129–42.
- 1991. 'Intertextualities in Arcadia.' In The Poetry of Allusion, ed. R. Jacoff and J.T. Schnapp, 131–44. Stanford, CA: Stanford University Press.

Jacoff, R., and J.T. Schnapp. 1991. The Poetry of Allusion: Virgil and Ovid in Dante's 'Commedia.' Stanford, CA: Stanford University Press.

Jacomuzzi, A. 1972. Il palinsesto della Retorica e altri saggi danteschi. Florence: Olschki.

Kaster, R. 1978. 'Servius and *idonei auctores.' American Journal of Philology* 99: 181–209.
Kelly, D. 1997. 'The *Fidus interpres*: Aid or Impediment to Medieval Translation and *Translatio*?' In *Translation Theory and Practice in the Middle Ages*, ed. J. Beer, 47–58. Kalamazoo: Western Michigan University.
Kelly, L.G. 1997. 'Medieval Psalm Translation and Literality.' In *Translation Theory and Practice in the Middle Ages*, ed. J. Beer, 161–72. Kalamazoo: Western Michigan University.
Kirwan, C. 2001. 'Augustine's Philosophy of Language.' In *The Cambridge Companion to Augustine*, ed. E. Stump and N. Kretzman, 186–204. Cambridge, UK: Cambridge University Press.
Kleinhenz, C. 1988. 'Virgil, Statius, and Dante: An Unusual Trinity.' In *Lectura Dantis Newberryana*, ed. P. Cherchi and A.C. Mastrobuono, 1: 37–55. Evanston: Northwestern University Press.
– 1995. '*Paradiso* XXX.' In *'Divine Comedy,' Introductory Readings III: 'Paradiso,'* ed. T. Wlassics, 456–69. *Lectura Dantis virginiana* 16–17. Charlottesville. University of Virginia.
– 1997. 'Dante and the Bible: Biblical Citation in the *Divine Comedy*.' In *Dante: Contemporary perspectives*, ed. A. Iannucci, 74–93. Toronto: University of Toronto Press.
– 2007. 'Perspectives on Intertextuality in Dante's *Divina Commedia*.' *Romance Quarterly* 54(3): 183–94.
Lansing, R. 1977. *From Image to Idea: A Study of the Simile in Dante's 'Commedia.'* Ravenna: Longo.
Lazzerini, L. 1996. 'Bonagiunta, il nodo e la vista recuperata.' In *Operosa parva per Gianni Antonini*, ed. D. De Robertis and F. Gavazzeni, 48–54. Verona: Valdonega.
Ledda, G. 2002. *La guerra della lingua: Ineffabilità, retorica e narrativa nella 'Commedia' di Dante*. Ravenna: Longo.
Levenstein, J. 1996. 'The Pilgrim, the Poet, and the Cowgirl: Dante's Alter-*Io* in *Purgatorio* XXX–XXXI.' *Dante Studies* 114: 189–208.
Lewis, C.S. 1956. 'Dante's Statius.' *Medium Aevum* 25: 133–9.
Lombardi, E. 2007. *The Syntax of Desire: Language and Love in Augustine, the Modistae, Dante*. Toronto: University of Toronto Press.
– Forthcoming. 'Augustine and Dante.' In *Reviewing Dante's Theology*, ed. M. Trehorne and C. Honess.
Longen, E.M. 1975. 'The Grammar of Apotheosis: *Paradiso* XXX, 94–99.' *Dante Studies* 93: 209–14.
Manetti, G. 1987. *Le teorie del segno nell'antichità classica*. Milan: Bompiani.

Marchesi, S. 2001a. 'Dante's Vertical Utopia: *Aulicum* and *Curiale* in the *De vulgari eloquentia*.' In *Utopianism/Literary Utopias and National Cultural Identities: A Comparative Perspective*, ed. P. Spinozzi, 311–16. Bologna: Cotepra–University of Bologna.
- 2001b. 'La rilettura del *De officiis* e i due tempi della composizione del *Convivio*.' *Giornale Storico della Letteratura Italiana* 178: 84–107.
- 2002. 'Dante, Virgilio (e Agostino) di fronte ai sette candelabri. *Purgatorio* 29.43.' *Electronic Bulletin of the Dante Society of America*. Available at http://www.princeton.edu/~dante/ebdsa.
- 2004. *Stratigrafie decameroniane*. Florence: Olschki.
- 2010. 'Ermeneutica del "segno," ermeneutica della storia.' In *Esperimenti Danteschi – Paradiso 2010*, ed. T. Montorfano, 61–86. Milan: Marietti.
- Forthcoming, 2011. 'Lucan at Last: the Lesson of the *Bellum civile* in Dante's *Divine Comedy*.' In *The Brill Companion to Lucan*, ed. P. Asso. Leiden: Brill.

Marigo, A. 1968. *Introduzione Commento* to Dante Alighieri, *De vulgari eloquentia*. 2nd ed. Florence: Le Monnier.

Markus, R.A. 1957. 'St. Augustine on Signs.' *Phronesis* 2: 60–83.

Marsili, A. 1986. *Lucano e Dante*. Lucca: Pacini Fazzi.

Martinez, R.L. 1983. 'The Pilgrim's Answer to Bonagiunta and the Poetics of the Spirit.' *Stanford Italian Review* 3: 37–63.
- 1995. 'Dante and the Two Canons: Statius in Virgil's Footsteps (*Purgatorio* 21–30).' *Comparative Literature Studies* 32: 151–75.

Masciandaro, F. 1972. '*Inferno* I–II: Il dramma della conversione e il tempo.' *Studi Danteschi* 49: 1–26.

Mazzocco, A. 1993. *Linguistic Theories in Dante and the Humanists: Studies of Language and Intellectual History in Late Medieval and Early Renaissance Italy*. Leiden: Brill.

Mazzoni, F. 1960. 'Il canto XXXI del *Purgatorio*.' In *Lectura Dantis Scaligera*, 2: *Il Purgatorio*, 1139–84. Florence: Le Monnier.
- 1965. 'Saggio di un nuovo commento alla *Divina Commedia*: Il canto IV dell'*Inferno*.' *Studi Danteschi* 42: 29–206.
- 1967. *Saggio di un nuovo commento alla 'Divina Commedia': 'Inferno' – Canti I–III*. Florence: Sansoni.
- 1997. *Il 'trascendentale' dimenticato*. In *Omaggio a Beatrice (1290–1990)*, ed. R. Abardo, 93–132. Florence: Le Lettere.

Mazzotta, G. 1972. 'Dante's Literary Typology.' *Modern Language Notes* 87: 1–19.
- 1979. *Dante Poet of the Desert: History and Allegory in the 'Divine Comedy'*. Princeton: Princeton University Press.

- 1993. *Dante's Vision and the Circle of Knowledge.* Princeton: Princeton University Press.
- 2005. '*Inferno*: The Language of Fraud in Lower Hell.' In *Patterns in Dante: Nine Literary Essays.* ed. C. Ó Cuilleanáin and J. Petrie, 169–87. Dublin: Foundation for Italian Studies.

McCormack, S. 1998. *The Shadows of Poetry: Virgil in the Mind of Augustine.* Berkeley: University of California Press.

Mengaldo, P.V. 1968. Introduction to Dante Alighieri, *De vulgari eloquentia.* Padua: Antenore.

- 1978. *Linguistica e retorica di Dante.* Pisa: Nistri Lischi.

Merleau-Ponty, M. 1964. 'An Unpublished Text by Maurice Merleau-Ponty: A Prospectus of His Work.' Trans. A.B. Dallery. In *The Primacy of Perception,* ed. J.M. Edie. Evanston: Northwestern University Press.

Miller Ortiz, J. 1986. 'The Two Faces of Dido: Classical Images and Medieval Interpretations.' *Romance Quarterly* 33: 421–30.

Minnis, A. 1988. *Medieval Theory of Authorship: Scholastic Literary Attitudes in the Later Middle Ages.* Philadelphia: University of Pennsylvania Press.

Minnis, A., and I. Johnson. 2005. *The Cambridge History of Literary Criticism.* Vol. 2. Cambridge: Cambridge University Press.

Minnis, A., and A.B. Scott. 1991. *Medieval Literary Theory and Criticism, circa 1100–1375.* 2nd ed. Oxford: Clarendon Press.

Moevs, C. 2005. *The Metaphysics of Dante's 'Comedy.'* Oxford: Oxford University Press.

Moore, E. 1896. *Studies in Dante, First Series: Scripture and Classical Authors in Dante.* Oxford: Clarendon Press.

Moretti, G. 1995. *Acutum dicendi genus: Brevità, oscurità, sottigliezze e paradossi nelle tradizioni retoriche degli Stoici.* Trento: Dipartimento di scienze filologiche e storiche.

Muresu, G. 1979. *Dante politico: Individuo e istituzioni nell'autunno del medioevo.* Turin: Paravia.

Murphy, J.J. 1974. *Rhetoric in the Middle Ages.* Berkeley: University of California Press.

Musa M. 1966. 'Le ali di Dante (e il Dolce Stil Novo): *Purgatorio* XXIV.' *Convivium* 34: 361–7.

Nardi, B. 1960. *Dal 'Convivio' alla 'Commedia.'* Rome: Istituto Storico Italiano per il Medio Evo.

- 1961. 'Osservazioni sul medievale *accessus ad auctores* in rapporto all'epistola a Cangrande,' in *Studi e problemi di critica testuale: Convegno di Studi di Filologia Italiana,* 272–305. Bologna: Commissione per i testi di lingua.
- 1967. *Saggi di filosofia dantesca.* Florence: La Nuova Italia. Second edition.

Nasti, P. 2007. *Favole d'amore e 'saver profondo': La tradizione salomonica in Dante*. Ravenna: Longo.

Negri, L. 1925. 'Dante e il testo della *Vulgata*.' *Giornale Storico della Letteratura Italiana* 85: 288–306.

Nohrnberg, J.C. 1996. 'The Descent of Geryon: The Moral System of *Inferno* XVI–XXXI.' *Dante Studies* 114: 129–87.

O'Donnell, J.J. 1983. Unpublished Introduction to Augustine's 'City of God.' Available at http://www9.georgetown.edu/faculty/jod/augustine/civ.html.

Padoan, G. 1959. 'Il mito di Teseo e il cristianesimo di Stazio.' *Lettere Italiane* 11: 432–57.

– 1970. 'Il canto XXI del *Purgatorio*.' In *Nuove letture dantesche*, 2: 183–204. 3 vols. Florence: Le Monnier.

Pagani, I. 1982. *La teoria linguistica di Dante*. Naples: Liguori.

Paparelli, G. 1960. '*Fictio*: La definizione dantesca della poesia.' *Filologia Romanza* 7: 1–83.

Paratore, E. 1968. *Tradizione e struttura in Dante*. Florence: Sansoni.

Parodi, E.G. 1915. Recensione a 'F. Flamini, *Le opere di Dante Alighieri* (Livorno: Giusti, 1910).' *Bullettino della Società dantesca italiana* 22: 265–9.

Pease, A., ed. 1935. *Publi Vergili Maronis Aeneidos: Liber Quartus*. Cambridge: Harvard University Press.

Pertile, L. 1993a. 'Dante's *Comedy* beyond the *Stilnovo*.' *Lectura Dantis* 13: 47–77.

– 1993b. 'Il nodo di Bonagiunta, le penne di Dante e il Dolce Stil Novo.' *Lettere Italiane* 46: 44–75.

– 1998. *La puttana e il gigante*. Ravenna: Longo.

Petrocchi, G. 1997. *Vita di Dante*. Bari: Laterza.

Pézard, A. 1952. 'Rencontres de Dante et de Stace.' *Bibliothèque d'Humanisme et Renaissance* 14: 10–28.

Picone, M. 1977. 'Dante e il Mito di Narciso: Dal *Roman de la Rose* alla *Commedia*.' *Romanische Forschungen* 89: 382–97.

– 1992. 'La *Lectio Ovidii* nella *Commedia*: La ricezione dantesca delle *Metamorfosi*.' *Le forme e la storia* 4: 35–52.

– 1993a. 'Dante e il canone degli *auctores*.' *Rassegna Europea di Letteratura Italiana* 1: 9–26.

– 1993b. 'L'Ovidio di Dante.' In *Dante e la 'bella scola' della poesia*, ed. A.A. Iannucci, 107–44. Ravenna: Longo.

– 1994. 'Intertestualità dantesca: La riscrittura di Ovidio.' *Nuova secondaria* 11: 22–66.

– 2005. 'La teoria dell' "*auctoritas*" della "Vita nova."' *Tenzone* 6: 173–91.

Press, G.A. 1980. 'The Subject and Structure of Augustine's *De doctrina christiana*.' *Augustinian Studies* 11: 99–124.
– 1981. 'The Content and Argument of Augustine's *De doctrina christiana*.' *Augustiniana* 31: 165–82.
– 1984. '*Doctrina* in Augustine's *De doctrina christiana*.' *Philosophy and Rhetoric* 17: 98–115.
Raimondi, E. 1977. *Metafora e Storia: Studi su Dante e Petrarca*. 2nd ed. Turin: Einaudi.
Renucci, P. 1954. *Dante disciple et juge du monde gréco-latin*. Paris: Les Belles Lettres.
Rigo, P. 1994. *Memoria classica e memoria biblica in Dante*. Florence: Olschki.
Ronconi, A. 1958. *Interpretazioni grammaticali*. Padua: Liviana.
Rossi, A. 1981. '*A l'ultimo suo*: *Paradiso* XXX and Its Virgilian Context.' *Studies in Medieval and Renaissance History* 4: 39–88.
– 1985. '*Miro gurge (Par*. XXX, 68): Virgilian Language and Textual Pattern in the River of Light.' *Dante Studies* 103.
– 1989. 'The Poetics of Resurrection: Virgil's Bees (*Paradiso* XXXI, 1–12).' *Romanic Review* 80: 305–24.
Rossi, L.C. 1993. 'Prospezioni filologiche per lo Stazio di Dante.' In *Dante e la 'bella scola' della poesia: Autorità e sfida poetica*, ed. A.A. Iannucci, 205–24. Ravenna: Longo.
Rostagno, E. 1925. 'Dante e il testo della *Vulgata*.' *Studi Danteschi* 10: 122–7.
Ruff, N. 1994. '*Regina, Meretrix*, and *Libido*: The Medieval and Renaissance Dido.' In *Acta Conventus Neo-Latini Hafniensis*, 875–81. Binghamton, NY: Medieval & Renaissance Texts and Studies.
Ryan, C.J. 1982. 'Virgil's Wisdom in the *Divine Comedy*.' *Medievalia et Humanistica* 11: 1–38.
Sarteschi, S. 2002. *Per la 'Comedìa' e non per essa soltanto*. Rome: Bulzoni.
Scarano, T. 2001. *Postfazione* to J.L. Borges, *Nove saggi danteschi*, 159–76. Milan: Adelphi.
Schildgen, B.D. 2001. 'Dante's Utopian Political Vision, the Roman Empire, and the Salvation of Pagans.' *Annali d'Italianistica* 19: 51–69.
Schnapp, J.T. 1997. 'Lucanian Estimations.' In *Seminario Dantesco Internazionale / International Dante Seminar 1: Atti del primo convegno tenutosi al Chauncey Conference Center (Princeton, 21–23 October 1994)*, ed. Z.G. Barański, 111–34. Florence: Le Lettere.
Scott, J.A. 1965. 'Dante's "Sweet New Style" and the *Vita Nuova*.' *Italica* 42: 98–107.
– 1977. '*Paradiso* XXX.' In *Dante Commentaries*, ed. D. Nolan, 159–80. Dublin: Irish Academic Press.

- 1979. 'Dante's Francesca and the Poet's Attitude towards Courtly Literature.' *Reading Medieval Studies* 5: 4–20.
- 1983. '*Monarchia* III, iv, 10.' In *Miscellanea di Studi in onore di Vittore Branca: Dal Medioevo al Petrarca*, 185–92. Florence: Olschki.
- 1995. 'Dante's *Convivio* as Pathway to the *Comedy*.' *Dante Studies* 113: 31–56.
- 1996a. 'Dante's Miraculous Mountainquake.' *Electronic Bulletin of the Dante Society*. Available at http://www.princeton.edu/~dante/ebdsa/js.html.
- 1996b. *Dante's Political Purgatory*. Philadelphia: University of Pennsylvania Press.

Scrivano, R. 1992. 'Stazio personaggio, poeta e cristiano.' *Quaderni d'Italianistica* 13: 2175–97.

Sebastio, L. 1993. 'Lettura di una rima dantesca: *Se Lippo amico se' tu che mi leggi*.' In *Dante in Lettura*, ed. G. De Matteis, 171–94. Ravenna: Longo.

Shapiro, M. 1982. '*Purgatorio* XXX: Arnaut at the Summit.' *Dante Studies* 100: 71–6.

- 1990. '*De vulgari eloquentia*': *Dante's Book of Exile*. Lincoln: University of Nebraska Press.

Shaw, P. 1981. '*Paradiso* XXX.' In *Cambridge Readings in Dante's 'Comedy*.' Ed. K. Foster and P. Boyde, 191–213. Cambridge: Cambridge University Press.

Shoaf, R.A. 1978. '*Auri sacra fames* and the Age of Gold (*Purg.* XXII, 40–41 and 148–150).' *Dante Studies* 92: 195–9.

Singleton, C.S. 1958. *Dante Studies 2: Journey to Beatrice*. Cambridge, MA: Harvard University Press.

- 1977. *Dante's 'Commedia': Elements of Structure*. 2nd ed. Baltimore, London: Johns Hopkins University Press.

Sowell M.U., ed. 1991. *Dante and Ovid: Essay in Intertextuality*. Binghamton, NY: Medieval and Renaissance Texts and Studies.

Spiegelberg, H. 1979. 'Augustine in Wittgenstein: A Case Study in Philosophical Stimulation.' *Journal of the History of Philosophy* 17: 319–27.

Spitzer, L. 1959. 'Speech and Language in *Inf.* XIII.' *Romanische Literaturstudien 1936–1956*. Tübingen: Max Niemeyer Verlag.

Stefanini, R. 1991. '*Purgatorio* XXX.' *Lectura Dantis Virginiana* 9: 90–104.

Steinberg, J. 2006. *Accounting for Dante: Urban Readers and Writers in Late Medieval Italy*. Notre Dame, IN: University of Notre Dame Press.

Steiner, G. 1975 *After Babel: Aspects of Language and Translation*. Oxford: Oxford University Press.

Stephany, W.A. 1983. 'Biblical Allusions to Conversion in *Purgatorio* XXI.' *Stanford Italian Review* 3: 141–62.

Stillinger, T.C. 1992. *The Song of Troilus: Lyric Authority in the Medieval Book*. Philadelphia: University of Pennsylvania Press.

Stock, B.1996. *Augustine the Reader: Meditation, Self-Knowledge, and the Ethics of Interpretation.* Cambridge, MA, and London: Belknap Press.
– 2001. *After Augustine: The Meditative Reader and the Text.* Philadelphia: University of Pennsylvania Press.
Stone, G.B. 1994. 'Dante's Averroistic Hermeneutics (On "Meaning" in the *Vita Nuova*).' *Dante Studies* 112: 133–59.
Storey, H.W. 1989. 'The Other Sword of *Purgatorio* XXX.' *Dante Studies* 107: 85–99.
Stull, W., and R. Hollander. 1991. 'The Lucanian Source of Dante's Ulysses.' *Studi Danteschi* 63: 1–52.
Tavoni, M. 2010. 'Volgare e latino nella storia di Dante.' In *Dante's Plurilingualism: Authority, Knowledge, Subjectivity*, ed. S. Fortuna, M. Gragnolati, and J. Trabant, 52–68. London: Legenda.
Thompson, D. 1978. 'Dante's Virtuous Romans.' *Dante Studies* 96: 145–62.
Took, J. 1990. 'Dante and the *Confessions* of Augustine.' *Annali d'Italianistica* 8: 360–82.
Tracy, D.W. 1990. 'Charity, Obscurity, Clarity: Augustine's Search for a True Rhetoric.' In *Morphologies of Faith*, ed. M. Gerhart and Anthony C. Yu, 123–43. Atlanta: Scholars Press.
Trone, G.A. 1995. 'The Cry of Dereliction in Purgatorio XXIII.' *Dante Studies* 113: 111–29.
Ussani, V. 1903. 'Il testo lucaneo e gli scolii bernensi.' *Studi italiani di Filologia Classica* 11: 46–51.
Vecchi, G. 1958. 'Temi e momenti d'arte dettatoria nel *Candelabrum* di Bene da Firenze.' *Atti e memorie della Deputazione di Storia Patria per le Province di Romagna* 10: 113–68.
Vecchio, S. 1994. *Le parole come segni: Introduzione alla linguistica agostiniana.* Palermo: Novecento.
Vinay, G. 1959. 'Ricerche sul *De vulgari eloquentia* I e II.' *Giornale storico della letteratura italiana* 136: 237–74 and 367–88.
Warner, L. 1995. 'The Dark Wood and the Dark Word in Dante's *Commedia*.' *Comparative Literature Studies* 32: 449–78.
Watson, G. 1982. 'St. Augustine's Theory of Language.' *The Maynooth Review* 6(2): 4–20.
Weiss, R. 1942. 'Links between the *Convivio* and the *De vulgari eloquentia*.' *Modern Language Review* 37: 156–68.
Weithman, P. 2001. 'Augustine's Political Philosophy.' In *The Cambridge Companion to Augustine*, ed. E. Stump and N. Kretzman, 234–52. Cambridge, UK: Cambridge University Press.
Wei Wei,Y. 2003. 'Embodiment in the *Commedia*: Dante's Exilic and Poetic Self-consciousness.' *Dante Studies* 121: 67–93.

Werner, S. 1994. 'On the History of the *Commenta Bernensia* and the *Adnotationes super Lucanum.*' *Harvard Studies in Classical Philology* 96: 343–68.
Wetherbee, W. 1988. 'Dante and the *Thebaid* of Statius.' In *Lectura Dantis Newberryana*, vol. 1, ed. P. Cherchi and A.C. Mastrobuono, 71–92. Evanston: Northwestern University Press.
Whitfield, J.H. 1981. 'Dante and Statius: Purgatorio XXI–XXII.' In *Dante Soundings*, ed. D. Nolan, 113–29. Dublin: Irish Academic Press.
Wingell, A.E. 1981. 'The Forested Mountaintop in Augustine and Dante.' *Dante Studies* 99: 9–48.
Wlassics, T. 1975. *Dante narratore: Saggio sullo stile della 'Commedia.'* Florence: Olschki.
Zetzel, J.E.G. 1981. *Latin Textual Criticism in Antiquity*. New York: Arno Press.
Zumthor, P. 1981. 'Intertextualité et mouvance.' *Litterature* 41: 8–16.

Index

Achilles 119
Actium 163
Adam 37, 150, 158
Aeneas 16, 18, 154–5, 157–8, 165, 180, 182, 185, 189–90, 192–3
Allegory 6–7, 14, 70–3, 75–7, 80, 84, 86–8, 109, 115–16, 131, 142, 147, 149, 169
Amore (Love, personified) 70, 114, 144–8, 152, 219n, 221n
Amos 93
Anchises 190, 192, 224n
Ando, C. 205n
Angels 17, 31–2, 41, 103, 134–5, 175, 184, 187–9, 195
Aquinas, Thomas 6, 196
Aristotle 92, 127, 159, 214n, 216n
Armour, P. 222n
Ascoli, A.R. 4, 153, 198n, 200n, 203n, 207n, 209n, 212n, 221–2n
Astraea 131, 190
Auerbach, E. 210–11n
Azzetta, L. 209n

Babel 23, 28, 39, 104–6
Barański, Z.G. xii, xiv, 4, 11, 67, 83, 88, 199n, 207n, 208n, 209n, 211n, 217n, 221n
Barchiesi, A. 223n
Barolini, T. xv, 4, 87, 197n, 199n, 205n, 207n, 214n, 216n, 217n, 220n
Barthes, R. 200n
Beatrice 11, 17, 44–5, 54, 70, 86, 103, 115, 132, 147–8, 155, 158, 175, 178–80, 182–7, 194–6
Bembo, Pietro 199n
Bene da Firenze 89–90
Benvenuto da Imola 146, 169
Bible (Scripture) xiii, 6–11, 13–15, 41, 88–95, 98–101, 103–6, 110, 133–41, 143–53, 171, 175
Bloom, H. 14, 120, 214n
Boethius 115–16, 180, 211n, 224n
Boethius of Dacia 202n
Bologna 34, 40
Bonagiunta (da Lucca) 221n, 222n
Botterill, S. 213n
Brunt, P.A. 223n
Brutus 157, 161, 164, 166, 169

Cacciaguida 52, 57
Caesar 156, 161–9, 174, 223n, 224n

Carrai, S. 208n
Carroll, J.S. 59
Casella 101–3
Cassius 166, 169
Cato 16, 102, 154, 156, 158, 162, 164–71, 173–4, 219n, 223n, 224n
Cavalcanti, Guido 44, 112
Cestaro, G. 201n, 214n, 215n
Charlemagne 158
Chiamenti, M. 216–17n
Chiavacci Leonardi, A.M. 227n
Christ 52, 55, 59, 62–3, 93, 120, 124–5, 131, 135, 142–3, 148, 155, 158, 166, 170, 175, 188–9, 205n, 206n, 208n, 223n
Church 61, 91, 106, 143, 150, 155, 221n
Cicero 94–5, 123, 162–3, 210n, 211n, 215n, 218n, 223n, 224n
Cincinnatus 157
Cocytus 47
Cogan, M. 216n
Constantine 158
Contini, G. 201n
Cornelius (consul) 217n
Corti, M. 199n, 203n, 214n
Cowan, B. 214n
Cremona 33
Cristaldi, S. 208n
Curtius, E.R. 133
Curtius (Marcus) 157

D'Andrea, A. 207n
David (as author of the Psalms) 99, 101, 103, 151
Davis, C.T. 4, 197n, 222n
Decii 157
Demons (devils) 31, 59
De Robertis, D. 113, 207n, 208n, 212n, 213n

Dido 16–17, 154, 174, 176, 179–84, 225n, 226n
Driope 129
Dronke, P. 199n, 208n, 211n

Earth 12, 21, 54, 56, 103, 135, 149, 152, 155–6, 158, 160, 167, 174, 186, 188, 190, 192–3, 195, 223n
Eden, K. 219n
Egypt 101, 142–3
Eliot, T.S. 209n
Elysian Fields 189–90, 192, 193
Empire 17, 34, 150, 155, 158–61, 163, 165–7, 169, 184, 221n, 222n
Empyrean 17, 56, 60, 185–7, 195
Ennius 123–4, 224n
Epicureanism 190–1
Eurydice 177

Fabricius 157
Fictio 7, 9, 69–70, 81–2, 86, 181–2, 198n
Florence 40, 48, 170
Forese, Donati 102
Fosca, N. 173
Freccero, J. 4, 197n, 205n, 207n, 217n, 222n, 225n, 227n
Frederick II (Emperor) 171
French (*oïl*) 24, 77, 201n
Freud, S. 67
Frontinus 99
Fulgentius 190–1, 194
Furius Camillus 157

Gabba, E. 223n
Glaucus 54
Glenn, D.C. 213n
Grayson, C. 36–7, 201n, 208n
Greek (language) 23, 28, 51, 92, 97–8, 106
Guinizzelli, Guido 34, 215n

Hannibal 158
Hawkins, P. 4, 197n, 200n, 214n, 215n
Hebrew (language) 23, 28, 98, 101, 106, 201n, 216n, 219n
Hebrus 177, 179
Hector 165
Hegel, G.W.F. 35
Hera 224n
Hero 174
History xiii, 4, 6–7, 9, 16, 29, 44–5, 80, 84–7, 104, 131, 134, 136, 143, 148, 154–60, 162–3, 165–7, 169–70, 174–5, 181–3, 208n
Hollander, R. 88, 119, 208n, 209n, 213n, 214n, 217n, 221n
Holmes, O. 226n
Holy Spirit 61, 139–40, 144, 146, 148–53
Homer 97–8
Horace xv, 36–7
Houston, J. 208n
Hugh of St Victor 219n
Hypsipyle 215n

Ineffability (topos) 43–6, 51, 53, 58–9, 61, 133
Isidore of Seville 43–4, 201n, 204n
Italian (language) 24, 32, 68, 72
Italy 32–3, 40, 164–5

Jews (Judaism) 28, 124–5, 137, 142–3, 148, 215–16n, 219n
Job 151
Judas 166, 171
Jupiter 55
Justinian 155, 158

Kelly, D. 216n
Kelly, L.G. 211n
Kleinhenz, C. 212n, 214n

Latin (*gramatica*) xv–xvi, 14, 21–30, 35–40, 42, 51, 68–9, 81–2, 96–103, 106, 111, 113, 128, 137, 175, 178
Latini, Brunetto 77
Leander 174
Lethe 103, 174, 189
Libya 170
Limbo 118–19, 128, 165–6, 170, 177
Lippo (Pasci de' Bardi) 207n
Livy 99
Lombard (vernacular) 33
Lombardi, E. 205n, 206n
Lucan 99, 155, 162–5, 169–71, 219n, 223n, 224n
Lucretia 167–8

Machiavelli, Niccolò 199n
Maenads 177
Manfredi 212n
Manichaeism 18, 134, 191–2, 194, 227n
Marc Anthony 163
Marcellus 175, 184
Markus, R.A. 205n
Mary (The Virgin) 131, 190
Matelda 174, 212n
Matthew (Evangelist) 151, 221n
Mazzoni, F. 203n, 208n, 224n
Mazzotta, G. 4, 197n, 199n, 205n, 207n, 214n, 220n, 221n, 222n, 224n, 225n, 226n, 227n
Mengaldo, P.V. 36–7, 74–5, 82, 89–90, 198n, 201n, 202n, 208n, 211n, 224n
Mercury 155
Merleau-Ponty, M. 65–6, 73
Metaphor 6, 18, 49, 51, 68–71, 73–5, 81, 83, 85, 89–90, 95–6, 102, 111–13, 116, 120, 123–4, 136, 138, 142–6, 149, 195–6, 204n, 205n, 208n, 213n, 214n, 220n, 221n, 222n, 226n
Minnis, A. 198n, 207n, 214n

Modena 163
Modistae xiii, xv, 27, 38, 51
Moevs, C. 198n, 200n, 208n, 226n, 227n
Moon 36, 53–4, 150
Moore, E. 215n, 225n
Moses 150–1
Mucius Scaevola 157
Munda 163
Musa, M. 222n
Muses 49–50, 55, 58, 122

Narcissus 226n
Nardi, B. 35, 199n, 214n, 221n, 222n
Neo-positivism 20, 35, 60–1
Nero 164–5, 224n
Nietzsche F. 134
Nimrod 100–1, 104

Octavian (Augustus) 158, 163, 223n, 224n
O'Donnell, J.J. 215n, 222n
Orosius 99
Orpheus 177, 179, 184
Ovid 17, 54, 99, 129, 174, 179, 216n, 225n, 226n

Pagani, I. 201n
Paparelli, G. 82, 198n, 208n
Paratore, E. 213n, 214n, 224n
Parnassus 174
Parodi, E.G. 201n
Paul, St 93, 137, 150–1, 217n, 219n
Pertile, L. 217n, 221–2n
Perugia 163
Peter, St 57, 147
Petrocchi, G. 200n, 216n
Pharsalus 163
Picone, M. 213n, 225n
Pier della Vigna 16, 169–73

Platonism 192–3, 227n
Pliny (the Elder) 99
Pollio 131
Polydorus 129
Pompeius (Sextus) 163
Press, G.A. 210n
Proserpina 174
Prosimetra 5, 14, 66, 76, 78, 84–7, 112–15
Provençal (*oc*) 5, 24, 85, 201n, 212n
Pulvillus 157

Quintilian 91, 94, 218n

Regulus 157
Ricoeur, P. 107–8
Rigo, P. 203n
Republic (Roman) 157, 159, 161, 163–7, 169–71, 174
Rome 16–17, 28, 97–8, 131, 137, 154–74, 184, 190, 216n, 222n, 223n, 224n
Rossi, A. 191, 226n

Sallust 162
Scarano, T. 213n
Scartazzini, G.A. 59
Scipio 158
Scott, J.A. 199n, 213n, 220n, 223n
Scyros 119
Servius 200n, 214n, 227n
Shapiro, M. 225n
Shaw, P. 226n
Sicily 40
Sign 11, 19, 20, 25, 27, 28, 30, 32, 34–5, 41–2, 44–5, 47, 53, 56, 60, 62, 65, 78, 86–7, 89, 105, 107–8, 114, 116, 124, 127, 129, 134–6, 144–5, 151–3, 157, 174, 176, 182–3, 199n, 203n, 221n, 223n
Simonetti, M. 217n, 218n

Singleton, C.S. 169, 198n
Solomon, King 106, 207n
Sordello 121
Statius 14–15, 99, 109–10, 117–26, 128–33, 140–1, 143–4, 152, 174–6, 182–4
Stillinger, T.C. 208n
Stoicism 21, 90, 170, 172–3, 191
Storey, H.W. 225n
Stull, W. 224n
Sun 150, 188

Tapsus 163
Thebes 48, 118–22, 129–30, 213n
Torquatus 157
Trone, G.A. 212n

Ulysses 204n, 224n
Utopia 39

Valerius 157
Vecchio, S. 212n

Vernacular (Italian) 5, 9, 13–15, 22–8, 32–40, 48, 66, 68–9, 71–4, 77–8, 81, 83, 87, 96, 98, 100–1, 111–13, 175, 178
Virgil
– author: iv, 14–17, 99, 110, 117, 119, 124–5, 127, 129, 131, 140–1, 152, 155, 169, 175–85, 189–94, 197n, 200n, 213n, 216n, 217n, 220n, 222n, 224n, 225n, 226n
– character: 14–15, 18, 100, 110, 117, 119, 120–32, 144, 173–9, 182–4, 195–6 , 204n, 214n, 215n, 216n, 225n

Warner, L. 219n
Weiss, R. 201n
Wetherbee, W. 215n
Wittgenstein, L. 19–22, 30–1, 35, 100
Wlassics, T. 220n

Zumthor, P. 10

www.ingramcontent.com/pod-product-compliance
Lightning Source LLC
Chambersburg PA
CBHW030311080526
44584CB00012B/527